D0084647

The Glamour
of Grammar

The Glamour of Grammar

Orality and Politics and the Emergence of Sean O'Casey

Colbert Kearney

Contributions in Drama and Theatre Studies, Number 92

GREENWOOD PRESS
Westport, Connecticut • London

Library of Congress Cataloging-in-Publication Data

Kearney, Colbert.
    The glamour of grammar : orality and politics and the emergence of Sean O'Casey /
Colbert Kearney.
       p.   cm.—(Contributions in drama and theatre studies, ISSN 0163–3821 ; no. 92)
    Includes bibliographical references (p.   ) and index.
    ISBN 0–313–31303–2 (alk. paper)
    1. O'Casey, Sean, 1880–1964—Criticism and interpretation.   2. Politics and
literature—Ireland—History—20th century.   3. Political plays, English—Irish
authors—History and criticism.   4. O'Casey, Sean, 1880–1964—Political and social views.
5. Oral tradition—Ireland.   6. Ireland—In literature.   I. Title.   II. Series.
PR6029.C33 Z6566   2000
822'.914—dc21   00–025110

British Library Cataloguing in Publication Data is available.

Library of Congress Card Number: 00–025110
ISBN: 0–313–31303–2
ISSN: 0163–3821

First published in 2000

Greenwood Press, 88 Post Road West, Westport, CT 06881
An imprint of Greenwood Publishing Group, Inc.
www.greenwood.com

Printed in the United States of America

The paper used in this book complies with the
Permanent Paper Standard issued by the National
Information Standards Organization (Z39.48–1984).

10 9 8 7 6 5 4 3 2 1

Copyright Acknowledgments

The author and publisher gratefully acknowledge permission for use of the following material:

Excerpts from the plays *The Shadow of a Gunman* (1925), *Juno and the Paycock* (1925), and
The Plough and the Stars (1926) by Sean O'Casey. Used by permission of Faber and Faber Ltd.,
publishers.

Excerpts from "Since Maggie Went Away" (1918) by Sean O'Casey and letters (1975, 1980, 1989)
of Sean O'Casey. Copyright © by The Green Crow Company Limited. Used by permission of
Macnaughton Lord Representation Ltd.

For Sally, Clíona, and Maeve

Contents

Introduction

The part-time actor Gabriel Fallon remembered arriving for a rehearsal of O'Casey's first Abbey play, *The Shadow of a Gunman,* in April 1923:

As I reached stage level my ear caught some of the richest Dublin dialogue I had ever heard, at least on the stage of the Abbey Theatre. It was spoken by F. J. McCormick with the proud consciousness of origin that marks the true-born Dubliner.[1]

Reviewers had their doubts about O'Casey's stagecraft and criticised his tendency to mix comic and tragic ingredients, but there was no denying the effect of the play or the appeal of the satire for an audience who, jaundiced by years of political violence, howled with laughter at the antics of his pretentious, self-deluded characters. An experienced playgoer, Joseph Holloway, judged that the structural weaknesses were balanced by the 'truth and human nature' depicted and by 'telling dialogue of the most topical and biting kind.'[2] The play was an immediate success, and the author was welcomed as a new and exciting talent.

And so it has been ever since, not only with *Shadow* but with *Juno and the Paycock* and *The Plough and the Stars.* Academics have slowly shed their neo-classical inhibitions and come to admire O'Casey's structural skills. Actors and producers have adopted every conceivable perspective on the characters. Unperturbed by critical debates, theatrical feuds, or changing political cultures, audiences, especially Dublin audiences, have established and maintained O'Casey's Abbey plays as among the most popular of the century. (The same cannot be said for the later plays, which, for whatever reason and despite good productions and a growing willingness to accept nonrealist forms of theatre, have never come close to achieving the same popularity or inspiring the same proud sense of ownership.) The ultimate mark of O'Casey's popular success is the acceptance of his phrases into common usage. Many of those who describe the world as 'in a state o' chassis' or humorously philosophise on the nature of the moon and stars or praise the goodness of 'a darlin' man' may not know that they are quoting O'Casey. Maybe, in one sense, they are not: the chances are that O'Casey did not invent these phrases *ex nihilo* but actually heard them himself. Early audiences would have recognised that almost every line of an O'Casey play could have been heard on the way to the theatre: part of the dramatist's talent was to edit and distill ordinary Dublin working-class speech in order to produce dialogue that was exceptionally rich but always acceptably 'true' to the communal style on which it was based.

O'Casey is not only a popular success; he has also achieved academic canonisation. There has been an *O'Casey Annual*, a *Sean O'Casey Review,* and several volumes listing productions, reviews, and scholarly research. Almost every aspect of his life and work has been scrutinised in lecture and learned publication. Strangely enough, if any element of O'Casey's plays has been relatively neglected, it is the nature of his language.

As early as 1952, in *Drama from Ibsen to Eliot*, Raymond Williams ridiculed the (largely English) tendency to gush with an enthusiastic lack of precision about the language of O'Casey's plays. Williams was shrewd enough to watch his step, knowing how dangerous it was 'to speak from outside so intense and self-conscious a culture,' but he confidently dismissed most of that talk about 'Elizabethan richness' as devoid of critical content.[3] A socialist who had fought in World War II, he was obviously irritated by the ratio of words to deeds in these plays of the Irish revolution and could not readily discover the relevance of the verbal display to the dramatic action. In a later version of the book—*Drama from Ibsen to Brecht* (1968)—he was less dismissive of those linguistic colours against which he remembered reacting 'very bitterly'; he could now see the dramatic force of a contrast between modes of language:

What is at issue, always, is the relation between the language of men in intense experience and the inflated, engaging language of men avoiding experience. It is a very deep disturbance, which I suppose comes out of that confused history. But what seems to happen, as O'Casey goes on, is the hardening of a mannerism which overrides this crucial and difficult distinction.[4]

Though generally well disposed to O'Casey, Williams could not conceal his exasperation at 'the endless, bibulous, blathering talk.'

In 1969, in his introduction to the O'Casey volume in the Modern Judgement series, Ronald Ayling took issue with Williams and argued that O'Casey's language, far from being irrelevant or merely ostentatious, frequently served as a dramatic reflection of a character or a central theme.[5] Almost ten years later, Bernice Schrank wrote an essay on *The Shadow of a Gunman* that developed ideas found in Williams and Ayling and argued that 'the language the characters use in *The Shadow of a Gunman* is an integral part of the play's overall vision of chaos.' Schrank underlined the sophisticated patterning of the play by showing how the characters exist in relation to various forms of linguistic behaviour, such as talking as a substitute for action or manipulating language in order to create 'a super-self.' In an interesting footnote Schrank referred to the work of Williams and Ayling and then concluded:

Ayling's and Williams' seminal remarks are the sum total of critical treatment of O'Casey's dramatic language to date. To my knowledge there are no extended studies of any of O'Casey's plays from the point of view of language.[6]

Apart from an essay by Robert Hogan that traces the development of O'Casey's language from 'the outer edge of comic realism,' to the more 'poetic' of the later plays,[7] I am not aware of any since.

Although always fascinated by the use of Dublin working-class speech in Joyce and O'Casey and Behan, it was only when I had undertaken *The Writings of Brendan Behan* that I was forced to make some effort to describe that speech. Behan's *Borstal Boy* struck me as a tour de force that re-created in literature the sense of an oral delivery. It struck me that many of the great passages were written in flagrant disregard of the conventions of 'good' writing: the piling up of clauses in elongated sentences, the dependence on stock turns of speech and clichés, even the use of expletives and other phrases that made no literal sense at all. Yet close textual analysis had convinced me that the narrative was immensely sophisticated.

Finishing the book only increased my desire to understand why, how, and to what extent the language of an oral tradition differed from that of a literate tradition. With this in mind I went back to books in modern Irish that were essentially transcriptions of oral narration, I looked again at what Synge had found so irresistible in the folk imagination of the west of Ireland, and I read about the oral tradition in Ireland and elsewhere; but it was only when I encountered Walter Ong's *Orality and Literacy* that I found a series of confidently clear answers to questions that had been baffling me for years.[8]

With Ong in mind, I returned to Joyce and Synge, Behan and O'Casey, and eventually this study began to take shape. What I have tried to do initially is show how and why an oral culture extending back into prehistory continued to flourish in inner-city Dublin at least as late as the early decades of this century. My next task was to look at O'Casey's relation to this tradition because, of course, he grew up in a highly literate household; of importance here were O'Casey's political dedication to the working class and his lifelong conviction, the central thesis of the Abbey plays, that the working class had been duped by bourgeois Nationalists into rejecting a genuine revolution in favour of a Nationalist uprising that brought them nothing but suffering and death. A study of the early plays suggests that O'Casey, unconsciously, saw this duping in terms of illiterates and semiliterates being dazzled by men whose literary education set them above ordinary working-class people. Chapter 3 looks at O'Casey's literary career up to 1922, noting the strikingly 'oral' tone of his early essays into print and, later on, the influence of Shaw on his first attempts at writing plays. In fact, Chapter 4 begins by arguing that, in a sense, *The Shadow of a Gunman* got out of the author's control, that the play still bears the marks of a Shavian 'play of ideas' that was taken over by linguistic exuberance of Tommy Owens and successive verbal fantasists.

Chapters 4 to 6 deal, in turn, with the three Abbey plays. I cannot lay sufficient stress on an important disclaimer: never for a moment do I suggest that O'Casey is writing explicitly about the oral/literary opposition or that the tenement-dwellers of Hilljoy Square are conscious that their linguistic abilities derive from their oral heritage. What I have tried to do in each case is to locate the language of characters in an oral tradition, emphasising the sheer power of that language and suggesting that much of what seems strange to an educated reader—including 'the endless, bibulous, blathering talk'—would pass unnoticed in an oral community. I have also sought to establish an interesting motif: in each of these plays the character who is seen to peddle the most dangerous delusions is an outsider whose literacy and educated speech mark him off from the denizens of Hilljoy Square. In the final chapter, which is really an epilogue, I look at examples of the language of the Abbey plays in which, anticipating the language of the later plays, O'Casey refuses to be circumscribed by rules of working-class speech and insists on the dramatist's traditional right to create a more 'poetic' form.

If there is any value in this study, credit is due to two teachers who, were they alive, would have ensured that it was less imperfect. It was my good fortune to encounter Eugene Watters at primary school and to enjoy his inspirational company until he died in 1982; a fine writer of plays, poems, and fiction in Irish and English, he spoke with unique authority about the distinctive qualities of each language. I was also lucky to meet Alan Bliss at University College Dublin when he was developing his interest in Irish and Hiberno-English, an interest that was to produce seminal works such as 'The Language of Synge' and *The English Language in Ireland* as well as many conversations over pints in Kehoe's of Anne Street and in the Mayo Gaeltacht.

It is a pleasure to acknowledge my indebtedness to my friend and colleague Ger FitzGibbon, with whom I have been discussing O'Casey for more years than either of us would care to count; I have never ceased to learn from him. It is a sad duty to note the death of Bob Hogan, who read this book in draft and made characteristically sharp observations; like all students of Irish drama, I am indebted to him. I am also indebted to the Arts Faculty of University College Cork, for a grant that enabled me to consult the O'Casey material in the Berg Collection of the New York Public Library.

Finally, and most important of all, thanks to my mother and late father for giving me a head start over most other scholars in this particular field.

NOTES

1. Gabriel Fallon, *Sean O'Casey, The Man I Knew* (London: Routledge and Kegan Paul, 1965), 5.

2. Joseph Holloway, *Joseph Holloway's Abbey Theatre*, ed. Robert Hogan and Michael J. O'Neill, (Carbondale: Southern Illinois UP, 1967), 215f.

3. Raymond Williams, *Drama from Ibsen to Eliot* (London: Chatto and Windus, 1964), 169ff.

4. Raymond Williams, *Drama from Ibsen to Brecht* (Harmondsworth: Penguin Books, 1968), 164.

5. Ronald Ayling, ed., *Sean O'Casey: Modern Judgements* (London: Macmillan, 1969), 17–21.

6. Bernice Schrank, "'You needn't say no more": Language and the Problem of Communication in *The Shadow of a Gunman,*' in *O'Casey: The Dublin Trilogy: A Casebook,* ed. Ronald Ayling (London: Macmillan, 1985), 80.

7. Robert Hogan, *'Since O'Casey' and Other Essays on Irish Drama* (Gerrards Cross: Colin Smythe, 1983), 45.

8. Walter Ong, *Orality and Literacy: The Technologizing of the Word* (London: Methuen, 1982).

Chapter 1

Hilljoy Square at the Turn of the Century

In almost every external way the history of Dublin in the nineteenth century is one of dilapidation. By 1800 an increasingly ambitious Anglo-Irish Ascendancy had remade the city into an architecturally splendid capital, noted for its bold thoroughfares and squares of elegant town houses. When the Act of Union, 1800, abolished the Dublin parliament and subsumed it into Westminster, it also removed the social and political energy that had placed Dublin among the ten largest cities in Europe. Those who had thronged Dublin for the social life of the parliamentary season now went to London instead. The days of the Anglo-Irish Ascendancy were numbered. In the course of the nineteenth century a Catholic middle class, freed from the more extreme constraints of legal repression, began to play a greater part in the social and political life of the city, but the combination of doomed Protestant Ascendancy and emergent Catholic bourgeoisie was unable to generate in Dublin the rate of development that characterised other European cities: three times during the century the census registered a drop in population, and in 1901 the figure was less than a quarter of a million.[1]

The most obvious manifestation of this change were the splendid Georgian town houses, for which the owners now had no personal use. Few Catholics could afford to buy them for themselves, and, as the market collapsed, the houses fell into the hands of landlords who filled them with as many tenants as possible. It did not make commercial sense to maintain these houses, and they gradually degenerated into tenements and, in many cases, into slum tenements, 'old, rotten, permeated with . . . physical and moral corruption.'[2]

One-third of the population of Dublin lived in appalling poverty, the consequence of under- and unemployment in a city that was industrially stagnant.

Dublin had, since the Union in 1800, declined in manufacturing and productive power. Chiefly an administrative and commercial city, its main source of employment lay in the restricted spheres of clerical work and unskilled labour. The ranks of the unemployed were continuously enlarged by the illiterate poor, the unskilled, those in seasonal or casual labour, and by the influx of rural migrants.[3]

In 1914 this third of the population was living in 5,000 tenement houses:

Nearly 26,000 families lived in 5,000 tenements, while over 20,000 families lived in one room, and another 5,000 had only two rooms. Of the 5,000 tenements, over 1,500 were actually condemned as not only unfit for human habitation, but condemned, in fact, as incapable of ever being rendered fit for human habitation. The total of Dublin's 'slum jungle' population came to about 87,000 people, or 30 per cent of that city's population of nearly 300,000. The living conditions of these slum dwellers approached the subhuman . . . . 'In nearly all of these dwellings the hallways are unlighted and nightly filled with waifs and strays of the city, men, women, and children, seeking a place to lay their heads. The reeking stench of these dens pollutes the air of the streets.'

From these festering tenements oozed all the fearful concomitants of Dublin slum life. Death, disease, immorality, insanity, crime, drunkenness, unemployment, low wages, and high rents rolled on in a seemingly interminable vicious cycle. The Dublin death-rate was fantastic . . . . The infant mortality figures for Dublin were appalling.[4]

Those who could afford to rent a room or rooms when adequately employed were forced to sublet to others in order to pay the rent during periods of shortage, and these others might, in turn, be obliged to sublet, and so on down the line until some buildings were literally swarming with adults and children in conditions that produced disease and despair of any improvement.

'Todd' Andrews was born in 1901 in Summerhill. Though this street was immediately adjacent to some of the worst slums and was itself 'quickly sinking into slums,' the Andrews family was lower-middle-class. His parents 'kept themselves to themselves' (meaning that they preserved themselves from contact with their social inferiors) and ran a dairy business in the house and extensive yard behind.[5] Though his father had a sentimental loyalty to working-class values, his mother would not allow Andrews to attend the local national school but insisted on sending him to the fee-paying convent school in Dominic Street, where his 'common' accent was mocked by his teachers and fellow pupils. But if the children of shopkeepers and civil servants felt he was the lowest of the low, he knew that there were many others further down. One of the girls employed by his parents often took him to her own home nearby:

She lived with her parents in one room in Gardiner Street. The stench of the house when you entered the hall was disgusting. Urine and excrement (visible as well as smelling) mingled with all the stinks that the human body can exude. There was no indoor lavatory and only one outdoor lavatory and one outdoor tap for the whole building. The room where the girl lived with her father, mother and two sisters, had two beds with old rags for bed clothes and no other furnishings except a table, a few chairs, a china dog, and statues of the Blessed Virgin and the Sacred Heart.[6]

From the evidence of his own street he could see the dire situation getting even worse: 'Dublin in the first decade of the century was probably the most pathetic and apathetic city in Europe. The slums kept on increasing and the poor got poorer and more degraded.'[7] The poor had no external amusements other than the pub and an occasional soccer match. They had no interest in politics, and their constant struggle was to feed and shelter their family. Before the arrival of Jim Larkin they accepted their miserable fate as the will of God. Andrews' Uncle Mattie, who lived with them in Summerhill and was relatively fortunate in that he was in secure employment as a timekeeper, had but one interest outside work: having paid for his rent on a Friday, he drank the rest of his money over the weekend. In 1909 Andrews' father received a legacy of £100: 'this small capital . . . enabled my father to leave Summerhill which, despite his affection for my grandmother, he found distasteful because of the drinking, disorder and general fecklessness there.'[8] Young Todd escaped to the polite security of a shop in the suburban village of Terenure, where he enjoyed many of the pleasures of rural life. Though his father was not a Nationalist, Todd was sent for a while to Patrick Pearse's school in Rathfarnam; he later changed to the Christian Brothers school in Synge Street and eventually went to university. But, as he himself knew well, Andrews was lucky to have been born into the lower middle class and to have parents who were relatively well-off and committed to improving the fortunes of their family. He may even have been unique among the children who were born in Summerhill in 1901; the vast majority were doomed to rot with the houses in which they lived.

The core of the problem was economic: in the Ireland of the time there was 'the curious paradox of . . . shortage of labour in the rural parts and an enormous surplus in the urban areas.' About half of the total male workforce was engaged in casual labour in the transport trade.[9] In 1914 more than three-quarters of the average working-class family's income went on food and rent. The death rate in Dublin was the fifth highest in the world. Dublin City Corporation was not particularly effective in changing the tenement system, partly because one-fifth of the members were themselves owners of tenements. Some efforts were made by charities in association with the Corporation, but the resulting cottages—artisan dwellings—were within the range only of skilled tradesmen.

One observer wrote in 1910:

What makes it easier to live at a low level, and harder to climb to a higher one, is the tenement house system with the communistic way of life . . . . It would be very inhuman not to admire the virtues these poor people display; but every virtue has its seamy side. The patient and cheerful endurance of poverty merges into apathy and even laziness; the easy and generous man who helps a friend in need is equally ready to rely on him in turn; to improve one's position and become really independent would be a kind of treachery to the small community.[10]

Here was the classic poverty trap that not only condemned the poor to unremitting deprivation but increased the relative deprivation by cutting them off from whatever progress was being made elsewhere in the city and the world. Some advances were made in the provision of free primary education, but they were insufficient to spring the trap. There were isolated protests from within the ranks of the very poor but nothing of any significance before the arrival of Jim Larkin in 1907. Till then the fate of the poor had not figured very prominently in politics. The last quarter of the nineteenth century had been dominated by the larger issue of Home Rule with its implication that, given the right to administer itself, Ireland and all its people would prosper. Local politics were obsessed with national issues, a tendency that would continue well into the new century.[11]

Even after a century of Catholic emancipation, the social structure was extraordinarily rigid.

While the proportion of Catholics rose in medicine, law, teaching and banking, the overall rise was not dramatic and Catholics remained seriously underrepresented. Their rise to overrepresentation in municipal employment, in marked contrast to the trend in civil service employment, probably reflects the impact of political favour within municipal employment.[12]

What people had, they tried to hold, and this produced a society with minimal social mobility. This was especially true at the top and at the bottom of the scale. The son of a doctor was more likely to gain access to a teaching hospital than the son of a carpenter; similarly (and at least as blatantly) access to most of the skilled trades was limited to children and close relatives of members. People might move up or down a few degrees but seldom crossed the lines of class: if a member of the working class moved up in the world, it was most likely to be into another segment of the working class: 'The only groups which show any degree of inter-generational mobility are clerical white-collar workers, reflecting that this was an expanding and relatively new occupation, and semi-skilled workers.'[13] Here was a possible ladder for those at the bottom of the heap, for the children of casual labourers and hawkers and beggars, provided they acquired the necessary skills of reading and writing. But the way forward was really a vicious circle. In order to acquire the skills, it was necessary to have 'higher' education of some kind, and in order to pay for such 'higher' education, it was necessary to have the money that those at the bottom of the pile simply did not have; but 'although the education standard for many clerical jobs was only that of national—i.e. elementary school, few children of unskilled or semi-skilled workers reached this level.'[14] Though Ireland had had a state-supported primary school scheme since 1831, the schools never figured very seriously in the lives of the poor.

There were at least two reasons for this. In the first place, Catholics, following the lead of the hierarchy, always suspected the state schools of being anti-Catholic; second, the schools were never sufficiently well organised or equipped to overcome the suspicions of the poor, who did not need to go to school to learn 'the duties of respect to superiors, and obedience to all persons placed in authority.'[15] The poor had no great interest in attending schools that promised so little. Many children stayed away in order to help out at home; most working-class children would have started school at the age of seven, attended irregularly, and left school altogether at the age of ten.

Education as a path to upward mobility was not readily available to the poor, though it provided a limited avenue for skilled working class families and those of clerical background. Many of these families favoured the schools of the Christian Brothers because they had a reputation for achieving examination successes, but despite the fact that the

Christian Brothers provided secondary schooling free of charge—the only body doing so—few working class children continued their education.[16]

When Todd Andrews was at Synge Street, most of the pupils were working-class or lower-middle-class, but 'when the Secondary School stage was reached, a great number of the working class boys dropped out. Their family circumstances required that they should contribute to the family budget.'[17] Some of the boys who, like Andrews, were enabled to stay on—and, of course, one is speaking only of boys—made it to university, involved themselves in politics, and were in a position to play a prominent part in the political, economic, and social life of the Free State.

In 1881 almost a quarter of the population of Dublin city and county was totally illiterate, unable to read or write, and by 1891 the figure had fallen only to slightly more than one-fifth.[18]

At the bottom of the heap were the have-nots of the city, consisting of labourers, dockers, coal heavers, shop attendants, messenger boys and domestic servants. Even those who had regular work were seldom far above the poverty line and very many were below it. There was no security of employment and great numbers of them had no work at all. They sent their children to the National Schools for as short a time as possible and a great many emerged from these schools illiterate and remained so.[19]

One may safely assume that the incidence of illiteracy among the slum tenement poor was many times the general average.

Illiteracy statistics are notoriously difficult to interpret.[20] The term is popularly understood to mean a total inability to read or write, but there are many levels of illiteracy. There are, for example, those who can read but not write. Traditionally, pupils were taught to read before the teaching of writing began, and, given the short period that many spent at school in Dublin at the turn of the century, it is very likely that many emerged who were able to read but who had never been taught to write at all. Others would have learned enough to read posters or newspaper headlines but not enough to read, say, a novel or a lengthy article; others were capable of signing their names but would not have had the confidence to write anything more complex, especially if their economic fortune depended on it. Again, because of the stigma attached to illiteracy in the twentieth century, it is likely that some who were effectively unable to read complex material or to express themselves competently in writing would deny being illiterate in an absolute sense. The situation in Dublin during the early decades of the last century has not yet been scientifically assessed or analysed, but the central fact is irresistible: a considerable portion—my guess would be at least a half—of the slum dwellers were functionally illiterate in that they lacked the competence or the confidence to use the written word. It also seems safe to assume that, among those who had been introduced to literacy, the ability to read was much more common than the ability to write and that illiteracy was more prevalent among the old than among the young.

It is difficult for us not to see these people in terms of what they lacked. So strong is our sense of a literate culture stretching back to the classical Greeks that we must remind ourselves that they were, in fact, the final generations of an oral culture that had dominated human history. Far from being temporarily deprived of the advantages of literacy, they belonged to the vast mass of people who had never known literacy and whose oral culture was only beginning to give way to the culture we associate with contemporary Europe. Even the word 'culture' would not have been applied to the behaviour of the urban poor at the turn of the century; the comfortable assumption of those who considered such matters, the educated elite, was that literacy was the basis of culture. Things have changed a good deal since then, at least in terms of scholarship, and now we can appreciate not only the riches of oral cultures but also the enormous differences between our perception of the world and that of an oral community.

The tenements were not a primary oral culture, that is, a culture untouched by literacy. They were a part of a modern society that included educational systems, elaborate bureaucracy, formal education, mass publication of books and newspapers. Even if the most wretched were, as we have seen, unable to exploit these, they could not be unaware of them. Nor were they totally devoid of literary culture. Even in the tenements there were individuals who had, for one reason or another, been excited by books and who treasured their small libraries; perhaps they had slipped down the economic ladder and were emulating their parents, or perhaps some casual contact—theatrical, musical or political—had encouraged them. Many who could not themselves read depended on others to read for them.[21] What Walter Ong has observed of the late twentieth century was even more obvious at the turn of the century: 'Today primary oral culture in the strict sense hardly exists, since every culture knows of writing and has some experience of its effects. Still, to varying degrees many cultures and subcultures, even in a high-technology ambiance, preserve much of the mind-set of primary orality.'[22] The mind-set of working-class Dubliners was, for obvious historical reasons, overwhelmingly oral.

From about the sixteenth century onward it was English colonial policy to extirpate the native literary class and denigrate the native culture as barbarous. This class had enjoyed for centuries a powerful and prestigious position in Irish society, but, with the defeat of the princes who employed them, it survived in the persons of popular poets who were frequently in lowly employment and often vagrant. By 1800 the days of aristocratic patronage were a distant memory, and, with half the population speaking English, the break between the Gaelic poet and his audience was almost complete. The Gaelic tradition survived relatively intact in the *Gaeltachtaí* on the western seaboard, and, despite the change of language, its influence remained strong throughout the country.

From the very beginning the tradition had been predominantly oral; literacy was, as everywhere else, the preserve of an educated elite. One effect of English colonial policy was that the oral tradition survived to an extent that was rare, if not unique, in modern Europe. In Ireland anti-Catholic legislation proscribed the kind of developments in formal education that were taking place throughout Europe; instead of colleges and universities there were only hedge-schools where itinerant teachers taught a surprisingly wide range of subjects and that were crucial to those brave and ambitious young men who wished to qualify for a clerical education. But it would be wrong to assume that even those who never attended any kind of school were uneducated. It is true that they were illiterate, but a strong oral tradition of song, poetry, story, and historical and natural lore gave them a sense of themselves in the past and present. Nor were the poems and stories that were composed and transmitted orally from generation to generation qualitatively inferior to those published and preserved in print. Nor were the people for whom these poems and stories were performed a less sophisticated audience than the readership for whom modern literature was written. The Homeric poems assumed an illiterate audience, and the plays of Shakespeare, though they became available in written form, were composed for a largely illiterate audience. What oral audiences lack in literary awareness is compensated for in aural abilities to absorb and appreciate the most elaborate material. Strong traces of this tradition are to be found to this day in Ireland despite the gradual domination of literacy.

A writer has described the Irish-speakers of Connemara as follows:

[They] had retained the habit of taking pleasure in language. Speech was one of their passtimes. Many of them, men and women, were artists in words, delighting in making fresh combinations and minting fresh images from sea, sky, mountain, legend, and the details of craft and daily work. They transcended the drudgery of daily life in song, verse, sharp saying, and 'the wild oats of speech.'[23]

Oral culture is characterised by a sense of language as performance rather than description, of language as individual creation rather than standard medium, of language as generated by physically objective circumstances rather than by abstraction.[24] The bulk of what modern literates know is deposited in libraries. In an oral society knowledge is what you (or somebody beside you) can remember; culture in the sense of communal knowledge is not contained in libraries but in stories and formulas that somebody can recite—hence the crucial importance of memory and vivid speech that impresses itself on the memory. When I claim to know *Hamlet*, I mean that I have a good outline memory of the play and the criticism it has generated. When an illiterate says he knows a story or a poem, he is saying that he can repeat it word for word.

To this day Irish students may experience some confusion when faced with the different rules applied to Irish and English composition. In the Irish class the teacher will encourage them to enhance their work by including *corraí cainte*, idiomatic turns of phrase that are characteristic of spoken Irish; in the English class such phrases are disdained as clichés. This tells us a good deal about the differences between modern Irish and modern English, differences that were much more pronounced at the turn of the century before government agencies set about establishing a standardised, written form of modern Irish. In oral cultures, where so much depends on memory, great importance is attached to mnemonic formulas; in literate cultures, there is no such need to remember, and so the mnemonic formula is disdained in favour of originality of expression.[25] Even when written down, modern Irish, in contrast with modern English, is still essentially the language of an oral tradition.

Contemporary modern Irish is based on the recorded speech of the *Gaeltachtaí* at the turn of the century, that is, the speech of subsistence farming and fishing families in an oral community. Standard English for several centuries has been based on texts written by a university-educated elite. Irish is relatively rich in concrete nouns that reflect the physical experience of agriculture; the high incidence of abstract nouns in English reflects centuries of academic study. The mass circulation of printed material has led to a high value being placed on uniformity: the text must be instantly clear to readers of English throughout the world who have no access to the writer. In an oral community intellectual inquiry takes place in discussion, and consequently the language tends to be more dramatic than discursive; individual force is more important than adherence to conventional correctness, and this generates, among other things, a relatively plastic syntax. As we have seen, oral language makes more use of linguistic formulas; for the same reasons it also uses rhythm to an extent that would seem excessive in the speech (or the prose) of literates. Just as a literate society values those who write with individual colour and force, so an oral community values those whose speech is memorably striking in its concision or colour or fluency. Those who wish to improve their English go to universities; those who wish to improve their Irish head for the *Gaeltachtai* of the Atlantic seaboard.

In the course of the nineteenth century Hiberno-English preserved many of the stylistic features of Gaelic mainly because the culture of the speakers had in some important ways survived the change of language. There was only a limited awareness of reading and writing and little sense of a standard either in speech or in writing. The culture of the community was contained not in libraries but in remembered speech and especially in those ballads and stories and proverbs that were, to varying degrees, translations of the Gaelic or composed in the same moulds. Knowledge and information were transmitted by word of mouth. Entertainment was overwhelmingly domestic and consisted of singing, dancing, and narration. (The pub was also an important part of life where the arts of oral performance were not limited to the consumption of alcohol.) The vast majority of Irish people learned English by listening to others, and this meant that early Hiberno-English began as a direct translation of Irish in which elements of Irish pronunciation, syntax, and style survived more strongly than they would have done if people had studied it at school with grammars and texts.[26]

For obvious reasons there are few firsthand narratives of slum life, and this is why Andrews' book, though written at a distance, is invaluable. It is likely that James Stephens grew up in or near the tenements, but the local details of his early life are as vague as the date of his birth, 1880 or 1882. His first novel, *The Charwoman's Daughter* (1912), is set in a tenement, but though the poverty and squalor are described convincingly, the dialogue is, like the narrative itself, essentially standard. Stephens seems to have been one of the few who escaped up into the lower middle class by becoming a white-collar clerk: from 1896 till 1912 he worked as a typist in legal offices. He went on to become a prominent literary figure, but though he was interested in Irish legend and invented a conversational style based on speech, it was more a gently humorous literary style than one based on Dublin working-class vernacular, the voice of an educated Dubliner whose innate narrative abilities have been amplified by extensive reading:

From the time she opened her eyes in the morning her mother never ceased to talk. It was then she went over all the things that had happened on the previous day, and enumerated all the places she would have to go to on the present day, and the chances for and against the making of a little money.[27]

Stephens captures the prominent role of speech in this tenement—the mother always speaks aloud what literates would tend to think silently—but the narrator attributes lexic and syntactic features to her that no tenement-dweller would use:

When the subject of matrimony was under discussion her mother planned minutely the person of the groom, his vast accomplishments, and yet vaster wealth, the magnificence of his person, and the love in which he was held by rich and poor alike . . . . Mary Makebelieve's questions as to the status and appurtenances of a lord were searching and minute; her mother's rejoinders were equally elaborate and particular.[28]

Realism is but a small part of the novel, and the other element, a charmingly fanciful blend of the ordinary and the theosophical, became the dominant in Stephens' writing. His fiction always exuded the atmosphere of storytelling, and in the final decade of his life he abandoned writing in favour of the new oral medium, the radio talk. O'Casey thought *The Charwoman's Daughter* 'a very pleasingly written story, but scarcely true to slum life.'[29]

Ever since Macmorris asserted his nationality and Irish accent in Shakespeare's *Henry V*, writers have been attracted to the possibilities of Hiberno-English in comic dialogue. Maria Edgeworth is often credited with establishing both the dialect and the oral narrative in *Castle Rackrent* (1800) but elsewhere used Standard literary English. Writers such as the Banims, Lover, and Lever used Hiberno-English but only in comic dialogue. William Carleton (1794–1869) was probably the first major Irish writer of English who had firsthand experience of the oral tradition. Born into an Irish-speaking family in Tyrone—his mother was a singer, and his father a noted *seanchaí* (storyteller)—Carleton had actually lived the life of his fictional characters and spoken the dialect he put into their mouths: 'In undertaking to describe the Irish peasantry as they are, I approach the difficult task with the advantage of knowing them, which perhaps few other Irish writers ever possessed.'[30] Yeats considered Carleton the greatest Irish novelist of the century and the originator of modern Anglo-Irish literature. He published *Stories from Carleton* and made great use of Carleton's writings in his own extensive works on folklore.[31] Like Lady Gregory, Yeats was obsessed by the Irish oral tradition, seeing it as valuable in itself and also a useful means of escaping the overwhelming influence of the English tradition. Disdainful of modern rational philosophy, he embraced the traditional tales of the Irish poor as a form of imaginative expression that reached back in an unbroken line to the Homeric age and beyond. He never mastered the Hiberno-English dialect as well as, say, Lady Gregory, but he sought to introduce into his verse the colourfully concrete qualities of 'peasant' speech.

In *Beside the Fire* (1890) and his translations of Irish poetry, Douglas Hyde used Hiberno-English in order to give a fuller sense of the original Irish than he felt would have been possible in standard literary English, and it is likely that this experiment had a crucial influence on the career of Synge, the most perceptive student of the Irish oral tradition and the first to use it fully as a literary medium. Synge had studied Irish and could see how the imagination of an oral community persisted through the change of language, producing an English that was crucially different from the written or spoken standard of the day. The term 'oral culture' does not occur in the Preface to *The Playboy of the Western World*, but the language described has those qualities of physicality, richness, and exuberance that the literate immediately notices in the speech of an oral community, and Synge's studies enabled him to analyse it: 'In writing *The Playboy of the Western World*, as in my other plays, I have used one or two words only that I have not heard among the country people of Ireland, or spoken in my own nursery before I could read the newspapers . . . and I am glad to acknowledge how much I owe to the folk-imagination of these fine people.' Synge compared his own good fortune to that of the Elizabethan dramatists who also lived in a largely oral community during a period of linguistic cross-fertilization: 'This matter, I think, is of importance, for in countries where the imagination of the people, and the language they use, is rich and living, it is possible for a writer to be rich and copious in his words, and at the same time to give the reality, which is the root of all poetry, in a comprehensive and natural form.' Synge found contemporary drama either too intellectual, that is, too abstract, or too far removed from actual life: 'In a good play every speech should be as fully flavoured as a nut or apple, and such speeches cannot be written by any one who works among people who have shut their lips on poetry.' He was conscious that the situation in Ireland would soon change as modernisation altered both the imagination and the language of the people: 'In Ireland, for a few years more, we have a popular imagination that is fiery, and magnificent, and tender; so that those of us who wish to write start with a chance that is not given to writers in places where the springtime of the local life has been forgotten, and the harvest is a memory only, and the straw has been turned into bricks.'[32]

Synge's general reference is to rural Ireland, especially the far west and the mountains of Wicklow, an area that, though physically close to Dublin, was culturally closer to the west. Dublin city, the capital and centre of British rule in Ireland, was the most Anglicised, urbanised, and modernised part of Ireland. Dublin, founded by the Vikings and developed by the Normans and the English, had never been predominantly Irish-speaking. Irish had long since disappeared when the Gaelic League began to teach it again in the 1890s. But though the language itself was not to be heard, its residual influences made the speech of working-class Dubliners almost impenetrable to ears attuned to Received Pronunciation. At the turn of the century Dublin had two universities and a vital literary tradition, but they did not impinge on the lives of the poor, of whom, at most, only one-third were literate. As we have seen, there was almost no social mobility upward: the poor were almost hermetically sealed in their tenement ghettos. Their only contact with the better-off was in the capacity of service; the only way out of the tenements was with the army or on the emigrant ship. Consequently, though living in a modern city, the poor were socially isolated, and this forced them to preserve a culture that was, in many ways, closer to that of their rural counterparts (and, of course, to the very poor of other cities) than to that of the middle and upper classes around them. In no way was this more manifest than in the language they spoke and in their attitude to language, spoken and written.

Even if James Stephens was born and grew up in such circumstances (and, like everything else about his early years, he has shrouded this in whimsical mists), he was one of the few to escape the trap and, in his teens, find employment as a clerk-typist. James Joyce was part of a family moving in the other direction. From the high bourgeois splendour of a seaside house in Bray and a Jesuit boarding school, young James found himself living on the edge of the slums; but though the fall must have seemed catastrophic, the Joyces, for all the poverty and violence of their home, always managed to preserve some distinction between themselves and the working-class poor.[33] Joyce's Dubliners are almost all lower-middle-class, clinging tenaciously to respectability and their superiority to 'the rough tribes' of the working-class cottages and the brawling squalor of the tenements; and yet if anybody deserves the credit for introducing the oral tradition into Irish urban literature, it is Joyce.

Young Joyce was a highly self-conscious literary stylist who sought the purity of diction he associated with, among others, Jonson and Newman, but he was the son of a gifted raconteur from whom he may have inherited his fine ear and his delight in the rich, if rambling, conversation of the men in the Committee Room and in Mr. Kernan's bedroom. Perhaps no writer has caught the modulations of Dublin speech as well as Joyce, but the dominant tone of his Dubliners is lower-middle-class.

His desire for truthful representation led him to develop the free, indirect style of *Dubliners*: by infusing his narration with elements that Standard English (which insists, e.g., that 'if' be used to introduce an indirect question) would have rejected, Joyce allows the tones of the characters' voices to compete with the impersonal narrative. Here Maria, the precariously middle-class spinster of 'Clay,' encounters the impatience and the working-class sarcasm of the shop assistant:

Then she thought what else would she buy: she wanted to buy something really nice. They [her brother's family] would be sure to have plenty of apples and nuts. It was hard to know what to buy and all she could think of was cake. She decided to buy some plumcake but Downes's plumcake had not enough icing on top of it so she went over to a shop in Henry Street. Here she was a long time in suiting herself and the stylish young lady behind the counter, who was evidently a little annoyed by her, asked her was it wedding-cake she wanted to buy.[34]

The interior monologue is a development of this technique, but Stephen is highly educated, and Bloom is distinctly middle-class. Molly is more interesting, perhaps because her delivery owes so much to Nora Barnacle and her early years in Galway, the most Gaelic of Irish cities; but, in the context of this essay, more interesting still is the anonymous narrator of 'Cyclops,' whose language has all the hallmarks of the urban oral style: fluent, copious, rhythmic, dramatic, and sarcastically studded with formulas and references that link the speaker and his audience. Significantly, it is punctuated by passages of inflated and cliché-ridden prose, as if to suggest that the 'oral' narrative is preliterary and the interruptions postliterary.

Poor Bloom has just felt obliged to praise Blazes Boylan, his wife's manager, as 'an excellent man to organise,' and the narrator shrewdly infers more than Bloom has implied. Weldon Thornton failed to locate the remarks about the coconuts and the animal's chest in any dictionary of quotations or proverbs but suspected that they might be 'common Irish expressions.'[35] It is almost certain that they were common in Dublin at the time, less likely that they were, like the exotic apostrophe to Caddareesh, specific to the word-hoard of John Joyce. It is not necessary to be aware of their origins or even of their figurative logic because the meaning is crystal clear. The first two sentences make very little rational or literate sense (the gist is simply *Now I understand*) but are strikingly copious, delighting in the delivery itself and in the use of slang expressions that establish the intimacy between speaker and audience.

In order to appreciate the texture of the rhapsody, we must remember the circumstances: the speaker suspects that Boylan will make use of the musical concert to continue his affair with Molly. We must also bear in mind that the key word is 'organise,' a word that, as the speaker will demonstrate, combines the two meanings of music (the musical instrument) and sex (the sexual organ) in exactly the same way as Boylan's concert tour will. This double pun is echoed in the next phrase where the speaker uses a concealed quotation from a song, 'Phil the Fluter's Ball' ('with a toot on the flute and a twiddle on the fiddle-o'), to make another innuendo combining music ('flute' as musical instrument) and sex ('flute' as common slang for penis). Nor is our virtuoso finished with this trope. The phrase 'concert tour,' when spoken in a strong Dublin accent, is indistinguishable from 'concert whore,' a climactic chord on the music/sex theme.[36] Then follows a wonderfully compact and dramatised account of how Blazes Boylan's notoriously dishonest cheat of a father got his nickname, with the implication, of course, that his son is at least equally dishonest. He finishes with a final flourish on 'organise' and a coda that is, again, simply a bravura version of *Now we both understand*.

Hoho begob says I to myself says I. That explains the milk in the coconut and the absence of hair on the animal's chest. Blazes doing the tootle on the flute. Concert tour. Dirty Dan the dodger's son off Island bridge that sold the same horses twice over to the government to fight the Boers. Old Whatwhat. I called about the poor and water rate, Mr Boylan. You what? The water rate, Mr Boylan. You whatwhat? That's the bucko that'll organise her, take my tip. 'Twixt me and you Caddareesh.[37]

Typical of the oral performer from Homer to the present day, our narrator does not compose new phrases or expressions but orchestrates current phrases into a wonderfully rich and rhythmical texture of innuendo and insinuation that binds listeners to his every word by making them strain to follow the arcane sequence from nuance to nuance. Here is a narrative genius, and yet we find it credible that such artistry should be overheard in a pub.

Joyce's literary artistry shows itself in the general image of the bar as a cave of primitive bigotry and in the counterpoint of vernacular brutality and literatesque flatulence. Though the reader may feel comfortably removed from the sneering narrator, it is worthwhile noting that though he may seem morally and socially uncouth, he is undeniably a superb master of language: we may not like what he does with it, but he does it with a rare skill. What we have, of course, is Joyce's literary version of oral narrative, but only a writer who perceived and admired the brilliance of the speech could have reproduced its power in print.

In 1923, the year after the publication of *Ulysses*, the actor Gabriel Fallon entered the Abbey Theatre and heard 'some of the richest Dublin dialogue I had ever heard, at least on the stage of the Abbey Theatre. It was spoken by F. J. McCormick with the proud consciousness of origin that marks the true-born Dubliner.'[38] *The Shadow of a Gunman* was in rehearsal, and Irish audiences were about to be introduced to a dramatic version of the language and linguistic culture of the tenements. It was not the first Abbey play to be set in the Dublin slums—A. P. Wilson's *The Slough* had been produced in 1914[39]—but it was the first by a playwright who had intimate experience of the characters and conditions involved. O'Casey's Dublin trilogy is discussed in detail in later chapters, but before concentrating on O'Casey, it is helpful to see what a later dramatist made of the speech of the Dublin poor.

Brendan Behan was born on February 23, 1923, about a month before *The Shadow of a Gunman* went into rehearsal. He grew up in Russell Street, off the North Circular Road, in a tenement house owned by his paternal grandmother. Though, like his idol O'Casey, he identified himself with the tenement-dwellers, he was not, again like O'Casey, *of* the tenements. His maternal grandfather had been a prosperous grocer with two shops of his own, but these had been lost by the time he died in 1897; his paternal grandfather had been a foreman painter. However, middle-class comfort was a distant memory by the time Brendan was born, and, despite the fact that they lived rent-free and that his father was a tradesman painter, the Behans were what could only be described as poor. What distinguished the Behans from their neighbours was their culture. Brendan's father was extremely well read and claimed to have studied at a seminary. One of his maternal uncles was a prominent writer of Nationalist ballads and songs, including the Irish national anthem, and had worked as property man in the Abbey; another was P. J. Bourke, melodramatist, actor, and manager of the Queen's Theatre.

From infancy Behan was adored by his paternal grandmother, who introduced the child to the irresistible mixture of alcohol and the rich and racy conversation of her cronies. Behan never lost his love for the pub talk of elderly people, some of whom had been themselves or had had family in the Boer and Great Wars, and part of the reason was that the linguistic culture of these people was that of the old oral tradition; in turn, he became the greatest oral performer of the century in a city not short on competition. His writings, especially his journalism, teem with loquacious *oul' wans* whose only amusement was recounting and reliving the hilarious adventures of the locals in an outrageously imaginative language that was larded with songs, proverbs, traditional witticisms, and quotations. Behan's plays, most obviously his play for radio, *The Big House*, are indebted to his command of the older city speech, but seldom has an individual talent exploited an oral tradition as spectacularly as he did in his autobiographical novel, *Borstal Boy*.

From an early age Behan was a noted raconteur in the working-class Dublin tradition; in *Borstal Boy* he uses his literary skills to create the illusion of an oral narrative, and no reader can read the printed words without hearing the voice of young Brendan as he reenacts his adventures. Even a casual inspection reveals the linguistic skill beneath the apparently spontaneous delivery. Snobbery should not prevent the reader from recognising that this is essentially the same tradition as produced *The Iliad*. Take, for example, the moment when young Brendan, in Walton Gaol, Liverpool, prepares himself to launch a preemptive strike against a bully called James:

I was no country Paddy from the middle of the Bog of Allen to be frightened to death by a lot of Liverpool seldom-fed bastards, nor was I one of your wrap-the-green-flag-round-me junior Civil Servants that came into the IRA [Irish Republican Army] from the Gaelic League, and well ready to die for their country any day of the week, purity in their hearts, truth on their lips, for the glory of God and the honour of Ireland. No, be Jesus, I was from Russell Street, North Circular Road, Dublin, from the Northside, where, be Jesus, the likes of Dale wouldn't make a dinner for them, where the whole of this pack of Limeys would be scruff-hounds, would be et, bet, and threw up again—et without salt. I'll James you, you bastard.[40]

The frightened young warrior prepares himself psychologically for the coming battle, defining himself, first of all, in terms of what he is not and then *crescendo* by what he is and where he comes from; then he raises his passions by hurling verbal abuse at his enemy in what linguists call a 'flyting.'[41] Rhythm is at least as important as rationality, and the dominant rhythm is the same dactyl that powered Homer's verse. There is much here that does not make rational sense, but the emotional meaning is clear. This extract is typical in that it is characterised by inherited formulas and references. 'Wrap the Green Flag Round Me' was a popular revolutionary ballad; 'purity in their hearts, truth on their lips' was part of the motto of the Fianna, the warriors of ancient Ireland; 'for the glory of God and the honour of Ireland' is quoted from the Declaration of the Republic in 1916; 'wouldn't make a dinner for them' and 'et, bet, and threw up again' were popular working-class expressions. Typical of the oral performance, little is invented; the skill of the performer is in weaving together a brilliant texture of popular threads, reminding us that the original meaning of 'rhapsodize' was to stitch songs together.[42]

Behan's achievement is all the more remarkable because it was published as late as 1958 and written by one whose first piece of fiction appeared in 1936, when he was only thirteen. No Dublin writer since Behan has developed a literary style so rich in the technical virtuosity associated with oral culture, and that is partly because the old centre city working class ceased in 1930s to be the socially sealed unit it had been till then. Native governments set about clearing the slums and moving the inhabitants out into new suburbs: the Behans left for Crumlin in 1937. This diaspora and the increasing influence of education, literacy, newspapers, radio, film, television, and travel inevitably led to a dissipation of the old structures and the evolution of a new style that, though still bearing traces of orality, was much closer to the international English of the global village. Behan was lucky that Joyce and O'Casey had established the prestige not only of Dublin writing but also of working-class speech. He was also lucky that his early jaunts with his grandmother had given him a love for the old life that he never lost and a talent for the old talk that he could translate into print. Though forty-three years younger than O'Casey, his ear had been tuned among those who had been O'Casey's contemporaries and whose world was very close to the world of Hilljoy Square.

NOTES

1. Mary E. Daly, *Dublin, the Deposed Capital, a Social and Economic History* (Cork: Cork UP, 1984), 3.

2. Emmet Larkin, *James Larkin: Irish Labour Leader 1876–1947* (London: Routledge and Kegan Paul, 1965), 41.

3. Deirdre Henchy, 'Dublin in the Age of O'Casey: 1880–1910,' in *Essays on Sean O'Casey's Autobiographies*, ed. Robert Lowery (London: Macmillan, 1981), 36.

4. Larkin, 42.

5. C. S. Andrews, *Dublin Made Me* (Cork: Mercier Press, 1979), 14–16. In *Juno and the Paycock,* when Jack Boyles learns that he is to inherit money, he immediately orders his children to 'keep yourselves to yourselves for the future.'

6. Ibid., 32.

7. Ibid., 13.

8. Ibid., 22.

9. Larkin, 43f.

10. Henchy, 42.

11. Daly, 322.

12. Ibid., 127.

13. Ibid., 128.

14. Ibid., 135.

15. Martin B. Margulies, *The Early Life of Sean O'Casey* (Dublin: Dolmen Press, 1970), 14.

16. Daly, 136.

17. Andrews, 59.

18. Henchy, 60.

19. Andrews, 12.

20. See, for example, R. S. Scholfield, 'The Measurement of Literacy in Pre-Industrial England,' in *Literacy in Traditional Societies*, ed. Jack Goody (Cambridge: Cambridge UP, 1968).

21. Ibid., 312f.

22. Ong, 11.

23. Máirtín Ó Cadhain, *The Road to Brightcity*, trans. Eoghan Ó Tuairisc (Dublin: Poolbeg, 1981), 10.

24. See Ong, Chapter 3, on the 'psychodynamics of orality.'

25. See Ong, 22–24.

26. Alan J. Bliss, 'The Emergence of Modern English Dialects in Ireland,' in *The English Language in Ireland*, ed. Diarmuid Ó Muirithe (Dublin: Mercier Press, 1977), 17f.

27. James Stephens, *The Charwoman's Daughter*, with an introduction by Augustine Martin (Dublin: Gill and Macmillan, 1972), 12.

28. Ibid., 16.

29. Joseph Holloway, *Joseph Holloway's Abbey Theatre*, ed. Robert Hogan and Michael J. O'Neill (Carbondale: Southern Illinois UP, 1967), 233. Perhaps the most convincingly horrifying fictional account of slum tenement life is Paul Smith's *The Countrywoman* (London: Heinemann, 1962). Though set around the year 1920, fifteen years before the author's birth, and published when most of the tenements had disappeared, the novel obviously draws on personal experience in presenting the chaos of slum life and the language of the inhabitants. The controlling narrative is that of one who, like the author, escaped the slums and became a novelist and dramatist.

30. William Carleton, *Traits and Stories of the Irish Peasantry*, with a foreword by Barbara Hayley, 2 vols. (Gerrards Cross: Colin Smythe, 1990), xvii. Of his father, Carleton wrote: 'In fact his memory was a perfect storehouse, and a rich one, of all that the social antiquary, the man of letters, the poet, or the musician, would consider valuable' (viii).

31. See Mary Helen Thuente, *W. B. Yeats and Irish Folklore* (Dublin: Gill and Macmillan, 1980).

32. J. M. Synge, *Collected Works*, vol. 4, ed. Ann Saddlemyer (London: Oxford UP, 1968), 53f.

33. See, for example, Stanislaus Joyce, *My Brother's Keeper* (New York: Viking Press, 1958), 54.

34. James Joyce, *Dubliners* (Harmondsworth: Penguin Books, 1992), 98.

35. Weldon Thornton, *Allusions in Ulysses* (Chapel Hill: U of North Carolina P, 1968), 276.

36. Some might find this claim excessive simply because the speaker does not have an educated accent; nobody doubts that Shakespeare plays the same game with 'the Troyans' trumpet' when Cressida arrives at the Greek camp in *Troilus and Cressida*, IV, v, 64.

37. James Joyce, *Ulysses* (Harmondsworth: Penguin Books, 1992), 414.

38. Fallon, 5.

39. See discussion in Chapter 3.

40. Brendan Behan, *Borstal Boy* (London: Hutchinson, 1958), 81.

41. See Ong, 44.

42. Ibid., 59f.

Chapter 2

John/Johnny/Jack/Seaghan/ Seán/Sean

As readers of *Finnegans Wake* know well, in the General Election of April 1880, John Joyce, father-to-be of James, campaigned successfully for the Liberals and helped defeat the two sitting Conservatives, one of whom was Sir Arthur E. Guinness.

We went out soon after and had a thanksgiving meeting in the Rotunda Bar. I was cock of the walk that day and I will never forget it; I was complimented by everybody. I got one hundred guineas from each of the members. My God it was three o'clock in the morning and the excitement was great and I was the hero of it all because they said that it was I that won the election. By God Almighty, such drinking of champagne I never saw in my life! We could not wait to draw the corks, we slapped them against the marble-topped counter. The result was we were there drinking for about three hours and when we came out the question was what were we to do with ourselves at that ungodly hour of the morning. The Turkish Baths came into my mind and there I went after having any God's quantity of champagne. O dear, dear, God, those were great times.[1]

A few days before John Joyce's moment of glory—and not far from the Rotunda Bar—John Casey was born in Upper Dorset Street, the last child of Michael and Susan Casey. Though he would always identify himself with the tenement poor, the circumstances into which John was born were distinctly lower-middle-class. As a clerk for the [Protestant] Society for Church Missions, Michael Casey earned almost six pounds a month or about double the average wage of a manual labourer.[2] (John Joyce could never serve as a dependable measure, but it may be noted in passing that the gifts he received were the equivalent of three times a clerk's and six times a labourer's annual income.)

John Casey's early years were relatively comfortable: though lacking many of the physical comforts that young James Joyce took for granted, he enjoyed, and would have been aware of enjoying, a standard of living far ahead of that of the majority of the population of Dublin, the lower or working class. The Caseys were not merely middle-class by virtue of their father's income; they were Protestants and saw themselves as distinct from, and superior to, the Catholic majority among whom they lived. In the sectarian conditions of the time it was much easier for Protestants to get and stay ahead, for they were more acceptable to employers than Catholics.[3] The Dorset Street house in which John was born was a large house of at least three storeys in which Michael Casey was 'the sole listed tenant and rate-payer,' letting out rooms on behalf of the landlord. The ethos of the family was middle-class: the Caseys were acutely conscious of their own dignity, respectability, propriety, and providence and equally conscious of their position on the middle rungs of society. They lived in a comfort and cleanliness that were noted by those who visited them, and they were never short. It was a cultured household where the parents placed a high value on education and literature. They had their own furniture, including, at one stage, a piano, and Mrs. Casey delighted in flowers, a passion that her youngest son inherited and one that may have partly inspired his unlikely dream of becoming a painter.[4]

Michael Casey was regarded in the neighbourhood as a scholar, a mark of high respect for his exceptional proficiency in reading and writing. At the time of his marriage he was a clerk, and shortly afterward he began earning extra money as a teacher at the night school run by the Society for Church Missions; he must have impressed his employers because within a few weeks he was working as a clerk in their central office.[5] He had his own little library, which, though dominated by books on theology and religious history, also permitted Shakespeare, Scott, Dickens, Pope, Milton, and Keats.[6] How great an influence Michael had on his youngest son, who was only six when his father died, is difficult to gauge: there is no recognisable version of him in the plays, and the figure in the *Autobiographies* is dimly felt, a scholarly cripple doomed to inactivity and an early death due to a fall. The father's influence would have been felt most by the eldest child, Bella, who was nineteen when he died in 1886.

Bella (b. 1865) was sent to the fee-paying Central Model Schools in Marlborough Street, graduated with honours in four subjects, including French, and was 'an accomplished pianist.' She then went on to spend two years in Marlborough Street Teacher Training College, and in 1885 she was appointed to St. Mary's Infant School, Mountjoy Street, where she lived in an attached two-room flat.[7] To young Johnny, fifteen years her junior, Bella must have seemed like another and even more attractive mother: successfully studious and accomplished in 'high' culture and the arts, she was bound to realise the upward aspirations of the Caseys. Johnny was among her pupils at St. Mary's, and it was noted that his attendance improved and that his achievements in reading, spelling, and arithmetic were satisfactory.

Mick (b. 1866), Tom (b. 1869), and Isaac Casey (b. 1873) also attended the Model Schools. Mick and Tom graduated, perhaps with the help of extra tuition, and may have trained briefly for careers in teaching, but they lacked ambition and settled for easier lives in the Post Office. Isaac did not graduate: his academic career ended with the death of his father in 1886. For all that O'Casey has left us an image of his mother as proud and powerful, it seems that the death of the father had a profoundly unsettling effect on the family.

Three years previously, when Bella moved into her school flat, the rest of the family left Dorset Street for 9 Inishfallen Parade, a neat, two-storey house nearby. Perhaps this is evidence of economic belt-tightening as a consequence of the fall that crippled Michael Casey, but, whatever about his moral and cultural presence, the loss of his income should not have proved disastrous: the oldest sons, Michael and Tom, were in secure jobs with only their mother and Isaac and Johnny to support.[8] But in 1887 Michael and Tom enlisted in the army, a step down the social ladder for them and a double blow to their snobbish and widowed mother. Another blow followed in 1889, when Bella married a soldier. Susan Casey refused to attend the wedding but was willing to move with Isaac and Johnny into Bella's two-room school-flat. In 1890 Bella, now pregnant, gave up her job and the flat and moved, with Susan, Isaac, and Johnny, to 25 Hawthorne Terrace in East Wall, a move down the social scale but not traumatic: they had the three-room cottage to themselves, and Susan Casey kept it neat and clean and very respectable.

In 1893 Bella left to live with her husband, and the following year young Johnny was sent out to work. This must have disappointed his mother, who had seen his sister and brothers into 'higher' education. It is impossible to know for sure why Johnny was not allowed to continue at school. Maybe the money was not available or too scarce to spend on a child with severe eye problems; maybe the behaviour of the older children had made education seem more a luxury than an investment.

The next move, in 1897, was to 18 Abercorn Road, nearer the docks, another step down on the social scale but still respectable. Shortly afterward the screws of poverty began to tighten. Young Johnny was neither a consistent nor a committed worker. Then Isaac, who had seemed the steadiest, announced that he was going to marry a Catholic, appalling his mother, who once again boycotted one of her children's nuptials. Mick and Tom were recalled to the army for the Boer War, leaving only Susan and her darling Johnny; Susan was forced to take in washing for sixpence a week and a glass of porter.[9] The return of Tom to employment was only a temporary relief: in 1903 he too married a Catholic, and his mother marked the event in her customary way. In the same year Johnny, well read, of middle-class Protestant stock, seemed to dash any hopes of a recovery in the family fortunes by becoming a labourer on the Great Northern Railway (where he remained until dismissed in 1911).

In 1905 the family was again knocked back when Bella's husband was committed to the Richmond District Lunatic Asylum. This led to a crucial development: Bella and her five children moved across the social Rubicon into a tenement in Fitzgibbon Street, where she survived by scrubbing floors.[10] She lasted there until 1907, when, on the death of her husband, she and the children crowded into Abercorn Road, making an extended family of four adults and five children in the cottage. Now the Caseys experienced the crowding, if not the hunger and deprivation, of the slums. This situation lasted for a few months, and then Bella and the children moved out of the house and almost out of O'Casey's range of sympathy.

In 1914 Tom died of peritonitis. In 1915 Mick reenlisted in the army, and this left the household depending on Johnny, who was now Seán Ó Cathasaigh to his intellectual friends. In January 1918 Bella died, and her death had an enormous effect on O'Casey. In November 1918 Susan Casey died, and with her went any semblance of the family that had begun in Upper Dorset Street. It was time for Johnny to leave the nest and fend for himself, and this he eventually did late in 1920 at the age of forty. At that stage he was living with his brother Mick in increasingly unacceptable discord. There were many differences between the brothers: Mick was a loyal Tommy, and Seán was an Irish-speaking socialist agitator; Mick was an easygoing, companionable boozer, and Seán was a cantankerous abstainer with a history of taking offence; Mick had the security of his army pension and, now that their mother was dead, may have commented on the relative contributions of the two brothers to the household then and previously.[11] Whatever the cause of the war, the consequence was that late in 1920 O'Casey moved to a tenement room in Mountjoy Square and worked as a janitor in the Old Foresters' Hall in nearby Langrishe Place, Summerhill.

The house in Mountjoy Square was a tenement in the strict sense of rented accommodation, but it was very different from the tenement house in which O'Casey had been born. Mícheál Ó Maoláin, an old friend from the days of Larkin and the Citizen Army, sublet part of his room to O'Casey. In his account of the time he and O'Casey were together, Ó Maoláin makes no reference to the condition of the house, which suggests that it was not as bad as many of the slum tenements.[12] Nor does anything in *The Shadow of a Gunman* suggest that the circumstances were particularly squalid or impoverished. Yet this was as close as O'Casey ever came to experiencing the slum tenements firsthand.

O'Casey's treatment of Bella and her life in the *Autobiographies* is very interesting. With a super-Joycean honesty he describes the hatred he felt for Bella and her brood, whose hungry eyes pricked his conscience and whose bodies crammed the limited living space:

At times, a surge of hatred swept through him against those scarecrow figures asleep at his feet, for they were in his way, and hampered all he strove to do, and a venomous dislike of [Bella] charged his heart when he realised that for the romance of a crimson coat, a mean strip of gold braid, and corded tassels of blue, yellow, and green, she had brought him, herself, and all of them to this repulsive and confused condition.[13]

As Garry O'Connor noticed, the *Autobiographies* give the impression that Bella died at least ten years earlier than the actual date of her death in 1918. O'Connor suggests that perhaps O'Casey the autobiographer felt that 1918 was sufficiently supplied with important developments: his own emergence as a pamphleteer and the death of the most substantial figure of the early life, his mother.[14] But perhaps O'Casey's thinking was not quite so concerned with the distribution of material; perhaps, in his own mind, Bella had 'died' in some sense when the appalling consequences of her marriage became clear, especially when Beaver, her husband, was committed in 1905 and died in 1907. O'Casey's version of the marriage was tinged with the prejudice of brotherly feeling:

She had married a man who had destroyed every struggling gift she had had when her heart was young and her careless mind was blooming. He had given her, with God's help, a child for every year, or less, that they had been together . . . . Ah! faded into the forgotten past were the recitations of bits from Racine's *Andromaque* and *Iphigenie*, or from Scott's *Lady of the Lake*, the confident playing of waltz, schottishe, polka, and gavotte on a piano in a friend's house . . . . Now she went about everything like a near-drowned fly in a jar of water.[15]

Bella had died in the sense that she lost the life of refined culture and became a victim of the living death of hopeless poverty, drinking from jam-jars in a home of rags, bones, and bottles. The widowed Bella who took her children to Abercorn Road in 1907 was not the cultured young lady who had once dazzled her baby brother with her arts and accomplishments. Her social or spiritual 'death' was, if only in retrospect, the knell of the family that Michael and Susan Casey had created. Michael Casey had died when Sean was too young to suspect the full implications; Susan had lived into a ripe old age, sharing so much of her youngest son's early life that she seemed a part of it rather than a separate individual. Apart from Bella and Sean, none of the children inherited anything of the pride and ambition that characterised Michael and Susan in their different ways: the others were content with the security of easy jobs and the excitement offered by the army or the pub or amateur theatricals. If they, in O'Casey's eyes, fell from grace, the fall was gradual and without any great discomposure; but Bella's fall was almost primal in its catastrophic clarity. She was in the paradise of promise, the world of elegant accomplishments at her fingertips, when she was attracted to a good-looking young man in a uniform. O'Casey could never understand why; it was as if his childish sense of being betrayed by an adored sister for a stranger never lost its sting. The fingers that had flicked through French books, danced along piano keys, and directed the eyes of her pupils toward the light of knowledge—those same fingers were now scrubbing floors. Worse still, she wore white gloves, unable to abandon absolutely the sense that she was made for better things. Her fall had its pathetic side: even on her knees, she had hopes that her children would rise again, and her neighbours mocked her aspirations by referring to her as 'the Duchess.' But O'Casey was more aware of the grotesque tragedy of a soul that had once flown but had eventually fallen 'like a near-drowned fly in a jar full of water'—and all, as the writer of the *Autobiographies* pointed out with detailed cruelty, for a nobody dressed up as a soldier, a drummer boy who beat her into submission and squalor before he himself went mad. When Bella and her brood moved into Abercorn Road, O'Casey resented her claims on his own resources. He allowed Bella's youngest son, John, access to his precious books until he accused him of stealing a volume. (O'Casey was wrong; he was judging young John by his own youthful standards.) Books were the only way out of the physical and mental poverty trap; Uncle Jack was acutely aware of that, but he himself was still too close to the mire of poverty to suffer the loss of even one of his precious keys to freedom.[16]

O'Casey told Gabriel Fallon that his mother had taught him to read at an early age; he told Lady Gregory that he did not learn until he was sixteen. School records note that he achieved honours level in reading between the ages of eight and eleven; he himself later claimed that he had fooled the examiners by reciting the passages by heart.

Perhaps there is truth in all these statements: sight-reading would have been a major problem for the half-blind child, and there is evidence that young Johnny possessed remarkable ability to memorise passages that were only read to him once.[17]

The incontrovertible facts are that he grew up in a house in which great importance was attached to literature, inherited a love of literature, and became a great writer. Given the problems with his eyes, it was inevitable that his sense of literature would initially have been predominantly aural and oral; though her secular reading did not go beyond Dickens, his mother read the Bible for him so effectively that he memorised a considerable amount and never lost his delight in the sonority of the Authorized Version. A few days before he died, the almost blind O'Casey was still quoting the Bible and remembering its importance during his early years:

I wasn't able to read at the age of seven, because of my eyes, but like all children I could repeat anything if I heard it several times. The Bible was the important book in our house, and full of fine stories and mysterious words for a curious kid to imitate. I liked the sound of the words long before I knew what they meant, and it gave me a feeling of power to spout them in the house and in front of the other kids.[18]

His first public performances were in St. Barnabas' Church, where he was a constant volunteer when it came to leading the final prayer. A less than fervent admirer remembered him.

He sat behind us and we were afraid to turn around and look, but soon we heard his voice ringing out loud and clear, in that drawling, lilting way he had of speaking. He didn't read from the prayer-book as the others did, he just made up his prayer as he went along, using some biblical passages but mostly his own words about the glory of God. As I said, at the time my sister and I joked about how he would go on and on with it, but we were silly little girls then, and when I think of it all now it comes back to me as something very moving and beautiful. He would have made a great preacher.[19]

Here we have a rhapsody in which the oral performer weaves a text by stitching remembered quotations together with a fervent copiousness and a sense of sound and rhythm that must have seemed excessive to the more literate members of the congregation but that allowed him to relish the thrill of hieratic power.

As he grew older and managed to steal, buy, beg, or borrow books, Johnny read with the omnivorousness of one who had been for long denied a commodity he had always been led to prize above all others. Whatever he read became part of himself, as the Bible had become. Reading offered an escape, imaginative or economic, from the surrounding poverty trap, of which he became increasingly aware as he grew up. When he begrudged his nephew a single book, he was revealing his own desperate need to survive at all costs.

How else could young John escape the fate that had overtaken his mother and might still overtake his Uncle Jack? What of those who were even worse off than Bella and her children, those who had never even come into contact with a life higher than that afforded by the slums? What of those who had not even acquired the desire for a better life, who had come to accept their poverty and deprivation as natural and inevitable? Was there any hope for them? For the third of the population who lived below the poverty level and who spent three-quarters of their income on food and rent, there could be no 'higher' education and consequently no escape from the poverty trap.[20] They were trapped in their own wretched rooms, counting themselves lucky when they had adequate food, shelter, and clothing; for them the comfortable lives of lawyers and doctors must have seemed as remote as those of kings and queens. Before Jim Larkin, the fate of the poor did not figure in any political agenda: it was as if politicians, believing that the poor would always be with them, left them to the kind attentions and best efforts of charitable organisations.

Between 1900 and 1903 O'Casey was a committed member of his church and taught Sunday school, but when he failed to reconcile his religious beliefs with his emerging political passions, his Anglicanism gave way. The vacuum created by the fall of Parnell had been filled by many movements dedicated to the establishment of a distinctly Irish culture. O'Casey became involved in almost all the most important and invariably found himself at odds with the leadership and obliged to resign.

In the early years of the century O'Casey joined the Gaelic League, dedicated to the revival of the native language in Ireland, and became Seán Ó Cathasaigh: he learned to speak Irish fluently and taught Irish to other members of the Gaelic League while at the same time teaching Sunday school for the rector of St. Barnabas. He also played hurling and the bagpipes, bringing to both the same energetic lack of ability, and, no matter what the organisation, he always came to the fore as a natural organiser and secretary. At Gaelic League meetings he began to emerge as a political preacher: 'He speaks first, and very fluently and eloquently in Irish, then launches out into a violent Republican oration in English, stark and forceful, biblical in diction with gorgeous tints of rhetoric.'[21] His enthusiasm was noted by the Irish Republican Brotherhood (IRB), the successors to the Fenians, who were dedicated to achieving an independent Ireland by whatever means necessary. Around 1903 he was inducted into the IRB and became one of many who combined the nonpolitical League with the militant IRB. He sought recruits for both movements and, among other projects, campaigned to have the Church of Ireland make more use of the Irish language in its services.[22] Among those he recruited for the IRB was a young northern Protestant, Ernest Blythe, later to become minister for finance and, later still, managing director of the Abbey Theatre. Blythe was involved in O'Casey's efforts to Gaelicise the Church of Ireland, even though Blythe was uncomfortable with O'Casey's 'high' preference for the kind of ritual that 'low' Protestants associate with Catholicism.[23]

Between 1903 and 1911 O'Casey worked as a labourer for the Great Northern Railway. 'Irish Jack' was an unusual navvy: he was much better read and more culturally aware than his fellow workers and made no secret of his involvement with the Gaelic League and related organisations. In 1907/1908 he had met Frank Cahill, a teacher in the local Christian Brothers School and a raconteur whose stories would resurface later in O'Casey's plays. Cahill introduced O'Casey to the St. Laurence O'Toole Club, one of many clubs founded at the time to provide a culturally and ideologically suitable social life for Nationalists, many of whom would also be members of the Gaelic League, the Gaelic Athletic Association, and the IRB.[24] O'Casey found the atmosphere very congenial and was generally admired for his organisational zeal and his contributions to discussions, both serious and lighthearted, for he was a good comedian with a gift for mimicry and always ready with a song or poem. Some of his first writings were published in the club's manuscript journal.[25]

Blythe has left an interesting account of the Drumcondra Branch of the Gaelic League, where O'Casey did more than teach Irish.

On the first Sunday of the month the manuscript journal of the branch was read out and a regular feature was the comic short story written by Sean O'Casey. If it hadn't been for the short story, half the people would not have come to the reading. The central character of the series of stories was a supposed brother of the author whose name was Adolphus O'Casey. Poor Adolphus was forever climbing up the social ladder and getting friendly with people far more refined than himself. Normally Adolphus would be getting on fine and earning the respect of his rich friends when some accident would occur which would reveal the kind of man he really was; either that or he would make some gaffe that would disgust the swells just when they were about to grant him permission to marry their daughter. The short stories would leave everybody in stitches and wanting to hear more. Maybe the reason why we never suspected we had a future great writer in our midst was because all the stories were written with a branch of the Gaelic League in mind, that they were, so to speak, pieces of propaganda designed to assist the League's campaign against pro-Britishism. I don't believe it ever occurred to Sean at that time that he would ever become a famous writer. He had a fearlessly independent mind: but I never found any evidence to suggest that he thought of himself as exceptionally talented. Sean had no interest then in the theatre. Or if he did, he hid it from me. I often asked him to come with me to a play but he never came.[26]

There was no reason why O'Casey should keep any interest in theatre a secret from a close friend who was a regular theatregoer. Nor could even such a close friend have realised that the creator of Adolphus O'Casey would leave the Gaelic League because he considered it too snobbish, too concerned with maintaining bourgeois stability, and consequently unwilling to contemplate a genuine revolution that would demand social justice for the poor.

Almost inevitably, O'Casey's first printed piece was in a Nationalist periodical and was controversial in tone: this was an article on the subject of education in *The Peasant and Irish Ireland*, May 25, 1907, signed *An Gall Fada*, 'the lanky Protestant/foreigner.' It is rhetorical in the sense that it is more like the text of a speech than a piece of discursive prose or, in other words, shaped by a sense of sound rather than an abstract theorem. For the rest of his life he could never resist the attractions of controversy. He loved to embroil himself in disputes, and his method always owed more to street flytings than to the conventional essay, so much so that his opponents would frequently claim to find O'Casey's tirades incomprehensible and ask him to reply to their points rather than indulge his own fantasies. The style he evolved was so exuberantly dramatic, detailed, and allusive, so apparently intimate, spontaneous, and careless of the conventions of literary debate, that Orwell, for example, described the *Autobiographies* as written in 'a sort of basic Joyce, sometimes effective in a humorous aside, but . . . hopeless for narrative purposes.'[27]

The predominant tone of his first outing is that of a preacher, but the religious mode is undercut by Nationalist irony:

The Englishman, in the shape of the British Government, has lifted up his hands to bless us: yea, and we shall be blessed. Now shall the winter of our discontent be made glorious summer by this illustrious son of Britain . . . . Now can the Irish shout with a loud voice; now can they seriously break into solemn and joyous anthem of victory; now can they cast their caps into the air and cry with a deep and unanimous shout hallelujah, hallelujah![28]

Birrell, the chief secretary for Ireland, had admitted that the schools of Ireland were in a disgraceful condition and promised improvements, including the teaching of Irish in ways that, he hoped, would not antagonize the Gaelic League. O'Casey's reaction is to rhapsodize his utter contempt for any such statements of British benevolence. His next piece, in the same paper on July 6, was essentially a scheme to improve the efficiency of the Gaelic League in Dublin: here the zealous organizer took over from the mocking preacher, and the tone was quite restrained, if passionate. He finished with a plea: 'Let the Dublin Leaguers impartially judge this scheme of one whose strongest prayer and hope is for Ireland's regeneration.'[29]

When O'Casey was dismissed by the Great Northern Railway in December 1911, he had ampler opportunity to commit his thoughts to paper. Larkin's *Irish Worker* was the first Irish newspaper written for, and in the interest of, the working class, and between 1912 and 1914 O'Casey contributed 62 articles, including poems and songs, three translations from the Irish, press releases from various groups, and a regular series of notes relating to the Irish Citizen Army.[30] Though he had curbed his style somewhat from the days of *An Gall Fada*, he was still, even by the standards of the time, unusually colourful and extravagant in his imagery and his rhythm; his prose had a strong oral dimension, and the speaking voice—intimate, ironic, allusive, dramatic—overrode the demands of any written standard. He took offence at some remarks by one columnist who signed himself 'Euchan' and challenged him to public debate. Euchan's view was insufficiently Nationalist for S. O Cathasaigh who proclaimed:

by the fame of our forefathers; by the murder of Red Hugh; by the anguished sighs of the Geraldine; by the blood-dripping wounds of Wolfe Tone; by the noble blood of Emmet; by the death-wasted bodies of the famine—that we will enter into our inheritance or we will fall one by one. Amen.[31]

He was once accused by an opponent of losing his logic 'amidst his flowers of rhetoric,' and it is not difficult to see why anybody would be unsettled by a correspondent who begins: 'Are you ready, "Euchan"? On guard, then!'[32]

James 'Big Jim' Larkin had made his name as a labour leader in England, Scotland, and Belfast before he went to Dublin in 1907 to organise the port workers. O'Casey liked to remember his conversion to Larkinism as instant and total, but, as with so many of O'Casey's 'memories,' this is a little wide of the mark. As late as February 1913, writing in the *Irish Worker*, he was still to the right of Larkin, still very much the IRB Gaelic Leaguer: 'The delivery of Ireland is not in the Labour Manifesto, good and salutary as it may be, but in the strength, beauty, nobility and imagination of the Gaelic ideal.' A year later, writing of previous efforts to unite all Irishmen in a common bond, his Nationalism was a thing of the past:

Have not greater men than those who prance the National Stage of Ireland now, tried and failed to unite all Irishmen in a common bond? Davis tried and failed; so did Mitchel, and even O'Connell displayed at his meetings, on his breast ribbons of orange and green. The Gaelic League was to bring about this blessed consummation, and so was the Sinn Fein movement, and where all these failed we are asked to believe the Volunteer movement will succeed! There can be no unity amongst men save the unity engendered by a common heritage of pain, oppression and wage-slavery . . . . Personally, I hold the workers are beside themselves with foolishness to support any movement that does not stand to make the workers supreme, for these are the people, and without them there can be no life or power.[33]

The main reason for this conversion was the Lock-Out of 1913.

The summer of 1913 was a period of strike, reprisal, anger, demonstration, police brutality against the workers on the streets and in their homes; winter brought poverty and starvation among the poor. O'Casey was not much use in the violent confrontations but, as secretary of the Women's and Children's Relief Fund, he worked from dawn till dusk in an effort to ease the agony of the workers and their families. He was also a founder member and secretary of the Irish Citizen Army, which was intended to protect the workers against the police. Eventually, he was to leave the Citizen Army when he felt it had lost its way by yielding too much of its socialist identity to the Nationalists, but the opportunity offered by Larkin, the Transport Union, and the Citizen Army would always remain for him the lost opportunity, the moment when revolutionary Ireland went astray, beguiled by the slogans of a Nationalism he saw as essentially bourgeois and hostile to the interests of the workers and, consequently, to the true interests of Ireland. He, like Larkin, had done his best to lead the people in the right direction. Larkin was a brilliant orator who inspired hope and direction in Dublin's poor.

Here was the word En-Masse, not handed down from Heaven, but handed up from a man. In this voice was the march of Wat Tyler's men, the yells and grunts of those who took the Bastille, the sigh of the famine-stricken, the last shouts from those, all bloodied over, who fell in Ninety-eight on the corn slopes of Royal Meath.[34]

Despite the leadership of this Prometheus, the war for the working class had been lost. In the official history of the new state the Lock-Out of 1913 was of secondary importance, but O'Casey was among the handful of socialists who were convinced that the Nationalist victory had been a political disaster and would effect no real change, that the working class had been deluded into supporting a struggle that would leave them worse off than they had been beforehand. The opportunity for a real revolution had come in 1913 and had been missed.

In November 1913 the IRB established the Irish Volunteers in order to mobilise Irish Nationalists on a paramilitary level. This was a disaster for the Citizen Army, not only because the Volunteers attracted members away from the Citizen Army but, more damagingly still, because it subverted the idea of the Citizen Army as *the* revolutionary front of the Irish working class. O'Casey severed his remaining connections with the IRB. He understood the situation in terms of delusion and fantasy: the Nationalist leaders deluded the workers with their talk of liberation, and many of the workers fell for it. In January 1914 he wrote 'An Open Letter to the Workers in the Volunteers' in the *Irish Worker*.

Many of you have been tempted to join this much talked of movement by the wild impulse of genuine enthusiasm. You have again allowed yourselves to be led away by words—words—words . . . . Are you going to be satisfied with a crowd of chattering, well-fed aristocrats and commercial bugs coming in and going out of College Green?

In this and ensuing letters O'Casey examined and dismissed the claims of the Volunteer leaders to inherit the glorious tradition of Irish liberators and tried to show that the workers had been hypnotized and duped by the lies of their social superiors, who had no genuine concern for the working class: 'Workers, the leaders of this movement will try to cajole you with terms of Wolfe Tone and Mitchel whom they never knew, or did not understand.' Unless the workers awoke from the spell, they would be misled to their doom, failing to realise that 'it is good to die for one's friend, but foolish to die for one's enemy.'[35] All was in vain: on Easter Monday 1916, the Citizen Army made common cause with the Volunteers, and Larkin's successor, James Connolly, was executed and, shortly afterward, was popularly canonised as a saint of Irish Nationalism.

In the years that followed, O'Casey must have asked himself why things had gone as they had. Why had not Larkin and his supporters, including himself, succeeded in guiding the workers to a true sense of their own interests? The departure of Larkin for America in 1914 was not an adequate explanation. The fact was that the Nationalists had won the battle for the support of the majority of the revolutionaries despite being, in O'Casey's eyes, essentially middle-class in sympathy and aspiration and, consequently, hostile to interests of the working class. How had middle-class leaders won the battle for the hearts and minds of most working-class people?

There were some obvious reasons. The most powerful organisation in Ireland, the Catholic Church, was antisocialist: in September 1913 the *Irish Catholic* condemned the strikers as 'members of the very lowest and most degraded section of the unemployable class who came out from the slums attracted by plunder.'[36] In

Ireland, as in most countries at the time, the idea of a campaign 'to make the workers supreme' was too radical to win the workers or to woo the middle- and upper-class Nationalists away from the concept of a liberal democracy in which, mutatis mutandis, the structures of church and state would remain intact. Only by education could the workers come to see where their interests lay and how they might achieve a state in which they would no longer be the lower class. O'Casey's own education had not brought him straight to the truth: his road to socialism had been via Nationalism, and it had taken the trauma of 1913 to enable him to see that only true socialists like Larkin held the interests of the poor above all other considerations. Larkin knew the poor and could speak to and for them; but Larkin's words had not been strong enough to counteract those of the Nationalist leaders, such as Pearse.[37]

Pearse was a shy, religious, artistic man who was utterly dedicated to the Gaelic League and the de-Anglicization of Ireland. He was a poet and dramatist and also edited *An Claidheamh Soluis*, the organ of the League, until he retired to concentrate on running St. Enda's, the school he had founded in 1908. Pearse was a perceptive educator, and some who condemn his political activities still admire his efforts with the boys at St. Enda's. As late as June 1913 O'Casey helped Pearse with the publicity for a fund-raising fete at St. Enda's by writing to the *Irish Worker* and urging all to go and see Pearse's dramatic adaptation of a sequence from the Irish epic, *An Táin Bó Cuailgne*. He addressed his final remarks to Pearse himself: 'Our hopes are your hopes; your work shall be our work; we stand or fall together.'[38] Within the year O'Casey was denouncing Pearse as the worst of all the Volunteers because he had used the trams during the Lock-Out.[39] O'Casey must have known that he was not being totally fair to Pearse: Pearse had written with unusual insight into the plight of the tenement poor in Dublin, and, though he was not a great admirer of Larkin, he published his preference for Larkin against his capitalist opponent, William Martin Murphy.[40] But Pearse was an avowed Nationalist and would, like so many others, see separation from Britain as the necessary first step to all social progress.

Only in the last three years of his life did Pearse emerge as a prominent political activist, partly because he was the most eloquent spokesman for the idea of blood sacrifice. He believed that a new Ireland would be born out of the blood that he and like-minded patriots would shed, and his religious fervour led him to see patriotic self-sacrifice as an imitation of Christ, a form of martyrdom that, it was implied, would be rewarded in the next life. It was this aspect of Pearse's thought that O'Casey portrayed with such damning effect in Act Two of *The Plough and the Stars* as to be considered blasphemous by many in the audience. Though the idea of blood sacrifice may seem extreme in the West today, it is and always has been quite common in other cultures and was popular in Western Europe during the Great War. Bessie Burgess, the Protestant Unionist of *The Plough and the Stars*, holds views almost identical with those of Pearse, and, in fact, such sentiments found expression in the most unlikely mouths.

It is possible amongst your readers there are men and women who may, though thinking the rebellion an unwise one, cherish the ideals these men and women lived and died for, and it must be admitted that the most glorious thing that has happened during this carnival of blood-lust in Europe was the self-sacrifice and devotion of these men to a cause which they believed in.[41]

This was none other than Jim Larkin, then in America, giving his reaction to the 1916 Rising. He distinguishes between the 'carnival' of the Great War, in which working-class soldiers are duped by their officers to fight each other rather than the class system, and the 'glorious thing' that was the Easter Rising, in which, presumably, men and women freely chose to die for their ideals. From 1914 onward even Larkin had become increasingly Nationalistic.[42]

The majority of Irish people identified the struggle for self-improvement in terms of national movements: the Republicanism of the United Irishmen, O'Connell's constitutional crusades for Catholic Emancipation and the Repeal of the Union, the Nationalism of the Young Irelanders, the violent separatism of the Fenians, the parliamentary campaigns under Parnell and his successors for Home Rule, the Gaelic League's programme for cultural independence, the IRB plans for national independence, and so on. Of necessity, all these movements had been founded and directed by people who were middle-class: only those with some form of higher education could study developments outside Ireland and apply the results to Ireland. Larkin and Connolly, though of Irish descent, had grown up in Liverpool and Edinburgh, respectively, and this may have freed them from the most powerful ideological influence in Ireland, the oral tradition of Nationalism. The vast majority of Irish people, the less well-off, derived their Nationalism not from books and articles but from an oral tradition of poem and ballad, folklore and history and, more recently, melodrama. When, in the pieces from the *Irish Worker* quoted earlier, O'Casey referred to Red Hugh O'Donnell, Lord Edward Fitzgerald, Wolfe Tone, Robert Emmet, Daniel O'Connell, Thomas Davis, and John Mitchel, he could be absolutely certain that his readers (and even those illiterates for whom the pieces were read) would instantly understand the general references even if they had never read of these people in history books. An exceptionally strong oral tradition would have ensured that even the illiterate would be familiar with a version of Irish history that stressed the heroic continuity of *those who had died for Ireland* in the course of *700 hundred years of persecution*. Non-Irish people claim to be amazed at the extent to which contemporary Irish politics are attached to the past. This is at least partly due to the power of the oral tradition. Scholars use the term 'homoeostatic' to describe the manner in which members of an oral society have, by our standards, almost no sense of the past as separate from the present but live in a present that includes relevant memories of the past: life always is as it always was.[43] In popular Irish culture this facilitates the belief, for example, that the struggle for Irish freedom was always the same and that Brian Boru (d. 1014) and Patrick Pearse (d. 1916) would have shared the same national objectives. O'Casey certainly knew the power of poems and ballads: all his writings are littered with quotations, acknowledged and unacknowledged, and he himself achieved a certain fame as a balladeer.

A reading of the early plays would also indicate that O'Casey suspected another reason for the victory of the Nationalists over the socialists for the allegiance of the people. As I have already tried to show, the level of literacy in Ireland, where it existed at all, was very low by the standards of today. Very few working-class people, either urban or agricultural labourers, would have been capable of reading or writing complex material, and yet almost all of them would have been aware of the growing importance of literacy in the early twentieth century. Functional illiterates must have been increasingly aware of just how disadvantaged they were in a world increasingly dominated by newspapers, books, and bureaucratic files. Such people tended to put an extravagantly high value on the power of writing, which could, after all, change your life by getting you a clerical job, doubling your income, and enabling you to escape the squalor of the slums.

When a fully formed script of any sort . . . first makes its way from outside into a particular society, it does so necessarily at first in restricted sectors and with varying effects and implications. Writing is often regarded at first as an instrument of secret and magic power.[44]

To the very poor, beset by epidemics and unemployment, medical prescriptions and legal documents must have been much more than marks on paper, doctors and lawyers more than workingmen. Most of the Nationalist leaders were men of this superior class; a high percentage of politicians were lawyers. Pearse, for example, was a lawyer who wrote and spoke Irish and English, a schoolteacher who published poetry and prose in Irish and English. Viewed from the tenements (or the rural cabins), such men must have seemed of a higher race, and so they are represented in O'Casey's Abbey plays.

NOTES

1. See Richard Ellmann, *James Joyce,* new and rev. ed. (Oxford: Oxford UP, 1982), 17.

2. See Martin B. Margulies, *The Early Life of Sean O'Casey* (Dublin: Dolmen Press, 1970); Deirdre Henchy, 'Dublin in the Age of O'Casey: 1880–1910' in *Essays on Sean O'Casey's Autobiographies,* ed. Robert Lowery (London: Macmillan, 1981); Garry O'Connor, *Sean O'Casey* (London: Hodder and Stoughton, 1989), Chapter 1.

3. 'From childhood I was aware that there were two separate and immiscible kinds of citizens: the Catholics, of whom I was one, and the Protestants, who were as remote and different from us as if they had been blacks and we whites' (C. S. Andrews, *Dublin Made Me* [Cork: Mercier Press, 1979], 90). Dublin Catholics were also discriminated against by the Dublin United Tramway Company which had a policy of employing only country people as conductors and drivers (Andrews, 55).

4. See, for example, Garry O'Connor, 18f.

5. See Margulies, 12.

6. See Garry O'Connor, 16f.

7. See Hugh Hunt, *Sean O'Casey (*Dublin: Gill and Macmillan, 1980), 10.

8. O'Casey suggests that his elder brothers took advantage of the father's immobility by drinking and behaving in ways he would not have tolerated while healthy. See Sean O'Casey, *Autobiographies,* 2 vols. (London: Pan Books, 1980), I, 474.

9. Garry O'Connor, 36.

10. Margulies, 46ff.

11. In his *Autobiographies* (II, 31) O'Casey has a drunken Mick dismiss his literary ambitions as effete and pretentious.

12. See Mícheál Ó Maoláin, 'That Raid and What Went with It,' trans. Maureen Murphy, in *Essays on Sean O'Casey's Autobiographies*, ed. Robert Lowery (London: Macmillan, 1981), 103–122.

13. O'Casey, *Autobiographies*, I, 474.

14. Garry O'Connor, 104–106.

15. O'Casey, *Autobiographies*, I, 446f. There is an echo here of Stephen's anguish for his own sister in *Ulysses* (200). Part of O'Casey's anguish was transmuted into Mary Boyle, another young woman beguiled and brought down by a well-dressed fraud.

16. Margulies, 75f.

17. Hunt, 12.

18. E. H. Mikhail and John O'Riordan, eds., *The Sting and the Twinkle* (London: Macmillan, 1974), 156.

19. Quoted by Hunt, 21f.

20. Henchy, 38.

21. Desmond Ryan, *Remembering Sion* (London: Arthur Barker, 1934), 82.

22. See Margulies, 36ff.

23. See Earnán de Blaghd, *Trasna na Bóinne* (Áth Cliath: Sáirséal agus Dill, 1957), 105ff. O'Casey admitted reciting the rosary nightly, and Blythe expected him to convert to Catholicism (132).

24. Margulies, 49f. The parish in which O'Casey lived was, depending on whether you were a Protestant or a Catholic, St. Barnabas' or St. Laurence O'Toole's.

25. See Tom Buggy, 'Sean O'Casey's Dublin,' in *O'Casey Annual No. 1*, ed. Robert G. Lowery (Dublin: Gill and Macmillan, 1982), 95.

26. De Blaghd, 133, my translation.

27. Quoted by Bernard Benstock in 'Sean O'Casey as Wordsmith,' in Lowery, 233.

28. Reprinted in Sean O'Casey, *Feathers from the Green Crow*, ed. Robert Hogan (London: Macmillan, 1963), 2–6.

29. Ibid., 34.

30. See Robert G. Lowery, 'Sean O'Casey and the Irish Worker (with an index, 1911–14)' in *O'Casey Annual No. 3*, ed. Robert G. Lowery (London: Macmillan, 1984), 33–114.

31. O'Casey, *Feathers from the Green Crow*, 95.

32. Ibid., 90f.

33. Ibid., 95, 105, 107.

34. O'Casey, *Autobiographies,* I, 573.

35. O'Casey, *Feathers from the Green Crow*, 101f., 107.

36. Quoted by Mary E. Daly, *Dublin the Deposed Capital, a Social amd Economic History* (Cork: Cork UP, 1984), 115.

37. See, for example, Raymond J. Porter, 'O'Casey and Pearse,' in *Essays on Sean O'Casey's Autobiographies*, ed. Robert Lowery (London: Macmillan, 1981), 89–102.

38. Ibid., 94.

39. O'Casey, *Feathers from the Green Crow*, 107.

40. See Porter, 94ff.

41. *New York Herald*, May 22, 1916, quoted by Emmet Larkin, *James Larkin: Irish Labour Leader 1876–1947* (London: Routledge and Kegan Paul, 1965), 213f.

42. Larkin, 182f.

43. See, for example, Walter Ong, *Orality and Literacy: The Technologizing of the Word* (London: Methuen, 1982), 46ff.

44. Ong, 93. Literates should not feel superior: remember the awe we experienced when first hearing of the computer, word processing, and the Internet.

Chapter 3

O'Casey and the Theatre up to 1922

The whole tone of his letters is evidence of the spite which frustrated ambition engenders. In them is reflected the narrowmindedness, the shallowness and the pessimism which are the chief characteristics of the cynic and the sceptic.[1]

When he resigned from the Irish Citizen Army in July 1914, O'Casey seemed to have written himself out of Irish political life. In his own mind, he had remained loyal to Ireland and to socialism, but the majority of his former colleagues dismissed him as an embittered irrelevance, one of the 'Steps Committee' who stood outside Liberty Hall, mocking those who went in and came out.[2] He was utterly disillusioned. The 1913 Lock-Out had produced heroic resistance, but the opportunity for a socialist revolution had been lost, thanks mainly to the eclipse of the Citizen Army by the Irish Volunteers. In October 1914 Larkin left for America, where he would remain for almost a decade. The outbreak of the Great War made fundamental political debate almost impossible. Worse still, O'Casey knew that it would encourage those Nationalists who saw England's difficulty as Ireland's opportunity to stage an armed rebellion. Worst of all, perhaps, James Connolly, whose task was to protect the working class against such chicanery, was at least as ardent as the most enthusiastic IRB man in calling for rebellion.

O'Casey had ample time to nurse his grievances. The *Irish Worker* had ceased publication toward the end of 1914. He was unemployed and, as a prominent figure in the Lock-Out, unlikely to be employed. He was poor and in poor health: in August 1915 he was admitted to St. Vincent's Hospital for an operation on his neck. All he had was his pride and his reading. The extent of his ideological drift from his Gaelic League days is marked by his adoption of Shaw as his latest hero. He took no active part in the 1916 insurrection but was rounded up with other suspects and held for a night. After the surrender he helped a fellow member of the O'Toole Club smuggle rebels out of the city and into the relative safety of the countryside.[3]

   Unlike those friends and former comrades who were imprisoned or on the run,
O'Casey had to make a living, and it may have been this simple necessity as much
as anything else that directed him toward writing. In October 1917 he published a
pamphlet in memory of Thomas Ashe, an old friend and fellow piper who had been
fatally abused while imprisoned. The tone owes almost nothing to the literary
obituary or appreciation: O'Casey reenacts, rather than recounts, the fate of Thomas
Ashe. The mode is that of an Irish funeral oration or its antecedent, the *caoineadh,*
or traditional Irish lament in which the speaker frequently addresses both the dead
person and those responsible for his death:

Thomas Ashe, Thomas Ashe, take a last look at the Irish sky, for when these grim gates open
to let you forth, your strong body will be limp and helpless, your brave heart will faintly beat
in a final effort to live for the people, and your eyes will be too dim to see the kindly Irish
skies that have watched your life-long efforts to free your country and uplift her people. The
gate closes: Thomas Ashe is separated forever from his relatives, his friends, and the Irish
People—when once more they look upon him they find him dead![4]

An oration in print, intended to be read in the immediate aftermath of the appalling
event, it would have succeeded in moving the hearts of those at whom it was
directed.
   In April 1919 Maunsel & Co. published *The Story of the Irish Citizen Army,*
for which O'Casey was given fifteen pounds in advance. Even the publishers could
hardly have expected an objective account from a member of the 'Steps
Committee' who believed a great radical force had been wounded by the bourgeois
Volunteers and betrayed by its own leader, Connolly. The style is less emotional
than that of *The Story of Thomas Ashe* and is closer to the popular journalism of the
day. O'Casey moves awkwardly from the dramatic to the discursive and is at his
weakest when attempting a standard literary style. For example, when Captain
White arrives in Lucan to establish a company of the Irish Citizen Army, the
precious tone is hopelessly out of tune with the radical moments described:

After a very pleasant tea in a local restaurant, the Captain motored to a suitable place in the
vicinity of the village, and, standing on the car seat, waited a few moments while a shy and
obviously timorous crowd of about five hundred people gathered around the car, and
displayed a demeanour of such ominous quietude that plainly revealed to us that the Irish
Citizen Army had a long and energy exhausting struggle in front of it before the rural
workers would become sufficiently class-conscious to understand the elementary principles
of Labour thought and aspiration.[5]

O'Casey is much more effective when he gives rein to his own rhapsodic
tendencies, as in his description of Larkin appearing at a window in Liberty Hall
to announce the foundation of the Citizen Army. Occasionally, there is too much
'colour,' as when the 'Artist Sun had boldly brushed the sky with bold hues of
orange and crimson, and delicate shades of yellow and green, bordered with dusky
shadows of darkening blue, which seemed to symbolise . . .' But at times
O'Casey's rhapsodic instinct serves him rather well, as when there is prolonged
applause for Larkin, and then 'the lusty cheers died away to a droning echo, which

was followed for a few moments by a silence that was so strangely sincere that the mass of people resembled the upright figures of an assembly in the shady and silent regions of the dead.'[6] It is hardly surprising that O'Casey's inner eye was sharper than those external organs that troubled him all his life or that his literary instinct, shaped by his experience of the Bible, Shakespeare, Boucicault, and political oratory, was to regard the written word as a script to be performed in front of an imagined audience.

By 1917 O'Casey had met and fallen in love with Maura Keating. It was unusually late for a man to experience his first love, and O'Casey floundered, both in the physical affair and in verse. They went on walks together in the countryside around Dublin, and he wrote her songs to be sung to popular airs.

> The sweet wild-rose, the sweet wild-rose,
> that loved to see us there,
> And seemed to bid us hope, now droops
> and tells me to despair;
> The linnet sings his song unheard,
> perched on a leafy spray—
> Ah! my heart is filled with woe, with woe,
> Since Maggie went away.[7]

The years 1917 and 1918 were filled with songs, romantic songs to Maura and political satires of the kind he loved to sing himself at the Laurence O'Toole Club. In 1918 he published three collections, *Songs of the Wren Nos. 1 & 2*, and *More Songs of the Wren*. That same year saw the deaths of Bella and Susan Casey. The tortured affair with Maura continued until the end of 1919, but by then O'Casey had discovered what was to be the major passion of his life, writing plays. It might seem a radical change of direction for a man in his late thirties who had achieved a local reputation as a socialist pamphleteer and writer of popular songs, but the demand for socialist analysis had fallen with the rise of Sinn Fein, and the muse of his romantic verse had deserted him. And in many ways the theatre had been his first love, the dramatic his instinctive mode of expression.

O'Casey had grown up at a time when theatre as a form of popular entertainment was at its peak in Dublin.

During the last decade of the nineteenth century and the early years of the twentieth century, amateur drama was all the rage. Dublin bristled with dramatic societies, partly inspired by the greater frequency of visiting theatre companies from overseas, now made possible by improvements in rail and steamship services, partly by the growth and popularity of melodrama, notably the plays of Dion Boucicault and the patriotic dramas presented at the Queen's Theatre.[8]

This new passion swept through the O'Casey household, and Isaac in particular was stagestruck. He was a regular at the Queen's, and in 1891 he took his brother Johnny, then aged eleven, to see his first professional production, *The Shaughraun*. The standard fare at the Queen's was distinctly Nationalist. Boucicault's 'Irish' plays, while proposing a romantically comic conclusion of the Anglo-Irish problem, could still assert the moral nobility of the fight for Irish freedom. The works of J. W. Whitbread were more aggressively Nationalist, celebrating the patriotic self-sacrifice of men such as Lord Edward Fitzgerald and Wolfe Tone and advancing 'a myth of Irish heroism that reigned for decades in the popular imagination.'[9]

Shakespeare was, by universal consent, the greatest dramatist who ever lived, but young Johnny was torn between the Elizabethan grandeur of Shakespeare and the more immediate appeal of Boucicault. The language of Boucicault was closer to his own, as were the characters and the humour to the life around him, and, not least, there were the patriotic gestures that fired the emotions of the audience. It is a critical commonplace that Boucicault's melodrama left an indelible mark on O'Casey's work. It is also probable that the Nationalist element of the Queen's plays helped young Johnny free himself from the loyalism of the Casey family. Lord Edward Fitzgerald, Wolfe Tone, and Robert Emmet had also been Protestants, but here they were, in gloriously dramatic style, giving all so that Ireland might take its place among the nations of the earth.

In 1894 Isaac, not content with merely reading or attending plays, erected a stage in the living room at Hawthorne Terrace and supervised performances in which the family, including Johnny, and their friends took part. When Isaac began to parade his talents on public, if rather primitive, stages, young Johnny was close by. Shakespeare and Boucicault were the main fare: in an extract from *Henry VI Part Three*, Johnny played King Henry to Isaac's Richard of Gloucester. In Isaac's case the family tendency to truculence was not fully satisfied by swaggering on the stage, and he acquired a reputation for being 'difficult': he moved from the Townsend Dramatic Society to the Liberty Hall Players and spent some time at the Mechanics Theatre, site of the future Abbey Theatre, in Abbey Street. Here Johnny had the honour of playing the part of Father Dolan in *The Shaughraun* at short notice (and remembered it ironically when he was banned from the Abbey Green Room). In 1898, after a season with a touring company, Isaac gave up his theatrical career and became a clerk, but by then he had done more than anybody else to bring Johnny into the mysteries of the theatre.

By his late teens O'Casey had absorbed vast quantities of Shakespeare and Boucicault into his capacious memory and had experienced the dramatic effect from both sides of the curtains. He had seen plays performed in living rooms, in refurbished stables, in workingmen's clubs, and in the Queen's. He had also seen the visiting Benson Company performing Shakespeare, and he was reading widely, spending every available penny on books: 'The first serious book I ever bought was a shilling copy of the Globe edition of Shakespeare, and I learnt Hamlet, Macbeth and Julius Caesar by heart.'[10] It seems to have been instinctual with him not only to memorize what he learned but to internalize it so thoroughly that it became an intrinsic part of his perception, his personality, and his style of expression.

Other ideas and other words were changing him even more: before the turn of the century he had begun to interest himself in the Irish language and the ideal of a genuinely independent Ireland, a shift that perhaps originated in his absorption of the story of Ireland through the melodramas. O'Casey was not one to toe any line, and in 1907 he was almost expelled from the Drumcondra Branch of the Gaelic League for defending Synge's *Playboy* (which he hadn't seen) against the wrath of offended Nationalists.

Frank Cahill was very interested in drama, and eventually a Dramatic Club developed within the O'Toole Club. Even when he had broken his connections with all other Nationalist organisations, O'Casey remained a member of the O'Toole Club and used his talents for singing and storytelling in an effort to keep things going in the aftermath of the Rising when the old idealism had given way to death, imprisonment, and fear.[11] He must have fancied his English accent because he played a naive English tourist in Moylan's *Naboclish* at the Empire Theatre in November 1917 and, probably in 1921, a Cockney burglar in a production of Bernard Duffy's *Special Pleading* in the old Foresters' Hall off Mountjoy Square.[12]

O'Casey told Gabriel Fallon of the crucial moment when he decided to become a playwright. In a vignette that is suspiciously well staged, even to the lighting, O'Casey recalled that he and Frank Cahill were walking home from the Abbey Theatre and had come to the parting of their ways at the Five Lamps. Cahill insisted that O'Casey could write a better play than the one they had just seen; O'Casey pushed back his cap, looked up at the sky, and spoke: 'So help me God, Frank, I will!'[13]

Unfortunately, Fallon did not ask which play O'Casey had seen with Frank Cahill; nor is there any mention of the incident in the *Autobiographies*. Fallon wondered if the play was *Blight* (1917) or James Stephens' *The Wooing of Julia Elizabeth* (August 1920). David Krause is confidently detailed when he writes that it was in the company of old friends William and Ann Kelly that O'Casey went to the Abbey for the first time to see *Blight*.[14] Garry O'Connor is more cautious, wondering if Frank Cahill was a fourth member of the party and describing *Blight* as 'one of the first plays O'Casey claims to have seen' at the Abbey.[15] If Stephens' play is a possibility, then it is much more likely that the play that excited O'Casey to emulation was Corkery's *The Labour Leader*, which was produced at the Abbey in September 1919 and which O'Casey liked.[16] It would be unwise to read too much into the re-created scene at the Five Lamps. *Blight* fits neatly into the traditional chronology: shortly afterward O'Casey wrote his first play, *The Frost in the Flower,* and subsequently his earliest surviving play, *The Harvest Festival.* On the other hand, *The Frost in the Flower* does not seem to have remotely resembled *Blight*, while *The Harvest Festival* has much in common with *The Labour Leader*. Against that, *The Frost in the Flower* dealt with Frank Cahill in a way that would hardly have led him to encourage O'Casey to write another. Ultimately, it seems safest to accept the scene by the Five Lamps as one that owed more to dramatic imagination than to factual accuracy. It may even be that, consciously or unconsciously, O'Casey was obscuring, rather than illuminating, what actually happened.

One fact seems sound: O'Casey did see *Blight* at the Abbey in December 1917. Equally certain is the assumption that he, in whatever way, would have been impressed by a play that pleaded for a more humane attitude to those languishing in the slum tenements and that represented tenement conditions, characters, and speech convincingly.[17] *Blight* is popularly considered the first play to deal seriously with the tenement poor, but that achievement belongs to A. P. Wilson. Gogarty, like Stephens and Corkery, has always enjoyed a secure, if secondary, position in Irish literary history, but in 1914 Wilson seemed a likelier candidate for posthumous fame. He arrived in Dublin around 1910, probably from Scotland, and within a few years was manager of the Abbey Theatre and principal producer. His talents as a producer and his policy of producing new work were widely praised, and among the plays he produced in 1914 was *The Slough*, which he himself had written and in which he took the main part, Jake Allen, a lightly disguised version of Jim Larkin. It seems odd that O'Casey would not have noticed a play that Robert Hogan describes as 'the first notable play about the Dublin working man.'[18] Wilson was not a sympathetic outsider, like Gogarty or Stephens or Corkery; Wilson was involved with Delia Larkin in organising drama classes and productions for the Irish Transport and General Workers' Union, and his earlier short play, *Victims*, had been performed by the Irish Worker's Dramatic Club.[19] In fact, Wilson was none other than the correspondent for the *Irish Worker*, Euchan, who had found O'Casey's arguments so hard to understand. We may thus assume that O'Casey was aware of Wilson's theatrical career, at least in the years 1912–1914. The qualification is required by the fact that Wilson departed the Irish scene as meteorically as he had arrived. In 1915 he resigned from the Abbey after a row with Yeats, and shortly afterward he returned to Scotland and obscurity, leaving behind only two published works, *Victims* and *Poached*. *Victims* is remarkable as the first play set in a tenement and featuring working-class men. *The Slough* is remarkable for many reasons, not least the use of Jim Larkin and the very recent Lock-Out as central character and topic. The *Evening Herald* critic thought the play contained 'two scenes that put it away and beyond anything seen at the Abbey.' The *Irish Times* reviewer noted that Wilson had adopted

the point of view . . . of the 'under-dog.' The author does not intrude his sympathies to the detriment of the play, which is not used to point a moral. Its tragedy is relieved by a good deal of humour, and its well-connected incidents in which many instances make the heart beat fast with excitement.[20]

The one shortcoming mentioned in all the surviving reviews concerned the language:

He fails to get the Dublin dialect correctly; his younger characters particularly, have not the authentic note of the Dublin tenement; but this is a fault that would hardly be noticed outside of Dublin; and in the essentials of character and motive he is strictly true to life. His women are especially good: the worn old mother, trying to keep together a family of squabbling children and a drunken husband.[21]

The structural similarities with O'Casey are striking, but Hogan wisely resists the temptation to claim Wilson (or Gogarty) as an influence on O'Casey, 'for when a dramatist uses a family as a microcosm of urban decay, similarities are simply inevitable.'[22] Dissimilarities are equally obvious. O'Casey would not hesitate to intrude his sympathies and point a moral. Above all, O'Casey would capture the true flavour of Dublin working-class speech as no dramatist had ever done before him. The most interesting aspect is probably O'Casey's silence. It is hard to believe that O'Casey did not know of Euchan's life outside the pages of the *Irish Worker*. If he did know of *The Slough*, it is hard not to wonder if O'Casey was loath to accept that a fellow Larkinite had first represented the tenements on the Abbey stage almost a decade before *The Shadow of a Gunman*.

Whatever the inspiration was, in 1918 O'Casey submitted *The Frost in the Flower* to the O'Toole Club, and it was rejected because its central figure was a satirical portrait of Frank Cahill, whom O'Casey, who had a lifelong talent for losing friends, was beginning to find unsatisfactory. O'Casey submitted it to the Abbey, which rejected it on the grounds that, though it was 'not far from being a good play,' the central character had a tiresome tendency to be overcritical.[23] One suspects that this central character was some version of O'Casey and that the play was his means of achieving over his still Nationalist opponent the kind of total victory that was not possible in actual debates. Isolation and rejection, far from dampening his ardour, induced a Shavian arrogance. In a notebook he had begun a dialogue entitled *The Crimson Cornkrakes* in which Shaw was not only the subject matter but also the presiding genius: one of the two speakers, J (the author's initial, perhaps?) scores easily and eloquently against a rather limited interlocutor. In the same notebook was an outline for a play to be entitled *The Harvest Festival.*[24]

O'Casey spent the summer of 1918 on this play and sent it to the Abbey, along with a revised *Frost in the Flower*, in 1919. They were rejected but not dismissed: 'We are sorry to return the plays for the author's work interests us but we don't think either would succeed on the stage.'[25] For all its weaknesses, the play is surprisingly competent and shows the influence of Shaw in its elaborate stage directions and its set pieces in which conservative common sense is exposed by a series of witty jabs. In late 1919 he asked Shaw to lend his imprimatur by writing a preface to a collection of political essays. Shaw's refusal was robust: O'Casey should stand on his own two feet; the essays were overwritten; O'Casey should establish his own political position rather than criticising everybody else's because 'objecting to everyone else is Irish, but useless.'[26] Though Shaw's criticisms of the political essays were well founded, his final point did not apply to *The Harvest Festival*, which clearly espoused socialism and did so through the speeches of a character who was something of an ideal version of the dramatist himself.

The raw material had been in O'Casey's mind for some time and would be reworked later in *Red Roses for Me*: a young Dublin socialist is killed during a strike, and, despite the best efforts of the Rector, his corpse is not allowed into the church, which is decorated for a harvest festival. O'Casey divides the action quite efficiently into three acts and moves the characters about reasonably well. The Mother, her poor neighbour, and the Rector are sufficiently well drawn and complex to generate dramatic sympathy; the pompous, middle-class Protestants are tolerable as satirical cartoons. The main weaknesses are associated with the central character, Rocliffe. Just as O'Casey's demolition of the Frank Cahill character had unbalanced the earlier play, here O'Casey's unqualified enthusiasm for the *idea* of such a labour leader prevents him from achieving the minimal level of complexity necessary for such a play.

Jack Rocliffe is an artificial character, closer to Shavian drama than to Dublin life. A working-class Protestant, he is obsessed with his reading and uses his literary knowledge and his ability to speak literary English as his principal weapon against his class enemies. His opening line is a question addressed to a bricklayer: 'What singular inducement prompted her to leave your sweet society?'[27] Having encouraged the tradesman to read Swinburne, he confounds the Curate with the studied ease of a debating society champion who has one eye on his audience:

Allow me to point out, sir, that you have quoted the Catechism incorrectly. The phrase is not, in that state of life unto which it has pleased God to call you, but in that state of life unto which it shall please God to call you. [13]

His characteristic form of speech is a lecture, delivered with a confident sense of balance and rhythm that owes more to careful drafting than to impromptu conversation. This intellectual arrogance is ultimately exposed by his Mother, based on Susan Casey. Asked by a worker if she is not cheered to learn of the revenge taken on Jack's murderer, she strikes a chord deeper than anything her son has reached: 'I don't know, Bill. I don't know; maybe he, too, was the only son of some poor, old, heartbroken mother' [65]. Here we have the first draft of the greatest dramatic moment O'Casey would ever produce, Juno's sense of a common humanity that transcends ideological division.

Linguistically, the play is overwhelmed by Jack's compulsive exercise of oratory as if it were a magic wand or, at least, a weapon. His power of language enables him to inspire his working-class comrades and downface his middle-class enemies. Mrs. Duffy's comments are interesting:

Bedad, an' he's what you may call a speaker, too. I was listenin' to him last night an' he standin' on a brake, & if you had heard him. Sure, he knocked the divil out of all the rest of them that had their collars and ties. He has a power of books, Mrs Rocliffe. I don't know how he manages to read all them. [28]

By 'power of books' Mrs. Duffy means that Jack possesses a large number of books, but subconsciously she may be suggesting (and the reader/audience inferring) that Jack derives his strength from his extensive reading. It is a power that never leaves him: when mortally wounded, his eloquence is the last part of him to fade as his socialist philanthropy acquires a religious tone.

Most of the dialogue is in Standard English. The speech of the ordinary working-class characters is effectively rendered, but the circumstances are not conducive to comic exchanges. The only exception is at the beginning of the original version where the working-class expressions of Tom Nimmo, a Catholic bricklayer and proto-Fluther, contrast with the bourgeois propriety of his Protestant employer. When, for example, she suggests that the cabbages would look well around the pulpit during the Harvest Festival, he replies that 'they'd look better smokin' on a dish makin' a fine collar for a pig's cheek' [6]. But the creation of such comic dialogue was not a priority, and O'Casey cut this opening in his revised version. There is no suggestion that O'Casey is in any way critical of his hero's application of his reading to the lives of the people around him, a view he would modify severely within a few years when he cast a colder eye on Davoren and the Covey.

In his next dramatic effort O'Casey returned to what he saw as the key moment in Irish history, the struggle between Labour and the Nationalists that preceded the 1916 Rising and about which he had written extensively in the *Irish Worker* and *The Story of the Irish Citizen Army*. *The Crimson in the Tri-Colour* was first submitted to the Abbey in late 1921, shortly before the ratification of the treaty that ended the War of Independence; it has not survived, but it is possible to learn a good deal about it from the comments of O'Casey and others.

O'Casey remembered it as 'a "play of ideas" moulded on Shaw's style' with characters based on Arthur Griffith and William O'Brien and on the originals of the Covey and Fluther.[28] Lady Gregory was impressed and, according to her journal for April 15, 1923, 'wanted to pull [it] together and put it on' in order to give O'Casey experience.[29] Because Yeats was so unsympathetic to the play, Lady Gregory's report (copied by Lennox Robinson and given to O'Casey) was more restrained. With editing, 'we might find a possible play of ideas in it.' It was 'the expression of ideas that makes it interesting'; the 'personal interest,' especially the sexual relations between characters, was not 'worth developing.' Her qualms about producing the play were based on the power of the ideas expressed:

But we could not put it on while the Revolution is still unaccomplished—it might hasten the Labour attack on Sinn Fein, which ought to be kept back till the fight with England is over and the new Government has had time to show what it can do.[30]

(Lady Gregory records that when, on November 10, she told O'Casey that the play would weaken the Sinn Fein position in the Treaty negotiations, he replied that 'if that is so I would be the last to wish to put it on.'[31] O'Casey himself makes no mention of such an unselfish attitude.)

Yeats was predictably unsympathetic to 'this discursive play': he also anticipated that it would generate passionate political intensity, but of the kind he loathed:

[It] is so constructed that in every scene there is something for the pit & stalls to cheer or boo. In fact it is the old Irish idea of a good play—Queens Melodrama brought up to date would no doubt make a sensation—especially as everybody is as ill-mannered as possible, & all truth considered as inseperable [*sic*] from spite and hatred.[32]

Having made his antipathy quite clear, Yeats said that he did not care whether it was produced or not.

Shaw would hardly have been pleased to hear his style described as 'Queens melodrama,' but, if we lend sufficient weight to Yeats' qualification, *brought up to date*, it may not be unfair: both sides of a question are presented, but O'Casey, remembering the powerful political effect that Queen's melodrama had had on himself and the ordinary workers in the audience, appeals as much to the passions as the intellect. In this Shavian debate the Nationalist position is represented by a character based on Arthur Griffith, originator of Sinn Fein and condemned by O'Casey for his attacks on Larkin. The treacherous tendencies within Labour are represented by a 'mean and despicable' Union leader, based on William O'Brien, who replaced Larkin in the ITGWU and whom O'Casey described as a 'big sharp shit.' The hero of the piece is Kevin O'Regan, one of those semimystical figures who, like Jack Rocliffe, come to socialism via poetry and philosophy.[33]

Surrounding these were 'domestic' characters, including a Mr. and Mrs. Budrose (whose characters Lady Gregory admired) and their daughter, Eileen, who is courted by two men, Kevin O'Regan and Shemus O'Malley. As unimpressed as Lady Gregory by O'Casey's ability to handle sexual relations, Yeats reported:

At the end of Act II Kevin O'Regan is making very demonstrative love to Eileen Budrose . . . . In Act II without a word of explanation one finds him making equally successful love to Nora. In Act III one learns for the first time that Eileen has married Shemus O'Malley. We have not even been told that they were courting . . . . Regan talks constantly of his contempt for organised opinion & suddenly at the end we discover him as some kind of labour leader—one organised opinion exchanged for another. It is a story without meaning—a story where nothing happens except that a wife runs away from a husband to whom we had not the slightest idea that she was married, & the Mansion House lights are turned out because of some wrong to a man who never appears in the play.[34]

It sounds as if Kevin O'Regan is the intellectual who initially discourses on his philosophical isolation before being converted to the Labour movement. Perhaps it was the Nora character who convinced him to give up his pursuit of individual self-improvement (associated with his courtship of Miss Budrose?) in favour of unselfish devotion to the uneducated people of his own class? Does Eileen eventually see that she has made the wrong choice and run away from her husband? Does the play end in sudden darkness out of respect for an offstage Larkin figure who has been abused by the O'Brien figure?

All this is mere guesswork, but there is substantial evidence to establish an intellectual morality play in the Shavian manner but with Dublin accents. The key movement is the change in the central character from a contemptuous dismissal of all political parties, to an acceptance of his destiny as a Labour leader. This movement is traced through a series of arguments that would have excited the passions in the Dublin of 1920/1921. The intellectual battle is mirrored in sexual exchanges. The general tone is witty as the hero scores epigrammatic points over his opponents. There is, as in *The Harvest Festival*, an element of domestic farce centred on Mother Budrose and her husband. The attempt to introduce a romantic side plot, never to be one of O'Casey's strong points, was unsuccessful; Lady Gregory seems to suggest cutting all of it. The play lacked pace: too many debates put too great a strain on the plotline. The characterisation was faulted: again, one presumes that the main characters tended to be allegorical representations of their ideologies.

It is likely that the script submitted by O'Casey contained a scene in which socialism is discussed outside a convent. Certainly, the revised draft, submitted in 1923, contained such a scene, which was criticised by Abbey director Michael Dolan, who suggested that the discussion be relocated inside a pub.[35] (O'Casey remembered Dolan's advice when writing Act Two of *The Plough and the Stars*, but later on, in *The Silver Tassie,* he reverted to some extent to his earlier inspiration by using a monastery as background for the blasphemy of modern war.) It seems reasonable to guess that the scene in *The Crimson in the Tri-Colour* used the convent background to emphasise, as O'Casey and Larkin frequently did, the spiritual aspect of socialism.

Another point that, like *The Harvest Festival*, links the lost play with the later O'Casey is the presence of what might be termed a positive hero: though the play could not end with the dawn of socialism in Ireland, the audience is invited to see socialism vindicated in the emergence of Kevin O'Regan as a leader of his people. It is as if he had heeded the advice Shaw had given him in late 1919 to avoid the 'Irish' vice of 'objecting to everyone else.'

While waiting for the Abbey's decision on *The Crimson in the Tri-Colour*, O'Casey wrote a one-act piece entitled *The Seamless Coat of Kathleen*. Even he can hardly have been surprised when the Abbey rejected it as 'too definite a piece of propaganda' for April 1922 and suggested that O'Casey might try Liberty Hall. The play is almost certainly related in theme and tone to a short prose piece of the same name that O'Casey had published in *Poblacht na hÉireann* on March 29, 1922. The prose piece, subtitled 'A Parable of the Ard-Fheis,' is O'Casey's whimsically snide contribution to the major political crisis of the day. The 'seamless coat' is an ironic reference to the unity of Ireland, territorial and ideological, at a time when the country had been partitioned, and civil war was imminent. O'Casey's mockery was fuelled by his sense of vindication: now all must see what he had always claimed, that romantic Nationalism led not to freedom but to division and violence. One can only assume that the dramatised parable was allegorical in mode and farcical in tone, presenting Kathleen as the victim of Nationalist factions.

Well, he had done his best to get a word in edgeways. He had written a one-act play, satirising the contesting parties and putting Labour against the wall for its stupid and selfish pursuit of jobs, instead of flinging themselves between the opposing guns, calling out the question of which of you will fire first![36]

Later on in 1922 he began to write a play called *On the Run*. It was accepted by the Abbey in February 1923, on condition that he change the title to *The Shadow of a Gunman,* and produced a month later.

O'Casey now began to see himself as a professional dramatist. He quickly completed two one-act plays, *The Cooing of Doves* and *Kathleen Listens In*. The first, rejected by the Abbey, was almost certainly inspired by Michael Dolan's advice to set a wild political discussion in a pub. The second was accepted and produced on October 1, 1923, at the end of a triple bill that also included *The Man of Destiny* and *The Rising of the Moon*. O'Casey recalled that it was a disastrous failure, but some of the reviews were quite good, and it may be that the first-night audience was slightly baffled by the nature of the play. Those who came along expecting something in the vein of *The Shadow of a Gunman* were bound to be disappointed, for *Kathleen Listens In* is a farcical allegory.[37]

The material is related to that of *The Seamless Coat*. In the new independent Free State a range of men, including the Free Stater, the Republican, the Business Man, the Farmer, and Jimmy the Workman, are clamouring for the love of Kathleen, the daughter of (Miceawl O) Houlihan, but her only interest is in 'listening in' to the radio; meanwhile, the Orangeman appears outside, signifying the partition of Ireland. There is also the Man in the Kilts, representing the Irish language: the men pay lip service to this ridiculous figure but dismiss him behind his back: 'That oul cod's crocked; it won't be long till he snuffs it!' [287].[38]

Kathleen and her father are modernising and have little time for tradition: when men serenade her with ballads, Kathleen scorns them: 'Oh, for God's sake go away, an' done [*sic*] be annoyin' me. I have to practice me Fox Trots and Jazzin' so as to be ladylike when I make me deboo into the League of Nations' [282]. As one expects in a political satire, a good deal is tied to the time, but it is all carried off with great pace and exuberance.

There are in-jokes in almost every line. Musical parody abounds, looking back to O'Casey's performances in the O'Toole Club and forward to the late plays.

> Wrap the green flag round me, Joe,
> To die 'twere far more sweet,
> Than to be sacked out o' me job,
> An' sent to walk the street. [280]

The courtship of Kathleen becomes opera buffa:

[*Kathleen comes out, Mrs. O Houlihan holding her arm. They all bow.*]
The Republican. Me own sweet, little red little rose!
The Free Stater. Me own fair, little Drimin Donn Deehlish!
The Farmer. Me clusther o' little brown nuts, me heart's longin' for you.
The Business Man. I'll crown thee with gold an' I'll crown thee with silver, sweet little beautiful pulse o' me heart.
Jimmy. The people's flag is deepest red—
Tomaus. For God's sake, man!
The Free Stater [*singing*]. There's a dear little colleen that lives in our isle—
The Republican. She's as fresh an' as fair as a daisy—
The Farmer. An' she's bless'd with a tear an' she's bless'd with a smile—
Tomaus. Faith, some day, yous'll all dhrive her crazy!
The Business Man. An' we all, big an' small, lov'd her well thro' th' ages—
Jimmy. An' I'd love her more for an increase in wages!
All. An' it's dear little Kathleen, sweet little Kathleen, dear, little sweet, little Kathleen of Ireland!
Sheela. Oh Kathleen, aren't they a lovely lot o' gentlemen?
Kathleen. Oh, I've heard this too ofen, ma; I'm gettin' sick of it; . . . it's all codology. [292]

The direction *singing* should apply to the six subsequent lines, for the song is a parody of the popular 'The Dear Little Shamrock.'

There was much in O'Casey's cultural constitution to push him toward allegory, from his early immersion in the Bible, to his more recent interest in expressionist plays put on by the Dublin Drama League.[39] There was a strong element of allegory and symbolism in the oral and literary tradition of Irish separatism where references to Kathleen Ni Houlihan and her four green fields were instantly understood. O'Casey would have been familiar with the *aisling*, a species of poem that represented Ireland as a beautiful young woman oppressed by an English tyrant and hoping to be liberated by her lover across the seas, normally the Stuart Pretender. The Free Stater addresses Kathleen as his 'Drimin Donn Deehlish,' a reference to a famous song in which Ireland is figured as 'sweet brown cow.' Mangan's translation, 'Silk of the Kine,' was well known, as was Mangan's translation of 'Róisin Dubh' into what became one of the anthems of Irish separatism. (Garry O'Connor believes that *The Robe of Rosheen* and *The Seamless Coat of Kathleen* were two names for the same play, just as Rosheen and Kathleen were interchangeable names for Ireland.[40]) The most celebrated use of this tradition in the recent past was when Maud Gonne electrified audiences in Yeats' *Cathleen Ni Houlihan,* and it may be that the very fame of this play encouraged O'Casey to parody the hallowed *aisling* by transmuting it to a modern farce where solemnity was replaced by skits and the noble tones of ancient days by the lively vernacular of contemporary Ireland. It may even be that O'Casey was still smarting from Yeats' dismissal of *The Crimson in the Tri-Colour* and that his one-act play was his first shot in the direction of his illustrious colleague.

What is beyond doubt is that *Kathleen Listens In* marks O'Casey's position of absolute disdain for all cultural and political formations in Ireland at the end of the Civil War and the beginning of the Free State: Jimmy the Workman enjoys no privilege as the spokesman for Irish Labour but shares the common farcical fate. O'Casey had, at one time or another, been a convinced member of all the groups that were now bickering among themselves and quoting pieties at each other while getting down to the serious business of amassing power and wealth. But he had seen through the misleading words and false promises, and had never fallen for all that talk about freedom. He had anticipated the carve-up by bourgeois Nationalists of all shades, and this strengthened his faith in his own 'integrity.' There was nothing or nobody left deserving of his loyalty except his art and the poor proletariat who, as he had foretold, would find no relief in a Free State characterised by commercial greed and religious repression. Perhaps that was why the play, which seems so harmlessly funny now, was received so tepidly. Gabriel Fallon remembered how

gradually it dawned upon some of us that we were taking part in a piece of blistering satire directed at everything and almost everyone in the infant State . . . . Hardly more than ten per cent of the audience laughed together. The effect on the stage was slightly unnerving. In a flash it became clear what was happening. You laughed when my party fell under O'Casey's lash; I laughed where your party caught it. Both of us tried to laugh when the other fellow's party was made to squirm. And then slowly but surely all the laughing died away. When the curtain came down there were a few dispirited hand-claps obviously intended for the players.[41]

What had happened to the advice given by his great hero and fellow dramatist Shaw to avoid the useless Irish habit of 'objecting to everyone else' and concentrate instead on working out his own positive position? O'Casey had followed Shaw's advice in *The Harvest Festival* and, as far as one can judge, in *The Crimson in the Tri-Colour*. What had made him change direction? To some extent he was simply indulging a natural inclination toward revue-style satire, an inclination polished by performances in the O'Toole Club and one to which he would return in his later plays, but perhaps the experience of *The Shadow of a Gunman* had taught him that he could make his position quite clear without having a character onstage as a mouthpiece.

NOTES

1. James MacGowan in the *Irish Worker*, March 14, 1914. Reprinted in Sean O'Casey, *Feathers from the Green Crow: Sean O'Casey 1905–1925*, ed. Robert Hogan (London: Macmillan), 115.

2. Garry O'Connor, *Sean O'Casey* (London: Hodder and Stoughton, 1988), 87.

3. Ibid., 91, 95. He would exploit the night in the church in *The Plough and the Stars*.

4. A second, revised, and expanded version is reprinted in O'Casey, *Feathers from the Green Crow*, 157–173.

5. Ibid., 2f.

6. Ibid., 21.

7. Ibid., 150f.

8. Hugh Hunt, *Sean O'Casey* (Dublin: Gill and Macmillan), 16.

9. Stephen Watt, *Joyce, O'Casey, and the Irish Popular Theatre* (Syracuse, NY: Syracuse UP, 1991), 59.

10. See Hunt, 17f.

11. See, for example, Garry O'Connor, 95f.

12. Ibid, 101f. and 129f.

13. Gabriel Fallon, *Sean O'Casey: The Man I Knew* (London: Routledge and Kegan Paul, 1965), 37.

14. Sean O'Casey, *The Letters of Sean O'Casey*, ed. David Krause, vol. 1, 1910–1941 (London: Cassell, 1975), 69.

15. Garry O'Connor, 102.

16. Ibid., 131f.

17. See Ulick O'Connor, *Oliver St. John Gogarty* (London: Jonathan Cape, 1963), 134–140.

18. There is no surviving copy of the unpublished script of *The Slough*, but manuscripts of the individual parts are in the National Library of Ireland. For information on Wilson and the Abbey production, see Robert Hogan, Richard Burnham, and Daniel P. Poteet, *The Modern Irish Drama, a Documentary History, Volume 4: The Rise of the Realists 1910–1915* (Dublin: Dolmen Press, 1979).

19. Delia Larkin's Irish Workers' Dramatic Company performed for the first time in public in December 1912, offering four one-act plays directed by Wilson. O'Casey worked for Delia Larkin as a janitor in Langrishe Hall in 1920/1921, during which time he played in *Special Pleading*. See Sean O'Casey, *Autobiographies*, 2 vols. (London: Pan Books, 1980), II, 60; Donal Nevin, ed., *James Larkin: Lion of the Fold* (Dublin: Gill and Macmillan, 1998), 428–437.

20. Hogan, Burnham, and Poteet, 342f.

21. Ibid., 345.

22. Ibid., 342.

23. See, for example, Garry O'Connor, 112. Neither this nor a consequent draft submitted to the Abbey has survived.

24. Ibid., 111.

25. See O'Casey, *Letters*, I, 92.

26. Ibid., I, 88.

27. Sean O'Casey, *The Harvest Festival*, with a foreword by Eileen O'Casey and introduction by John O'Riordan (Gerrards Cross: Colin Smythe, 1980), 9. Future page references in square brackets. Jack manages the distinction between 'will' and 'shall' with a facility uncommon among the Dublin working class [37]. It is clear from the incomplete revision of the first act, where the Jack character speaks with a pronounced working-class accent, that O'Casey had seen the dramatic weaknesses of Jack's perpetual pyrotechnics [67-86].

28. Sean O'Casey, *The Letters of Sean O'Casey*, ed. David Krause, vol. 2, 1942–1954 (New York: Macmillan, 1980), 33. *The Crimson in the Tri-Colour* was eventually turned down in November 1922. O'Casey rewrote it in the summer of 1923, but it was again rejected.

29. Augusta Gregory, *Lady Gregory's Journals*, ed. Daniel J. Murphy, 2 vols. (Gerrards Cross: Colin Smythe, 1978), I, 446.

30. O'Casey, *Letters*, I, 95.

31. Gregory, I, 309.

32. O'Casey, *Letters*, I, 102f.

33. O'Casey wrote to Jack Carney that the 'noble proletarian' later became the Covey, another indication of how O'Casey's faith in Labour deserted him in the early 1920s. See O'Casey, *Letters*, II, 33.

34. O'Casey, *Letters*, I, 102.

35. See Garry O'Connor, 146.

36. O'Casey, *Autobiographies*, II, 95.

37. See O'Casey, *Feathers from the Green Crow*, 273–276.

38. The numbers in square brackets refer to the text in O'Casey, *Feathers from the Green Crow*.

39. See Fallon, 14.

40. Garry O'Connor, 132.

41. Fallon, 14f.

Chapter 4

A Peculiar Aptness
for Character

To me the tragedy and comedy of life lie in the consequences, sometimes terrible, sometimes ludicrous, of our persistent attempts to found our institutions on the ideals suggested to our imaginations by our half-satisfied passions, instead of on a genuinely scientific history.[1]

The received wisdom is that, broadly speaking, O'Casey's career consists of three phases. During the first, up till late 1922, he was trying to find his own voice and style and wrote those apprentice pieces—*The Frost in the Flower, The Harvest Festival, The Crimson in the Tri-Colour*, and *The Seamless Coat of Kathleen*—that were rejected by the Abbey. The second phase is marked by a radical change of direction that the Abbey immediately recognised and encouraged: O'Casey dropped the didacticism of the early work and developed his abilities to create the convincing comic characters and colourful vernacular that drive the comi-tragic masterpieces of the Dublin trilogy: *The Shadow of a Gunman, Juno and the Paycock*, and *The Plough and the Stars*. The third phase begins with *The Silver Tassie* and involves the development of nonrealist techniques and extravernacular dialogue, which the Abbey rejected, leading to O'Casey's exile in England and his continued experiments with expressionist and 'poetic' modes. It is difficult to refute the broad lines of this proposition, and, for many, the ultimate proof is the box office: none of O'Casey's other plays—with the possible exception of *Purple Dust*, which ran for a year in New York—have ever achieved anything remotely resembling the popular success of the three Abbey plays. But while, viewed from a distance, this division into phases may hold, it would be naive to think that the boundaries between the various phases were other than blurred or that O'Casey was ever fully conscious of those changes of direction, which in retrospect seem so pronounced.[2]

In 1923, shortly after the success of *Shadow*, O'Casey told Joseph Holloway that 'he was strong on character and weak on construction and could write dialogue with ease.'[3] A year later, in March 1924, anticipating even greater success with *Juno*, O'Casey recalled

that when he started to write plays he thought he was a second Shaw sent to express his views through his characters, and was conceited enough to think that his opinions were the only ones that mattered. It was Lady Gregory who advised him to cut out all expressions of self, and develop his peculiar aptness for character drawing. At first he didn't take kindly to her advice, but afterwards on consideration felt she was right.[4]

What O'Casey had in mind was advice, not recorded in her *Journal*, that Lady Gregory had given him when he went to see her for the first time in November 1921 after the rejection of *The Crimson in the Tri-Colour*. During the opening run of *Shadow* in April 1923, he reminded her of the earlier meeting.

He says he sent us a play four years ago *Frost and Flowers* and it was returned, but marked 'Not far from being a good play.' He has sent others, and says how grateful he was to me because when we had to refuse the Labour one 'The Crimson in the Tri-Colour' I had said 'I believe there is something in you' and 'your strong point is characterisation.'[5]

In the reader's report, as we have seen, apart from the reference to Mrs. Budrose, Lady Gregory seems to suggest the opposite.[6]

A year later, in March 1924, when it was obvious that *Juno and the Paycock* would be an even greater success, O'Casey once again reminded Lady Gregory of her crucial advice.

'I owe a great deal to you and Mr. Yeats and Mr. Robinson, but to you above all. You gave me encouragement. And it was you who said to me upstairs in the office—I could show you the very spot where you stood—"Mr. O'Casey, your gift is characterisation." And so I threw over my theories and worked at characters, and this is the result.'[7]

O'Casey's version is quite clear: Lady Gregory directed him away from the Shavian didacticism of the early plays (in which he sought directly to 'express his views through his characters') and toward the indirect, character-based technique that brought him success and fame. Lady Gregory allows O'Casey's praise to speak for itself: she never suggests that she actually remembered the occasion that was fixed so indelibly in O'Casey's memory. Perhaps, now in her seventies, she had no detailed recollection of what turned out to be a crucial moment in the history of the Abbey. Perhaps O'Casey in his generosity was gilding the lily. The available evidence suggests that their first meeting was not quite as damascene as O'Casey described it.

On his own admission, when O'Casey began writing plays, he saw himself as 'a second Shaw.' Ideological considerations aside, it is not difficult to see why O'Casey was drawn to Shaw. They were both Dublin Protestant, self-taught socialists. Shaw delighted in exposing the intellectual shortcomings of his contemporaries, something O'Casey had been doing even before he had read a word of Shaw. For any aspiring dramatist, Shaw was an encouraging reminder of what self-belief and perseverance could achieve.

In 1938 O'Casey wrote to Horace Reynolds, an American academic:

I had been for a good number of years a member of the Irish Republican Brotherhood, & an ardent Nationalist. Then came the preaching of Jim Larkin and the books of Bernard Shaw. (By the way, it was a young Dublin Nationalist named Kevin O'Loughlinn, member of the third order of St. Francis, who introduced me to Shaw, by persuading me to read the sixpenny edition of John Bull's Other Island.) These two great men swung me over to the left, & I became critical of pure nationalism.[8]

Here the credit for O'Casey's enlightenment is shared by Larkin and Shaw with the slight suggestion that Larkin had come first; in *Drums under the Windows,* published in 1945, it is Shaw who changes O'Casey's life.

In the chapter entitled 'Hora Novissima,' O'Casey describes his growing lack of fervour for a Nationalist movement that had no real concern for the plight of the workers. It ends with a prophetic declaration that soon a new 'song of life' will be heard: 'And in the song will be the unfolding of the final word from the evolving words of the ages, the word of the modern, the word En-Masse.'[9] Two chapters later, in 'Prometheus Hibernica,' O'Casey discovers Larkin and the red banner to which he can give himself completely. He depicts Big Jim speaking from Liberty Hall and revealing the ultimate *logos*, the divine gospel of secular socialism. (The highest form of the word is that *spoken* by the modern messiah to his assembled people.) 'Aha, here now was the unfolding of the final word from the evolving words of the ages, the word of the modern, the word En-Masse, and a mighty cheer gave it welcome' [573]. The crucial chapter between the withering of Nationalism and the blooming of Larkinite socialism is entitled 'Green Fire on the Hearth,' and the central figure is Shaw.

In or around 1912 O'Casey read *John Bull's Other Island*, and the effect was just as traumatic as O'Loughlin had promised. In the *Autobiographies* it generates a surrealistic farce in which the statue of St. Laurence O'Toole, patron saint of Dublin, leans over from his perch on top of the Catholic Pro-Cathedral and comes off second best in debate with Shaw. In a fantasy that refers to *Back to Methuselah* (not completed until 1920) O'Casey climbs into the Garden of Eden, where Eve, like a true Shavian heroine, convinces Adam to leave the ease of Eden and seek 'a finer and firmer life' elsewhere for themselves and their unborn child. She is the Life Force and will partake in the evolution toward a better future; those who remain as they are in Eden will disappear like the dinosaurs.

Under the darkened sky, in the midst of a flash of lightning, Sean saw that the low brow, the timid eye, the shivering step of Adam had changed to the alert walk, the gleaming eye, the lofty brow, and the reddish thrust-out beard of Bernard Shaw. And Sean, bending low under the Golden Bough, followed close behind him. [572]

Shaw was the prophet, and O'Casey his disciple. Thanks to Shaw's dismissal of the Celtic Twilight, O'Casey was able to see Ireland as it really was. Thanks to Shaw's critique, O'Casey was ready to shed the vestiges of his Nationalism and commit himself totally to Larkinite socialism.

O'Casey had seen only one of Shaw's plays, a 1918 Abbey production of *Androcles and the Lion*, before he himself emerged as a dramatist. He couldn't afford to go to the Abbey regularly and so missed the brave production of *The Shewing-up of Blanco Posnet* in 1909 and, much more surprisingly, the six Shaw plays put on by the Abbey between September 1916 and May 1917. On the other hand, one may safely assume that O'Casey read as much Shaw as he could lay hands on.[10] It is not surprising that the influence of Shaw is visible in *The Harvest Festival* and detectable in references to the early scripts that have not survived.

The Shadow of a Gunman, originally entitled *On the Run,* is very loosely based on a raid made by British counterterrorist paramilitaries on the house in Mountjoy Square where O'Casey lived for a while with fellow Larkinite Mícheál Ó Maoláin. One of the tenants was a committed Republican who regularly hid IRA men on the run; when O'Casey arrived, it was assumed by the neighbours that he too was on the run. The raid took place in May 1921, and O'Casey began the play shortly afterward. O'Casey did not limit himself to what actually happened. No young female was killed. The character of Shields does not seem to bear any substantial resemblance to that of Ó Maoláin; on the other hand, there is much in Davoren to remind one of O'Casey.[11]

The opening of the play is, when allowances are made for the setting, pure Shaw. No reasonably well read student of plays could miss the marks of Shaw on the first page. It is one long stage direction, informing the reader with Shavian omniscience as to the minute particulars of the scene and the physiognomical and psychological traits of the characters. No experienced dramatist would dream of imposing such strictures on a producer because, if taken literally, they would make casting impossible. Shaw had added such wealth of detail in the published versions to help readers visualize the action, but it is not clear that O'Casey was aware of this.[12]

DAVOREN *is sitting at the table typing. He is about thirty. There is in his face an expression that seems to indicate an eternal war between weakness and strength; there is in the lines of the brow and chin an indication of a desire for activity, while in his eyes there is visible an unquenchable tendency towards rest. His struggle through life has been a hard one, and his efforts have been handicapped by an inherited and self-developed devotion to 'the might of design, the mystery of colour, and the belief in the redemption of all things by beauty everlasting.'* [3][13]

O'Casey feels it unnecessary to identify the source of the quotation, assuming, quite reasonably in 1922, that the company will immediately understand that Davoren is devoted to the ideals of Louis Dubedat, the utterly selfish painter-hero of Shaw's *The Doctor's Dilemma*, who dismisses traditional morality as a restraint that the modern hero must dispense with.

Davoren's companion in the tenement room, Shields, is described more succinctly, but the problems for the actor and producer are still considerable:

SEUMAS SHIELDS, *who is in the bed next the wall to the right, is a heavily built man of thirty-five; he is dark-haired and sallow-complexioned. In him is frequently manifested the superstition, the fear and the malignity of primitive man.* [3]

The experienced reader of plays would be reasonably confident what to expect. There will be a Shavian play of ideas, a debate in which the modern, enlightened, rationalist Davoren will confront and defeat the pre-enlightened, religious Shields in a series of mental jousts. The experienced reader, now joined by the dedicated playgoer, will feel absolutely vindicated as, for the remainder of the opening sequence, debonair Davoren exposes Shields' delusions and contradictions. The basic dramatic element is the setup: poor Shields talks himself into a ridiculous position, and Davoren is there to lead the laughter.

SEUMAS. I rejoice in the vindication of the Church and Truth.
DAVOREN. Bah. You know as little about truth as anybody else, and you care as little about the Church as the least of those that profess her faith; your religion is simply the state of being afraid that God will torture your soul in the next world as you are afraid the Black and Tans will torture your body in this.
SEUMAS. Go on, me boy; I'll have a right laugh at you when both of us are dead.
DAVOREN. You're welcome to laugh as much as you like at me when both of us are dead. [5f.]

Those who have read *The Harvest Festival* will certainly be reminded of Jack Rocliffe scoring at will; some may even recall Jack's condescending remark to Tom: 'Poor Tom, you suffer under a dual tyranny—afraid of your soul in the next world and afraid of your body in this.'[14] When Minnie arrives on the scene, Shavians will surely experience a twinge of recognition, suspecting that she may owe her first name and more to a minor character in *The Doctor's Dilemma*. Minnie Tinwell was a maid whom Louis Dubedat married and stayed with for as long as her money lasted. While the doctors are shocked at his immorality, the apparently amoral Dubedat maintains that 'the brave little lassie' was quite content with her lot:

Minnie Tinwell is a young woman who has had three weeks of glorious happiness in her poor little life, which is more than most girls in her position get, I can tell you. Ask her whether she'd take it back if she could. She's got her name into history, that girl.[15]

There is an outrageously egocentric honesty about Dubedat that is almost appealing, but there is no hint of such a saving grace in Davoren. Nobody can ask Minnie Powell if she was happy with whatever moments of happiness she derived from her dalliance with Davoren because by the end of the play she has been shot dead. If we extend the fiction beyond the final curtain, we may surmise that her heroic gesture earned her a local fame and perhaps even a ballad, but by then we are more likely to be appalled not only by her misconceived heroism but also, and perhaps even more, by Davoren's selfishness, a selfishness unmitigated by any Shavian élan vital.

Even before the end of Act One, the 'play of ideas' mode gives way to something much more broadly comical, which is described presently, but perhaps even more remarkable than the abandonment of the Shavian format in Act One is its resumption at the beginning of Act Two, where Davoren returns to his writing and Shields to his silly interruptions:

SEAMAS [*sleepily*]. Donal, Donal, are you awake? [*A pause.*] Donal, Donal, are you asleep?
DAVOREN. I'm neither awake nor asleep: I'm thinking. [24]

They discuss the relationship between the poet and the people. Shields believes that 'a poet's claim to greatness depends upon his power to put passion in the common people.' Davoren, while maintaining that the poet is ultimately the saviour of the people, rejects the idea of a democratic poet living to please an ignorant people. Returning to national issues, Shields thinks the fight for Irish freedom is a serious threat to the Irish people. Davoren attributes Shields' misgivings to simple selfish fear. Davoren, like a good Shavian, cannot understand why anybody should fear death, which is, after all, inevitable. Superstitious Shields finds his strength in religion:

SEUMAS. . . . There's a great comfort in religion; it makes a man strong in time of trouble an' brave in time of danger. No man need be afraid with a crowd of angels round him; thanks to God for His Holy Religion!
DAVOREN. You're welcome to your angels; philosophy is mine; philosophy that makes the coward brave; the sufferer defiant; the weak strong; the . . .
A volley of shots is heard in a lane that runs parallel with the wall of the back-yard. Religion and philosophy are forgotten in the violent fear of a nervous equality. [29]

Shields is not the only one who has been set up here, and with Davoren exposed as lacking, at the very least, self-knowledge, the Shavian debate collapses again. As in Act One, the play of ideas gives way to something else, and Davoren is associated with a primitive instinct for self-preservation rather than a 'belief in the redemption of all things by beauty everlasting'; far from representing any Life Force, he is seen as largely responsible for the death of the one character in the play who makes any claim on our admiration.

It is as if O'Casey set out to write one kind of play and ended up writing another. We can easily imagine the initial outline. The setting is a tenement in an area in which all common sense has been lost in an epidemic of political hysteria. Enter a sensitive and imaginative young man whose literary education, especially his reading of the radical atheist Shelley, has made him immune to the chimeras of Nationalism; he confronts the range of traditional political views available in a tenement house—young and old, male and female, Catholic and Protestant, Nationalist and Unionist—and, somewhat in the priggish manner of Jack Rocliffe, reduces them to impotence with his wit and wisdom.[16] There is no such play, but there is some evidence, not only the internal shifts I have mentioned, to suggest that the play changed in the course of composition.

In early October 1922, when he had drafted the first act and most of the second, O'Casey wrote in a letter: 'It deals with the difficulties of a poet who is in continual conflict with the disturbances of a tenement house, and is built on the frame of Shelley's phrase: "Ah me, alas, pain, pain ever, forever."'[17] A student offering such a summary of *The Shadow of a Gunman* would be unlikely to pass. O'Casey's abstract suggests that the disturbance is all one-way and avoids any reference to the fatal disturbance Davoren will cause in Minnie's life. Then there is the designation of Davoren as, simply, 'a poet'; generally, in a modern literary text and without any qualification, the term suggests intelligence, sensitivity, and a generosity that may border on the recklessly unselfish. Maybe O'Casey was keeping his cards close to his chest, but this does not sound like *The Shadow of a Gunman* as we know it today. What happened to change the direction and the tone of the opening (and of O'Casey's abstract) into a play that does superbly what Shaw had warned O'Casey to avoid?

In the letter just quoted, O'Casey described his unfinished play as a tragedy, adding, as if anticipating objections, 'at least I have called it so.' The stage history of the play questions the aptness of the label. It was, from the beginning, an uproarious success and is still guaranteed to have audiences howling with laughter most of the time. The first-night attendance at the work of an unknown author was predictably moderate, but by the third night the Abbey had the unusual pleasure of turning people away. The audiences revelled in the series of satirical character studies. At least one man thought it was 'a revue and not a play.' The notices were excellent but implied that the essential play, the satire, was hindered rather than helped by the element of tragedy towards the end. Holloway found the 'dramatic construction' deficient, but he admired 'telling dialogue of the most topical and biting kind' and 'the truth and human nature' it contained.[18] The audience, most of them increasingly disillusioned by the way the idealism of 1916 had degenerated into the vindictiveness and gangsterism of civil war, revelled in a play that constantly mocked political violence and presented those who supported it as idiots or worse. O'Casey must have felt vindicated in his political prescience and doubly pleased that he had found a way of expressing his views that the audience could accept and enjoy.

Yet there is at least one other piece of evidence to suggest that he had, to some extent, stumbled on this form. O'Casey was surprised at the changes that occurred between his conception of the characters and the interpretation of the actors, not an unusual experience for a dramatist at his first produced work. He told Holloway that he felt like a spectator at his own play, that 'the characters seemed strangers to me, but I enjoyed them.'[19] Nor was he, despite his grateful relief, entirely happy with the Abbey production. Having watched a performance in the August revival, he accused F. J. McCormick of 'making a hames' of the play by playing Shields as too sympathetic. McCormick had obviously paid more attention to his lines than to the opening stage direction. This is perhaps the clearest indication that the play produced was not the play O'Casey had envisaged.[20]

Despite the almost constant comedy, or maybe even because of it, *The Shadow of a Gunman* is, in many ways, O'Casey's most savagely pessimistic play. Most of the characters are contemptible in one way or another. There is no sign of hope that any external force, religious or political, can rescue these people from their errors. The most repulsive and reprehensible character of all is Davoren, the poet who claims that his vocation is to save the people. If he was conceived as a Shelleyan philanthropist, he was soon transformed into a pretentious, self-serving prig, basking in the admiration of those he despises. When Davoren falls, so too does the Shavian blueprint. Dispensing with the Shavian educator, O'Casey prefers to have Tommy Owens, Mr. Gallogher, Mrs. Henderson, and the other ludicrously opinionated fantasists condemn themselves out of their own mouths rather than have them exposed by a superior intelligence.

It would be wrong simply to identify him with the younger O'Casey, but there can be no doubt that Davoren was, at least in part, a self-portrait and an extremely vicious one at times. Was O'Casey aware of this? Take the poetry he is composing at the beginning or the verse he quotes for Minnie. What is the producer to do here? Allow the audience to decide on its merits? Or nudge them toward satirical laughter?

> One day, when Morn's half-open'd eyes
> Were bright with spring sunshin —
> My hand was clasped in yours, dear love,
> And yours was clasped in mine—
> We bowed as worshippers before
> The Golden Celandine. [12]

Literary specialists in the audience may find it amusing that Davoren writes this kind of stuff in 1920, the year of 'The Love Song of J. Alfred Prufrock,' but Minnie judges it 'lovely.' It would be very easy for the actor to subvert this jaded effort at Wordsworthian simplicity, but was the dramatist setting out to make Davoren sensitive or silly? This is a verse from a poem O'Casey had written several years earlier; in attributing the lines to Davoren, was O'Casey mocking his own misdirected efforts at romantic verse? The critical reader may think so, but, on the other hand, O'Casey published this and other early efforts at poetry in a collection, *Windfalls*, in 1934, when he was fifty-four years of age. Is it possible that O'Casey thought there was something of value in it? That Davoren had some literary talent?[21]

But a gift for dubious verse is the least of Davoren's shortcomings. Most modern audiences see him as pompous, manipulative, pretentious, selfish enough to allow a young woman to believe that he is brave, cowardly enough to have that woman risk her life for him, and priggish enough to be, in some important ways, unaffected by her death.

Inevitably, the student of O'Casey seeks some biographical reason for this viciously satirical assault on himself and all around him.[22] Had his move from home forced him to take stock? Did he see himself as a forty-two-year-old failure? He had no job, no prospects, no wife or family of his own. He had failed as a political activist, failed as a lover, and, apart from some minor publications, failed as a writer. He worked at this new play, *On the Run*, despite the fact that his previous efforts had all been rejected. One senses a powerful bitterness beneath the comic exchanges of *Shadow*, to say nothing of its grim conclusion; perhaps it was sufficient to wrench the play away from its original direction. Wherever the subversive energy came from, it enters the play in the form of Tommy Owens.

The key element in the play is not Maguire's bag of bombs but the illusion that Davoren is a gunman on the run. If the raid is the most significant action, then many of the characters (Tommy Owens, Mrs. Henderson, Mr. Gallogher, Mrs. Grigson) are incongruously irrelevant. What dominates and binds the play together is the rumour started in the pub by Tommy Owens and eagerly believed by the community. O'Casey's stage direction describes Tommy as *a hero-worshipper and, like many others, he is anxious to be on familiar terms with those who he thinks are braver than himself, and whose approbation he tries to win by an assumption equal to their own* [14]. Before we actually meet him, Minnie has told us something of Tommy Owens' style and pedigree. He is, to begin with, a 'gorgeous melodeon player,' a description that provokes a typical example of Davoren's pedantry:

DAVOREN. A gifted son of Orpheus, eh?
MINNIE [*who never heard of Orpheus*]. You've said it, Mr Davoren: the son of poor oul' Battie Owens, a weeshy, dawny, bit of a man that was never sober an' was always talkin' politics. Poor man, it killed him in the long run.[23]
DAVOREN. A man should always be drunk, Minnie, when he talks politics—it's the only way in which to make them important.
MINNIE. Tommy takes after the oul' fellow, too; he'd talk from morning till night when he has a few jars in him. [11]

Tommy is a small, thin man of twenty-five and, after a few drinks, has come to bask in the warmth of familiarity with the most prestigious heroic type of the day, the gunman. The audience assumes that the intellectual Davoren, fresh from his linguistic triumphs over Shields and Minnie, will have little trouble confounding Tommy; but Davoren can hardly get a word in, and when he does, it is easily manipulated by Tommy. For Tommy is much more than a mere hero-worshipper: he is the embodiment of popular Nationalist culture, the incarnation of oral tradition.

Davoren insists that he neither has nor wishes to have any connection with 'the politics of the day.' Tommy, a master of linguistic agility, understands him perfectly.

You needn't say no more—a nod's as good as a wink to a blind horse—you've no meddlin' or makin' with it, good, bad or indifferent, pro nor con; I know it an' Minnie knows it—give me your hand. [*He catches* DAVOREN'S *hand.*] Two firm hands clasped together will all the power outbrave of the heartless English tyrant, the Saxon coward an' knave. That's Tommy Owens' hand, Mr Davoren, the hand of a man, a man—Mr Shields knows me well. [*He breaks into song.*]

High upon the gallows tree stood the noble-hearted three,
By the vengeful tyrant stricken in their bloom;
But they met him face to face with the spirit of their race,
And they went with souls undaunted to their doom!

Minnie attempts to stop him, but Tommy overwhelms her with a shout:

> God save Ireland ses the hayros, God save Ireland ses we all,
> Whether on the scaffold high or the battle-field we die.
> Oh, what matter when for Ayryinn dear we fall!
> [*Tearfully*] Mr Davoren, I'd die for Ireland! [15]

A simple summary of Tommy's declamation, *he asserts that he too has the political convictions he attributes to Davoren*, would be hopelessly inadequate because it would miss the point that the medium is at least as important as the message, style at least as important as content, and it is the torrential flow that drowns Davoren and Minnie.

Tommy's speech would fit Fallon's description, 'some of the richest Dublin dialogue I had ever heard,' but, far from being charged 'with an intensity of meaning,' it is, in some ways, meaningless. Tommy's words add nothing to human understanding or expression. His entire speech consists of a series of what might be termed, expanding the normal usage slightly, quotations. The printed text does not acknowledge what the ear recognises in the theatre: the sequence from *Two firm hands* to *knave* is a quatrain of Nationalist verse celebrating Irish unity and denigrating English turpitude. O'Casey knew that such quotations were so intrinsic to the language of people like Tommy that, instinctively, he omitted conventional quotation marks, just as he had done in his own political journalism.[24] Even today Irish audiences would recognise Tommy's song as one of the most famous hymns of Irish Nationalism: 'The Song of the Manchester Martyrs' commemorated the final defiance of three Fenians hanged for their involvement in an attack in Manchester in 1867. In the lower classes Nationalist ideology was not transmitted by books or articles but in 'ballad and story, rann and song.' A quotation from a ballad had the power and status that literates would associate with key extracts from books. Tommy Owens is not, as we shall discover, totally illiterate, but he is a member of a community in which literacy is only beginning to establish itself. Tommy's speech is that of an oral society, characteristically full, formulaic, and consisting of verbal units that advertise themselves as the common property of the community. He begins with three formulations: 'you've no meddlin' or makin' with it, good, bad, or indifferent, pro nor con.' Modern literary education would disdain this as pleonastic and clichéd, but in an oral culture Tommy's overture would be acceptably copious and rhythmical, his formulas serving to emphasise the intimacy between speaker and interlocutor. In a manner of speaking, Tommy's overwhelming of Davoren is the victory of oral over literate speech; it also marks the overwhelming of the Shavian 'play of ideas' by a new form of comi-tragic satire that O'Casey would make his own.

Tommy Owens is a satirical caricature in a play about Irish politics, not a nostalgic evocation of an oral rhapsodist. O'Casey uses Tommy's linguistic mode to dramatise an important aspect of political life at that time. Such a total dependence on formulas and quotations suggests a perception that is utterly devoid of individual intelligence and critical ability. Tommy Owens is a *blower* in the sense that he is a passive medium through which traditional ideas simply blow, unhindered by any subjective resistance. Living in his tenement trap between the twin mirages of a noble past and a glorious future, unable to do anything because some vague force 'never gave me a chance.' Tommy surrenders to the alchemy of alcohol and 'talkin'' politics' that killed his father. He is *miles gloriosus hibernicus*, the public house hero talking his way to greatness in a manner that would be merely ridiculous were it not contributing to an atmosphere that proves fatally heady for one less passive than himself.

Tommy Owens is also a great comic creation, the first in a long line of blowers who express their idle fantasies in rhythmical rhapsodies of extraordinary colour and texture, using all the skills of their oral tradition to compose *other* lives for themselves as rich, passionate, and interesting as their actual lives in the tenements were poor, dull, and deadening. The comedy lies in the disparity between the heroic fantasy and the proletarian actuality, between the word and the fact. Tommy boasts that he is willing to make the ultimate sacrifice, to die for Ireland, but meanwhile he lives with his mother and works in Ross and Walpole's, waiting for some vague 'they' to give him a chance to show his mettle. Tommy has no need of a Davoren to reveal his ridiculous fantasies; he is more than capable of doing it himself. However much we despise Tommy's pretentious lies, we cannot but admire his verbal power and agility, and however much O'Casey the socialist agitator raged at Tommy and his likes for their refusal to face up to the facts of their situation, one suspects that O'Casey the dramatist was forced to admire their ability to compose fanciful scripts for themselves.

The theme of self-satirising/self-scripting is what fires such brilliant comic sketches as Mr. Gallogher and Mr. Grigson. Adolphus Grigson, the last of the residents to make his appearance in Davoren's room, conforms closely to the communal pattern. As befits an Orangeman surrounded by Catholics, Grigson finds his script in the highest level of language, the Word of God as found in Holy Scripture. He is to Unionism what Tommy Owens is to Nationalism: both recall the glories of the past, and both are so fervent in their commitments that mere speech fails them, and they launch into song. In Grigson's case, comic incongruity is highlighted by the two contrasting accounts of his behaviour in the presence of the Auxiliaries. His own quietly heroic account is an obvious example of self-scripting. Even before he begins, the audience is convinced of the truthfulness of Mrs. Grigson's account of her husband's humiliation, and this makes his own heroic saga superbly incredible.

'No bother at all,' says one of them, 'only this gun might go off an' hit somebody—have you me?' says he. 'What if it does,' says I; 'a man can only die once, an' you'll find Grigson won't squeal.' 'God, you're a cool one,' says the other, 'there's no blottin' it out.' [128]

The final phrase identifies the scriptwriter as Grigson himself.

Mr. Gallogher is less a character or personality and more a persona, a medium of speech. Again the comedy is generated by a series of disparities, notably that between legal jargon and the intrusive vernacular and between the attempted professional poise and the palpable fear of a pathetic little man who lives in terror of a neighbour. He enjoys in legal language a power so painfully lacking in his own life.

The name of the resident-tenant who is giving all this trouble and who, pursuant to the facts of the case aforesaid mentioned, will be the defendant, is Dwyer. The husband of the aforesaid Mrs Dwyer, or the aforesaid defendant, as the case may be, is a seaman, who is coming home shortly, and we beg The Irish Republican Army to note that the said Mrs Dwyer says he will settle us when he comes home. . . .

NB. If you send up any of your men, please tell them to bring their guns. I beg to remain the humble servant and devoted admirer of the Gentlemen of the Irish Republican Army.

Witness my hand this tenth day of the fifth month of the year nineteen hundred and twenty. [20][25]

Mr. Gallogher ventures his opinion that 'Mr Shields is a man of exceptional mental capacity, and is worthy of a more dignified position' [21]. As is, it is implied, Mr. Gallogher himself who, though merely employed by a harness maker in the Coombe, seeks a more dignified life through the medium of refined language. Unfortunately, at least in the eyes and ears of the audience, his efforts at self-improvement are hilariously inept.

When Davoren, modern man of letters, is confronted by these people, he is unable to control their verbal torrents and is usually reduced to silence. The dramatic paradox is that they, who are (each in his own way) in awe of Davoren the gunman, far from remaining respectfully mute, literally assault him with verbal display. (It is to Davoren the gunman rather than Davoren the poet that Gallogher brings the letter: he is not looking for textual criticism but for express delivery to the IRA.) Tommy brandishes the tokens of the power of national fidelity. Gallogher tries to appropriate the speech of his social superiors and also the most potent symbol of their power, the written document. While this might make him ridiculous in the eyes of Davoren (and of the audience), it has the opposite effect on his neighbours and produces a moment of outrageously high farce.

Mr Gallogher *prepares to read;* Minnie *leans forward to listen;* Tommy *takes out a well-worn note-book and a pencil stump, and assumes a very important attitude.* [18]

A fellow fantasist, when Tommy sees a lawyer about to read a submission, he immediately acts as clerk of the court. As far as the others, apart from Davoren, are concerned, Gallogher's letter is a brilliant success. Mrs. Henderson, Minnie, and Tommy are unable to contain their admiration for the opening flourish and nothing in the letter lessens their amazement. Minnie cannot believe her ears (or eyes):

MINNIE. It wasn't you, really, that writ it, Mr Gallicker?
MRS. HENDERSON. Sinn Féin Amháin: him and him only, Minnie. I seen him with me own two eyes when me and Winnie—Mrs Gallicker, Mr. Davoren, aforesaid as appears in the letter—was havin' a chat be the fire. [20][26]

But by then the audience is aware of Minnie's own literary ambitions.

The fascination with literature finds its most dramatic expression in the character of Minnie. The dramatist tells us that Minnie has 'an easy confidence' and 'a force and assurance beyond her years' [10], but she pays the ultimate price for the rumour that has swept through the tenement and been swallowed whole by people addicted to fantasies. She's a lively young woman of marriageable age and not one to hold back from what she wants. She sees Davoren as the ideal lover, combining the sensitivity of the poet with the virility of the freedom fighter, and she immediately begins to imagine herself linked with him in an ideal romance involving poetry and politics.

Minnie would 'love to be able to write a poem—a lovely poem on Ireland an' the men o' '98' [11]. This is hardly surprising; one might safely assume that at least half the verse she has heard would have consisted of those patriotic ballads through which the Nationalist gospel was transmitted and developed. Lacking the power of poetry herself, she would settle for being the subject of a poem. Though her understanding of poets and poetry is somewhat naive, her own experience of sexual relations has made her cagey; she doubts whether any man, even one who had sworn in verse to do so, would lay down his life for his lover. But having no personal experience of patriotic self-sacrifice, she accepts the claims of popular history that patriots willingly die for their country and instances Robert Emmet, whose 1803 rebellion was brief and futile but whose grandiloquent speech from the dock made Emmet among the most famous of all Irish patriots. Emmet was still a young man when he was publicly hanged, drawn, and quartered in Thomas Street, but his speech, in which he requested that nobody write his epitaph until Ireland took its place 'among the nations of the earth,' became a popular recitation at houseparties, and a printed version was a standard wall-hanging in Nationalist homes. There were at least two plays called *Robert Emmet*, one by Boucicault and one by H. C. Mangan,[27] but Minnie would not have needed to see them to know the historical precedent for the role that awaited her: to Davoren's Emmet she would be Anne Devlin, who remained loyal to Emmet even when tortured by the infamous Major Sirr and who went on to become one of the few women in the Nationalist pantheon.

Meanwhile, until such time as she can show her patriotic devotion to Davoren the freedom fighter, Minnie must settle for the literary attentions of Davoren the poet. With characteristic agility she makes Davoren promise that he will write a poem about her. The string of visitors prevents Davoren from getting down to the task immediately, and so, before she rushes back to work, Minnie settles for something different.

MINNIE. Sacred Heart, I've only ten minutes to get back to work! I'll have to fly! Quick, Mr Davoren, write me name in typewritin' before I go—just 'Minnie.'
[DAVOREN *types the name*]
MINNIE [*shyly but determinedly*]. Now yours underneath—just 'Donal.' [DAVOREN *does so.*] Minnie, Donal; Donal, Minnie; good-bye now. [23]

Nothing, not even the attention to Gallogher's legal letter, shows the community's worship of writing more than Minnie's cherishing of a piece of paper with two names typed on it. For her it is a charm that unites her with her patriotic lover who has not only the power of writing but also the latest technology with which to do so.

In order to make any kind of sense of Minnie's request and of the general atmosphere of Hilljoy Square, we must remember that, despite the influence of modern education, the culture of the Dublin tenements preserved 'much of the mind-set of primary orality.'[28] Specifically, we must remember that

> when a fully formed script of any sort . . . first makes its way from outside into a particular society, it does so necessarily at first in restricted sectors and with varying effects and implications. Writing is often regarded at first as an instrument of secret and magic power.[29]

Mr. Gallogher obviously believes that by assuming the literary style of a lawyer, he acquires some of the power and status associated with the legal profession, masters of the most flamboyantly arcane branch of writing. This belief is shared and supported by those of his neighbours, who are in awe of the document he has produced. Minnie prizes the piece of paper on which Davoren has typed their names because she sees it as much more than a piece of paper. For her it represents Davoren's power to confer a kind of immortality on her and is also an earnest of his affection for her. Just as she believes that all poems are literally true, so she believes in the physical implications of a scrap of paper on which her name is linked with that of Davoren. She carries it as a charm, an item of magic potency.

As Walter Ong reminds us, the English language preserves evidence of the early reaction to the new art of writing:

> the Middle English 'grammarye' or grammar, referring to book-learning, came to mean occult or magical lore, and through one Scottish dialectical form has emerged in our present English vocabulary as 'glamor' (spell-casting power) . . . .The futhark or runic alphabet of medieval North Europe was commonly associated with magic. Scraps of writing are used as magic amulets.[30]

The same connection between literacy and magic can be seen in the word 'spell,' while the word 'charm' derives from the Latin for poem, 'carmen.' The world of Hilljoy Square may at first seem a long way from medieval Britain, but as members of a secondary oral culture, sealed by poverty and social rigidity in their tenement reservations, the inhabitants are as dazzled by the glamour of grammar as Minnie is by Davoren, and their use of speech is much closer to that of oral societies than to that of their formally educated middle-class contemporaries.

It is more than likely, to judge from the stage directions and from his reaction to McCormick's playing of the part, that O'Casey originally conceived of Shields as the villain of the piece, the benighted buffoon whose self-contradictions are exposed by Davoren's incisive barbs, the primitive whose superstitious malignity would be contrasted with Davoren's rational philanthropy. He is the only one in the house who knows the truth about Davoren, but he does nothing to scotch the rumour, perhaps because he feels it will protect him against the landlord to whom he owes rent, perhaps because it appeals to his cynical sense of humour. Despite his belief in religion and superstition, he is utterly cynical in matters relating to his fellow countrymen and their politics. His cynicism is that of the ex-zealot and may owe something to his creator's loss of faith in national movements.[31]

I remember the time when I taught Irish six nights a week, when in the Irish Republican Brotherhood I paid me rifle levy like a man, an' when the Church refused to have anything to do with James Stephens, I tarred a prayer for the repose of his soul on the steps of the Pro-Cathedral.

Whatever idealism he once had has long since degenerated and been transformed into the ultimate scepticism: 'Upon me soul, I'm beginning to believe that the Irish People aren't, never were, an' never will be fit for self-government' [7]. His cynicism is even more pronounced at the beginning of Act Two, where he seems to feel no sorrow for Maguire, dismissing his death merely as a great inconvenience to himself. He is given the final lines of the play, where, typically superstitious, self-serving, and unfeeling, he attributes the death of Minnie to the tapping on the wall.

In the overall pattern of the play Shields represents an unwillingness to join the others in attempted escape from grim actuality into self-promoting fantasies. This is because he has passed through the stage of idealism and emerged a disillusioned cynic. In the other pattern I have been exploring, the linguistic culture of the play, Shields seems to represent somebody who is caught between the oral and the literate.

Shields is intensely, if not compulsively (and in the theatre, hilariously), literate. Seconds after waking up he is referring to Morpheus and annotating the reference with information gleaned from some classical dictionary. He instantly recognises Davoren's quotation from *Prometheus Unbound* and knows something about Shelley's life and opinions. When Davoren quotes from Shakespeare, Shields supplies not only author, play, act, and scene but speaker and addressee as well. This is the ostentation of a man still intoxicated by a recently acquired capacity, the extravagant display of an autodidact who has a faith in book learning that more experienced literates would find excessive, maybe even superstitious. But he is also a compulsive talker. A characteristic of the oral community member is an inability to settle for an interior life of thought where there is the opportunity for talk and conversation. Shields plagues Davoren, who would prefer to compose his own verse in his own mind:

SEAMUS [*stretching himself*]. Oh-h-h. I was fast in the arms of Morpheus—he was one of the infernal deities, son of Somnus, wasn't he?
DAVOREN. I think so.
SEAMUS. The poppy was his emblem, wasn't it?
DAVOREN. Ah, I don't know.
SEAMUS. It's a bit cold this morning, I think, isn't it?
DAVOREN. It's quite plain I'm not going to get much quietness in this house. [4]

A well-read man, conscious of the power of the written word, he remains a pedlar who 'will talk above an hour over a pennorth o' pins' [21]. Or so he would seem to modern readers. Audiences enjoy themselves by laughing at Shields' many shortcomings, but that is not the whole story; audiences also enjoy themselves by delighting in Shields' linguistic dexterity. He has some of the best lines in the play. (O'Casey wanted the audience to loathe Shields, but he had not yet learned, despite his familiarity with *Richard III*, that the audience's relations with characters are not based solely on moral judgments.) Shields' cynicism and cowardice are always interesting because he expresses himself so memorably in a language that is essentially oral in its colourful fluency and its technique of weaving formulas and references into a popular rhetoric. If he doesn't, like Davoren, aspire to the status of literary poet, it is perhaps because he is still content to be a rhapsodist in this predominantly oral community.[32]

The land of Saints and Scholars 'll shortly be a land of bloody poets. [5]

I suppose he [Maguire] was too damn lazy to get up; he wanted the streets to be well aired first.—Oh, Kathleen ni Houlihan, your way's a thorny way. [5]

A Helen of Troy come to live in a tenement! You think a lot about her simply because she thinks a lot about you, an' she thinks a lot about you because she looks upon you as a hero—a kind o' Paris . . . . she'd give the world an' all to be gaddin' about with a gunman . . . . I wouldn't care to have me life dependin' on brave little Minnie Powell—she wouldn't sacrifice a jazz dance to save it. [27]

Shields is wrong about Minnie's capacity for sacrifice, but his earlier analysis of the relationship between her and Davoren is perceptive. It is likely that he was equally incisive and equally striking in his diagnosis of a change in the Irish political climate:

An' you daren't open your mouth, for Kathleen ni Houlihan is very different now to the woman who used to play the harp and sing 'Weep on, weep on, your hour is past,'[33] for she's a ragin' divil now an' if you only look crooked at her you're sure of a punch in th' eye . . . . I believe in the freedom of Ireland, an' that England has no right to be here, but I draw the line when I hear the gunmen blowin' about dyin' for the people, when it's the people that are dyin' for the gunmen! With all due respect to the gunmen, I don't want them to die for me. [28f.]

In his ability to subvert the cliché and expose the fallaciousness of what passed currently for common sense, one of the hallmarks of Shavian drama, Shields anticipates some of Juno's great lines, and this, admittedly partial, identification is another indication of the complex role of Shields in the play. He is no simple *blower* like Tommy Owens, and when he hears that it was Tommy Owens' pub talk that has probably brought on the raid, he is understandably furious: 'Well, God blast the little blower, anyway; it's the likes ov him that deserves to be plugged' [35]. He is a selfish coward, but, apart from the competitive moment with Grigson, he has the minimal virtue of not laying claim to heroism.

His cynical rhapsodies integrate elements from the Irish past, literary and historical, that his audience would recognise. Balor, Banba, Dark Rosaleen, and Cuchulain (significantly mispronounced as 'Cuchullian') drop in like neighbours, while his sardonic modulation of the patriotic lines of Eithne Carberry and Thomas Davis makes his first exit unforgettable:

> Oh, proud were the chieftains of famed Inishfail.
> Is truagh gan oighear 'na vfarradh.
> The stars of our sky an' the salt of our soil—
> Oh, Kathleen ni Houlihan, your way's a thorny way! [10]

He is equally impressive weaving a sceptical pattern by crossing popular patriotic songs like 'The Jacket Green' and 'The Tri-Coloured Ribbon' with a British army uniform complete with war decoration:

> An' what ecstasy it ud give her if after a bit you were shot or hanged; she'd be able to go about then—like a good many more—singin', 'I do not mourn me darlin' lost, for he fell in his Jacket Green.' An' then, for a year an' a day, all around her hat she'd wear the Tricoloured Ribbon O, till she'd pick up an' marry someone else—possibly a British Tommy with a Mons Star. [27]

One can easily imagine F. J. McCormick rejoicing in these lines 'with that proud consciousness of origin that marks the true-born Dubliner, every nuance charged with an intensity of meaning.'[34]

There is nothing in Davoren's lines to excite such local pride. Davoren is the only one in the play whose grammar is not characterised by Irish dialectal forms and whose accent is normally free from the elisions that mark *and* and *-ing* in that of the others. (It is interesting that on two of the three occasions on which he uses elided forms, to the Auxiliary and to Shields when he learns of Minnie's fate, he is under pressure, and the implication is that his acquired accent gives way, and he lapses back into his original speech.[35]) One doesn't need to be conscious of any oral/literate contrast to notice that only Davoren could have spoken the following lines. The form (syntax and vocabulary), rather than the content, distinguishes it from the speech of the other characters:

> Bah. You know as little about truth as anybody else, and you care as little about the Church as the least of those that profess her faith; your religion is simply the state of being afraid that God will torture your soul in the next world as you are afraid the Black and Tans will torture your body in this. [5]

The opening exclamation 'bah' is typical. It would never have been heard in or around Hilljoy Square and obviously derives from Davoren's acquaintance with the upper classes of English literature.

In the absence of any evidence to the contrary, one assumes that Davoren is, like Jack Rocliffe, of Dublin working-class stock. If so, he is quite unusual in his atheism, literary ambition, and lack of involvement with any contemporary political formation, but remarkably similar to his creator. His speech is most obviously literary in its dependence on quotations from such writers as Shelley and Shaw, whose work had never passed into popular usage as had the ballads of the *Nation* or the *Melodies* of Thomas Moore; but there is surely no need to labour the point that Davoren's speech has been raised and refined by his desire to speak as he thinks his favourite writers would speak. In the following lines we detect a biblical formula, a reference to Shelley, and a taste for compound epithets reminiscent of O'Casey's own prose style: 'And you actually rejoice and are exceedingly glad that, as you believe, Shelley, the sensitive, high-minded, noble-hearted Shelley, is suffering the tortures of the damned' [5]. This is fair enough in the course of literary jousts with Shields, whose reading has equipped him to give as good as he gets by way of literary references; but such literary displays border on deception when directed at Minnie.

When Minnie praises Tommy Owens' skill on the melodeon, Davoren refers to Tommy as a 'gifted son of Orpheus,' knowing, presumably, that Minnie will not catch the allusion [11]. Far from adapting his conversation to Minnie's, Davoren parades his academic knowledge of botany: 'These are wild violets, this is an *Arum maculatum*, or Wake Robin, and these are Celandines, a very beautiful flower related to the buttercups' [11f.]. Fully aware that Minnie would 'love to be able to write a poem,' Davoren advertises his own abilities, and Minnie is predictably impressed. Similarly, seeing that Minnie is attracted to him because he is said to be a gunman on the run, Davoren confirms her delusion with a speech that owes more to his reading than to Dublin working class-speech: 'I'll admit one does be a little nervous at first, but a fellow gets use to it after a bit, till, at last, a gunman throws a bomb as carelessly as a schoolboy throws a snowball' [13].[36] Davoren makes no attempt to draw Minnie's attention to the fact that he is quoting from a more celebrated writer, Edward Fitzgerald, in the following:

My soul within art thou, Minnie! A pioneer in action as I am a pioneer in thought. The two powers that shall 'grasp this sorry scheme of things entire, and mould life nearer to the heart's desire.' Lovely little Minnie, and brave as well; brave little Minnie, and lovely as well! [14]

Davoren realises that Minnie is not simply attracted to the actual Donal Davoren but mesmerised to receive the attentions of a supposed gunman-poet: 'A gunman on the run! Be careful, be careful, Donal Davoren. But Minnie is attracted to the idea, and I am attracted to Minnie. And what danger can there be in being the shadow of a gunman?' [23]. He might just as well have wondered what danger there can be in dazzling an impressionable young woman with a display of high literacy and literary knowledge that she would equate with a 'secret and magic power.'

The modern audience shares Davoren's amazement that he, of all people, should be identified as a gunman on the run. Gradually, they conclude that the inhabitants of Hilljoy Square *want* to believe that he is a gunman because the presence of such an exciting figure brings an element of glamorous power to their otherwise drab lives. (Of course, this is precisely what leads Davoren to accept and confirm the fiction.) But why did Tommy Owens not focus this fantasy on Shields, who had actually been a member of the IRB? Or on Minnie, the only one with the requisite courage and commitment? Because, presumably, Davoren is an outsider, an unknown quantity, whereas the others are well known to the community. Davoren has no known past and is a recent arrival who does not go out to work, has no obvious income, and tries to keep himself to himself in his room. Davoren is not only an outsider in the sense of a recent arrival; he is also an outsider in his speech and in the arcane mysteries he pursues in his room. From the initial conversation with Minnie until the final details of the blood-stained paper found 'in her breast,' the audience is led to wonder if there is some connection between Davoren's literary activities and the fact that he is believed to be a gunman.

During the opening run and for many years afterward, audiences must have been startled when the curtain went up to reveal a tenement room and Davoren *sitting at the table typing*. A production set in the present would have to replace the typewriter with a word processor of such sophistication as would cause the audience (and the other characters) to raise their collective eyebrows at the sight of such advanced technology in such an unlikely setting. Basic literacy was only beginning to intrude on the predominantly oral culture of Hilljoy Square and was, as we have seen, associated with power. 'High' literacy, the ability to preserve one's words in written form, was viewed with the awe accorded to Mr. Gallogher's letter. The 'highest' literacy, the ability to print one's own compositions using the latest machinery, would surely have seemed so extraordinary as to be almost supernaturally powerful. So it may be that the inhabitants of Hilljoy Square found it easier to believe that Davoren was a gunman, that is, a member of an elite whose courage and the technology gave them the ultimate power of life and death, because they knew he had another power that was equally rare and equally awe-inspiring.

There is no consciousness of the oral/literary shift among the characters (nor was there, I would guess, in the dramatist's mind at the time), but it could easily be argued that language is the central theme of the play, talk the predominant action, reading and writing crucial elements of the dramatic pattern.

Mrs. Henderson exemplifies the communal addiction to linguistic display. When Mr. Gallogher articulates his carefully formed opinion of Shields, she comments:

MRS HENDERSON. Them words is true, Mr Gallicker, and they aren't. For to be wise is to be a fool, an' to be a fool is to be wise.
MR GALLOGHER [*with deprecating tolerance*]. Oh, Mrs Henderson, that's a parrotox.
MRS HENDERSON. It may be what a parrot talks, or a blackbird, or, for the matter of that, a lark—but it's what Julia Henderson thinks. [21]

In many ways this exchange is characteristic of the play. The theme is language, and the medium is a comic dialogue that draws attention to its own linguistic nature: 'low' dialect, pretentious speech, mispronunciation, misunderstanding. At the core is the malapropism, the ludicrous misuse of words, especially in mistaking a word for another resembling it. Malapropisms (named for Mrs. Malaprop, the creation of another Dorset Street dramatist, Richard Brinsley Sheridan) are almost always the consequence of a cultural aspiration that leads one to attempt a 'higher' level of speech than that which one's circumstances have provided. *The Shadow of a Gunman* is a series of variations on the theme of malapropism.

Endemic in this community, infecting everybody, with the possible exception of Shields, is a tendency to escape the deprivation of Hilljoy Square by assuming a role that either raises the people to a higher social level or connects them with the one excitement available, the Troubles. Davoren, Minnie, and Tommy Owens choose roles provided by history in the sense of the past as recorded in story and verse, orally and literally: Shelleyan poet (and, later, gunman), hero's faithful lover, fervent Nationalist. Minnie makes the fatal mistake of taking her role into the real world. The others lack her physical courage: for example, when Shields and Davoren are confronted by the threatening Auxiliary, they try to save their skins by quick-changing from Seamus and Donal to Jimmy and Dan, undoing years of Gaelic League Nationalism in an instant [38]. Shields and Davoren here demonstrate a skill in exploiting the power of words, but the general pattern is closer to malapropism.

I have already shown how Tommy Owens' political role is created by stitching together a series of 'quotations' from the popular tradition. O'Casey uses Tommy's oral tendencies in order to suggest a political tradition that lacks the critical ability to free itself from the past and face up to the facts of the present. Tommy's dependence on existing formulas suggests a lack of individual awareness, the absence of any subjective filtering of experience. It might even be said that Tommy does not quote popular history; popular history speaks through Tommy.[37] On one significant occasion, however, Tommy is less than neutral: 'Up with the barricades, up with the barricades; it's now or never, now an' for ever, as Sarsfield said at the battle o' Vinegar Hill, Up with the barricades—that's Tommy Owens—an' a penny buys a whistle' [16]. While this may pass over a modern audience as mere bluster, O'Casey would have expected his contemporaries to laugh derisively at anybody who did not know that Sarsfield's eloquent death at Landen in 1693 prevented him from leading the rebels at Vinegar Hill in 1798. The effect of this mistake is to suggest that Tommy is enslaved not only by an historical past but by a form of the historical past that is blatantly garbled.

Nor is Tommy unique in his malapropism, his inability to maintain the level of language to which he aspires. Mrs. Henderson is a Mrs. Malaprop with a Dublin accent. Mr. Gallogher's letter is funny precisely because of his failure to sustain a convincingly legal tone. Even those who are not biblical experts might expect that Mr. Grigson's reading would be imperfect, and they would be right. His favourite quotation is from the *First Epistle of Peter*, 13–17, where one is urged to accept the political system wherever one is; the other biblical instruction he values may also come from this Epistle, Chapter 3, verse 1, where wives are ordered to be in subjection to their husbands. He does not seem to have the same high regard for the remainder of the Epistle, which, apart from advocating virtue in general, contains four specific exhortations to sobriety (I, 13; IV, 3, 7; V, 8). Mrs Grigson's knowledge is very deficient—she refers to Peter's Epistle as a gospel—but it is unlikely that her husband's readings would have attracted her to closer study.

In this respect, what distinguishes Donal Davoren from Tommy Owens is the cultural convention that asserts that *Prometheus Unbound* is more prestigious than 'God Save Ireland.' However, compared to this popular patriotic ballad, which, at the very least, succeeds in doing what it set out to do, Davoren's own 'poetry' is painfully bad, and Davoren's self-satisfaction suggests that his understanding of

Shelley and of the nature of poetry is on a par with Tommy's grasp of Sarsfield's role in Irish history. At least Tommy's quotation from the Nationalist ballad manages the joining of hands more skilfully than Davoren's effusion to the celandine.

Minnie's reading of 'story-books' and her education in romantic Nationalism have shaped her dreams and enabled her to imagine a life more rewarding than that into which she has been born. If she is deceived by Davoren, she is also misled into a fatal form of malapropism by her critical naïveté. For her the poem is the literal truth; what happens in storybooks is the fact, a form of misreading for which she will later pay with her life.[38]

When Davoren realises that the house might be raided, his first thought is the letter addressed to the IRA that he accepted from Mr. Gallogher. He is grateful to God when he finds the letter and destroys it. When Minnie is shot, the other documentary evidence is only partly destroyed.

They were raidin' a house a few doors down, an' had just got up in their lorries to go away, when they was ambushed. You never heard such shootin'! An' in the thick of it, poor Minnie went to jump off the lorry she was on, an' she was shot through the buzzom. Oh, it was horrible to see the blood pourin' out, an' Minnie moanin.' They found some paper in her breast, with 'Minnie' written on it, an' some other name they couldn't make out with the blood; the officer kep' it. [44]

The forensic scientists will never discover what the audience knows: that Minnie has saved Davoren with her own blood. Had she lived, the paper would have led them to Davoren, but now that she is dead, he is safe. She had kept the paper close to her heart as an earnest of Davoren's love and truth, but she had mistaken her man. The paper was not a magic charm but a forgery that brought her to her death. Only in death can brave little Minnie banish Davoren the poltroon from her dreamworld of heroic love: her blood has blotted out his name.

The image of Minnie's blood staining the typewritten paper will probably strike the reader as redolent of Victorian melodrama, but it may have had a deeper, unconscious inspiration. Walter Ong has written:

One of the most startling paradoxes inherent in writing is its close association with death. This association is suggested in Plato's charge that writing is inhuman, thing-like, and that it destroys memory. It is also abundantly evident in countless references to writing (and/or print) traceable in printed dictionaries of quotations, from 2 Corinthians 3:6, 'The letter kills but the spirit gives life' . . . on to and beyond Henry Vaughan's assurance to Sir Thomas Bodley that in the Bodleian Library at Oxford 'every book is thy epitaph.'[39]

O'Casey would certainly have been familiar with the quotation from Paul, but it is unlikely he would have been consciously expounding it in 1922. Indeed, the idea of a connection between writing and death in *Shadow* might seem excessive were there not strong evidence in the later Abbey plays that O'Casey does associate 'high' literacy with deception and death. Leaving aside such metaphysical promptings, it is undeniable that in *Shadow* the major agent of disaster in Hilljoy

Square is an outsider who uses his cultural superiority to delude the community, one of them fatally.[40]

Shortly after the opening night of the play in April 1923, O'Casey knew he had written a play that was perfectly to the taste of the Abbey audience of the day. After all those years in the vocal minority, he was in tune with popular opinion. Had the Abbey audience learned to share O'Casey's reading of recent Irish history? No: the events of a few years later would show that O'Casey's anti-Nationalist views remained anathema to most. It was O'Casey's nihilism that touched the audience, who in 1923 had become thoroughly disenchanted with the degeneration of the national struggle from the high-minded heroism of 1916 down to the small-minded savagery of the Civil War. *The Shadow of a Gunman*, for all its farce, offers a cynically gloomy view of Irish life. (No wonder the actor and the audience warmed to Shields, the cynic within the play.) There is nothing to admire in this world of pseudoreligion, pseudophilosophy, pseudopoetry, pseudopolitics. The real gunman sets up his friend and is then shot while trying to shoot others. The other ambush makes a lot of noise, but the only certain consequence is the death of Minnie. Although Minnie shows courage, the audience knows that she was a silly girl who gave up her life for a cowardly liar. There is even the possibility that she was not shot cold-bloodedly by the alien Auxiliaries but mistakenly by the IRA she admired so much.

The play was structurally unsophisticated. For the most part, it is a string of comic 'turns,' and the telescoping of time that enables Maguire's death to get into the papers shortly after he leaves the house is an obvious weakness. But it had something special. Even at the time, Holloway saw that 'what it lacked in dramatic construction it certainly pulled up in telling dialogue of the most topical and biting kind . . . . Out of the crudeness . . . truth and human nature leaped.'[41] What is much clearer in retrospect is that O'Casey had stumbled on a new form in which he could express his feelings about the Nationalist revolution while holding the close attention of a largely Nationalist audience. The Abbey audience would not have stood for a post-Shavian lecture demonstrating the ideological superiority of atheistic socialism over Christo-heroic Nationalism. On the other hand, they were delighted to laugh at convincingly 'real' characters who represented the bizarre effects of Nationalist ideology on people with an in-built appetite for fantasy and self-delusion.

One wonders to what extent his own experience as a performer, his sense of what worked and what didn't in the theatre, had prevailed over his intention to write 'a play of ideas.' In *Shadow* he had dispensed with the use of a central character who exposes the failings of the others and had adopted the technique of creating characters (reminiscent of the dim-witted tourist and the bungling burglar he had played himself) who exposed their own failings.[42]

He also discovered in *Shadow* a dramatic form that enabled him to express his embittered view of recent Irish history in a way that delighted an audience who did not share his views. From the very beginning critics were uneasy about the manner in which O'Casey, brought up on Shakespeare and Boucicault, mixed comic and tragic elements. The *Irish Times* critic was academically pure in his reaction: this essentially satirical play would be improved if 'the small element of real tragedy' were removed from the ending.[43] Today we are more inclined to admire the manner in which O'Casey uses comedy in order to lull the audience into a false sense of security before shocking them into silence by confronting them with aspects of recent Irish life, notably, political killing, that were far from funny. Audiences, especially Dublin audiences, would laugh heartily at Tommy Owens because, though they might feel intellectually superior to, or distant from, his lack of intelligence, they were drawn into sympathetic identification with his colourful language. The shape of *Shadow* was that into which he would pour his feelings on the Easter Rising and the Civil War: hilarious laughter, followed by shocked silence, followed by another invitation to laughter, which the chastened audience must resist.

Mrs. Grigson's account of Minnie's death silences the audience and makes those who have been laughing feel guilty for their shortsightedness in thinking it was all a joke. The last words are given to Davoren and Shields.

DAVOREN. Ah me, alas! Pain, pain, pain ever, for ever! It's terrible to think that little Minnie is dead, but it's still more terrible to think that Davoren and Shields are alive! Oh, Donal Davoren, shame is your portion now till the silver cord is loosened and the golden bowl is broken. Oh, Davoren, Donal Davoren, poet and poltroon, poltroon and poet!

In one sense he seems to accept responsibility for his role in Minnie's death, but here, as elsewhere, the sense is overwhelmed by the style, the message by the medium, and the audience cringes as they realise that even Minnie's death has not changed Davoren: he is still parading his superior reading and vocabulary, sufficiently unshaken to quote *Ecclesiastes* and repeat the reference to Shelley's *Prometheus Unbound* with which he had glamourised his irritation in the opening moments of the play.

Underlining this idea of failure to learn or change is Shields' wonderful curtain-line in which he remarks *solemnly*: 'I knew something ud come of the tappin' on the wall!' [44]. The cynical Shields is more concerned with vindicating his own wisdom than with acknowledging his part in Minnie's death. In actual fact, his prediction was limited to his own family, but detailed truth is casually sacrificed in order to attribute the death of Minnie to some mysterious agency rather than to his own actions. Such a declaration would have excited laughter earlier on in the play, but surely nobody can laugh at it now that Minnie is dead.

So it had been in the political realm. The inhabitants of Hilljoy Square had been deaf to the appeals of those like Larkin (and O'Casey) who had urged them to embrace a rational socialist revolution that would have changed their own lives for the good. Instead, they had been dazzled by the old fantasies of a Nationalist revolution that promised them everything but brought them nothing but suffering. Yet even when, after 1913, after 1916, after 1919–1921, after 1922–1923, it should have been possible for them to see that Nationalism was merely a delusion, they continued to lend their support and continued to reject the commonsense appeals of organised Labour.

The poor of Hilljoy Square continue to delight in the one commodity in which they are rich, words. They have a belief in the capacity of words to change things, Tommy Owens insisting that the opening words of Mr. Gallogher's letter are 'a hard wallop at the British Empire' [18]. The Auxiliary is wiser than he knows when he describes the Irish as members of 'the seltic race that speaks a lingo of its own, and that's going to overthrow the British Empire—I don't think!' [38f.]. If talk could bring down the British Empire, the Dublin poor would have finished it many years previously.

NOTES

1. Shaw, quoted by C. B. Purdom, *A Guide to the Plays of Bernard Shaw* (London: Methuen, 1964), 158.

2. See Christoper Innes, 'The Essential Continuity of Sean O'Casey,' *Modern Drama* 3, 1990, 419–433.

3. Joseph Holloway, *Joseph Holloway's Abbey Theatre*, ed. Robert Hogan and Michael J. O'Neill (Carbondale: Southern Illinois UP, 1967), 217.

4. Ibid., 227.

5. Augusta Gregory, *Lady Gregory's Journals*, ed. Daniel J. Murphy, 2 vols. (Gerrards Cross: Colin Smythe, 1978), II, 446.

6. See extracts from Lady Gregory's report already quoted on page 41.

7. Gregory, II, 512.

8. Sean O'Casey, *The Letters of Sean O'Casey*, ed. David Krause, vol. 1, 1910–1941 (London: Cassell, 1975), 697.

9. Sean O'Casey, *Autobiographies*, 2 vols. (London: Pan Books, 1980), I, 556. Figures in text in square brackets refer to pages in second volume.

10. Ó Maoláin confirmed that O'Casey knew his Shaw backward. See Maureen Murphy, 'The Raid and What Went with It,' in *Essays on Sean O'Casey's Autobiographies*, ed. Robert G. Lowery (London: Macmillan, 1981), 103–122.

11. I return to this point on page 55f.

12. Notice the reference to 'the books of Bernard Shaw' in the letter to Horace Reynolds quoted earlier.

13. Throughout this study, references to the Abbey plays are given in square brackets after quotations, the numbers referring to pages in Sean O'Casey, *Seven Plays by Sean O'Casey*, a students' edition, with an introduction and notes by Ronald Ayling (London: Macmillan, 1985).

14. Sean O'Casey, *The Harvest Festival* (Gerrards Cross: Colin Smythe, 1980), 11.

15. G. B. Shaw, *The Doctor's Dilemma* (Harmondsworth: Penguin Books, 1946), 147f. Jack Rocliffe is almost certainly indebted to his reading of this play for his reference to Dante as 'the man who had been in Hell' (171).

16. Paradoxically, the apolitical Davoren is devoted to Shelley, whereas the activist Rocliffe preferred Swinburne.

17. O'Casey, *Letters*, I, 105.

18. See Holloway, 215f.; Garry O'Connor, 139f.

19. Holloway, 216.

20. See Garry O'Connor, 144. The history of the play in the theatre suggests that Shields is the dominant character and the part actors prefer. Most productions allow the comedy free rein, so much so that 'several recent productions have underlined the tragedy by closing the distance between Seamus and Donal.' See Bernice Schrank, *Sean O'Casey:*

A Research and Production Sourcebook (Westport, CT: Greenwood Press, 1996), 65ff. O'Casey must have experienced a similar surprise when he realised that audiences did not, as he himself did, see Johnny Boyle as the dramatic focus of *Juno and the Paycock*. See Gabriel Fallon, *Sean O'Casey: The Man I Knew* (London: Routledge and Kegan Paul, 1965), 19, 24.

21. By way of contrast, the Captain's verse in *Juno and the Paycock*, the work of one Mr. Buckley, is obviously intended to provoke derision. See Holloway, 245.

22. See, for example, Garry O'Connor, 136ff.

23. Notice the use of the singular 'it,' which suggests that what killed Owens Senior was the cocktail of drinking *and* talking politics.

24. See, for example, earlier, 25.

25. Legal jargon (which can still terrorise most nonlegal people today) seems to have been the form of writing that most impressed those whose grasp of literacy was precarious. In Daniel Corkery's *The Labour Leader* (Dublin: Talbot Press, 1927), for example, it is said in praise of a man that 'he can write a letter as good as any lawyer in Ireland' [27]. When Mrs. Henderson describes Gallogher's letter as 'as good as any letter decomposed by a scholar,' she seems to use 'scholar' generally to indicate a person of learning, that is, high literacy.

26. Perhaps O'Casey enjoyed the in-joke here, remembering the letter he had written to the Republican Court in 1921 on behalf of tenants in dispute with their landlord. See Tom Buggy, 'Sean O'Casey's Dublin,' in *O'Casey Annual No. 1*, ed. Robert G. Lowery (Dublin: Gill and Macmillan), 94.

27. See Stephen Watt, *Joyce, O'Casey and the Irish Popular Theatre* (Syracuse, NY: Syracuse UP, 1991), 76–88; Séamus de Búrca, *The Soldier's Song: the Story of Peader Kearney* (Dublin: P. J. Bourke, 1957), 46–49. A picture of Robert Emmet is given pride of place in the Clitheroes' home, 'in the centre of the breast of the chimney.' Emmet was also celebrated in Moore's *Melodies*. A popular ballad described him as 'the darling of Erin' who had 'died with a smile.'

28. I have argued this in Chapter 1, page 6.

29. See Chapter 2, page 30.

30. Walter Ong, *Orality and Literacy: The Technologizing of the Word* (London: Methuen, 1982), 93.

31. See Garry O'Connor, 136.

32. While Davoren prefers the 'high' Shelley, Shields prefers the popular poet or balladeer for 'his power to put passion in the common people' [25].

33. The title of one of Moore's *Melodies*.

34. Fallon, 5. Shields' language is so filled with references as to be very difficult for those who do not get the allusions; on the other hand, contemporary Dublin audiences would have felt a strong sympathy for one who spoke their own arcane language.

35. In Act Two Davoren says 'tappin'' but this is clearly an imitation of Shields [26]. O'Casey is not totally consistent. Shields' early lines are unmarked by accent.

36. The use of the impersonal 'one' was totally alien to working-class usage. One could argue that 'does be' was equally out of place in educated speech.

37. Cf. Lévi-Strauss' comment on myths. 'Nous ne prétendons donc pas montrer comment les hommes pensent dans les mythes mais comment les mythes se pensent dans les hommes, et à leur insu' [We are not, therefore, claiming to show how men think the myths, but rather how the myths think themselves out in men and without men's knowledge]. Quoted and briefly discussed in Edmund Leach, *Lévi-Strauss* (London: Fontana, 1970), 51.

38. Davoren tries to correct this view but his example—that 'Annie Laurie wasn't the sweetheart of Bobbie Burns'—is at least ironic because 'Annie Laurie' was not written by Burns but by William Douglas.

39. Ong, 81.

40. This marks a radical change from *The Harvest Festival*, where literacy brought death to its practitioner in a manner that could be represented as a form of martyrdom for the community.

41. Holloway, 215f.

42. See chapter three, page 37.

43. Quoted by Garry O'Connor, 140.

Chapter 5

Juno and the Cliché

In the summer of 1921 O'Casey moved into a room at 422 North Circular Road. His situation was far from ideal. The Kavanaghs on the floor beneath objected if he typed late at night. The Moores on the floor above him were Diehard Republicans and were regularly raided by the Free State Army; on at least one occasion O'Casey himself was awakened and questioned at gunpoint. Nor did the savagery cease when the Republicans declared a truce in May 1923. In September of that year, a Captain Hogan, who had shot a Free Stater, was captured and brutally tortured before being shot and dumped. He had been the boyfriend of Mary Moore, and his execution proved the last straw for Mrs. Moore, who had seen her family life destroyed and her sons and daughter arrested and imprisoned; she wandered out on a cold night and was found dead the following morning. To add to their woes, Mr. Moore had been listed as a beneficiary in a will in 1921, but the document was too vaguely written and allowed lawyers to argue until there was nothing left to distribute.[1]

There is no evidence in O'Casey's notebook that his original conception of *Juno and the Paycock* involved the Civil War. Annie, the daughter of the house, is on strike, but her mother goes out to work. When Juno leaves, Joxer enters and talks with Andy, presumably the original of Jack. At the end of the first act, the Schoolteacher is introduced, and we are told of the will. The second act includes Annie's affair with the Schoolteacher and the borrowing of money in anticipation of the legacy.[2]

The motif of the working-class girl caught between the attraction of a socialist boyfriend and that of a middle-class admirer may derive something from *The Crimson in the Tri-Colour,* where the daughter of the house, Eileen Budrose, was courted by two men, one of whom was or became 'some kind of labour leader.'[3] It may be that O'Casey originally imagined *Juno* as essentially based on class: just as Annie was dazzled and deluded by the Schoolteacher, so too was the family beguiled by the mirage of a legacy into assuming a pseudo-middle-class standard of living and collapsing into a black hole of debt. The fact that the barren will and the Civil War occurred at the same time in the lives of the Moores may have seemed more than a simple coincidence to a dramatist disenchanted with Irish politics; for hundreds of years the Irish people had been promised that the departure of the British, source of all their woes, would usher in a golden age, but they soon realised that, the British gone, their great expectations were disappointed, and they inherited nothing but more violence, more suffering, more sacrifice, more promises. The merging of the two plots, the tragedy of the Civil War reprisals and the bitter comedy of a poor family's aspirations, proved a stroke of genius.

However much he was influenced by the sad saga of the Moores, O'Casey's choice of dramatis personae was directed by technical considerations. The Boyle family is not only convincing as a Dublin working-class family but also effective as a dramatic quartet of voices representing key parts of the political spectrum. (O'Casey had done this more obviously and less effectively in *Kathleen*.) The Captain is too selfish to commit himself to any ideology; Juno has seen enough of politics to have an instinctive distrust of all ideology. Mary supports the socialist plan for the improvement of the working class. Johnny has already paid dearly for his allegiance to the Republic but, being a Diehard, denounces the very idea of compromise. Mary is connected with Jerry Devine, representing organised labour, and with Charles Bentham, who was probably identified with the new men of the Free State, eager to put an end to all civil strife so that they could get busy on the socioeconomic ladder. Joxer Daly and Maisie Madigan are typical residents of Hilljoy Square and would have been at home with the blowers and rhapsodists of *Shadow*.

In terms of dramatic history Joxer is the parasite to Boyle's *miles gloriosus*, the feed to Boyle's comedian; in the present context it is interesting to see him as perhaps the ultimate development of Tommy Owens, where Tommy's patriotic posturing has been reduced to the lowest degree of cynical self-interest, and his dependence on formulaic language has been amplified to an extent hard to imagine until one analyses it line by line. Here, for example, is a list from his first appearance, the numbers indicating his individual speeches:

1. Ah, that's a darlin' song.
2. It ud put years on me . . . when the cat's away, the mice can play!
2. A darlin' thing, a daaarlin' thing—the cup cheers but doesn't . . .
4. I'm in a desperate hurry, a desperate hurry.
7. He's an oul' butty o' mine—oh, he's a darlin' man, a daaarlin' man.
8. It's better late than never.
9. 'Ah,' says I, 'you're a darlin' man, a daaarlin' man.'
10. It's a long lane that has no turnin'.
11. God never shut wan door but He opened another!
12. We mighten' want them, an' then agen, we might: for want of a nail the shoe was lost, for want of a shoe the horse was lost, an' for want of a horse the man was lost—aw, that's a darlin' proverb, a daaarlin' . . .

This is by no means unrepresentative of Joxer's language, which is, literally, a catalogue of clichés. He has a treasury, or an arsenal, of brief quotations from verse, proverbs, and idiomatic saying, and he shows great dexterity in stitching them into his lines to suit the circumstances, please others, and preserve the mystery of his own mental processes. When Boyle the provider lists instances of clerical oppression in Irish history, Joxer flatters him with a supporting quote from 'The Heart Bowed Down,' an air from Balfe's *Bohemian Girl.*

BOYLE. Didn't they say hell wasn't hot enough nor eternity long enough to punish the Fenians? We don't forget, we don't forget them things, Joxer. If they've taken everything else from us, Joxer, they've left us our memory.
JOXER [*emotionally*]. For mem'ry's the only friend that grief can call its own, that grief . . . can . . . call . . . its own! [61]

When Boyle speaks of shaking hands with Father Farrell, Joxer comes up with an echo from the popular revolutionary song, 'The Rising of the Moon':

[*ironically*] I met with Napper Tandy, an' he shuk me be the han'! [32]

On discovering that Boyle's expected wealth has given him a more favourable opinion of the clergy's contribution to 'the fight for Irelan's freedom,' Joxer has no difficulty in coming up with a more harmonious quotation from a Nationalist ballad praising a dear priest:

[*fervently*]. Who was it led the van, Soggart Aroon?
Since the fight first began, Soggart Aroon? [69]

Boyle introduces Joxer to Bentham as a former Chief Ranger of a branch of the Irish National Foresters, which took its name from a popular patriotic song, 'The Dear Little Shamrock.' The ever-alert Joxer raises the level of his reference to match that of the educated Bentham when he adds: 'Nil desperandum, Captain, nil desperandum' [76].[4] Of course, it is all the more hilariously incongruous when Joxer fails twice to get beyond the second line of songs at the party. The implication is that Joxer only has 'the wind of the word,' that he is all right for a couple of lines or so but no more, that his knowledge of the verses he quotes so constantly is partial, his comprehension minimal.

Poverty has made Joxer a parasite who lives by his wits and will survive as long as he can flatter somebody like the Captain into generosity. He is the complete sponger, but though the audience may despise his cynical selfishness, they must admire his utterly amoral verbal agility. Though by no means short of cunning, Joxer is devoid of intelligence, the ability to filter, analyse, and estimate experience; there is a sense in which Joxer consists of the past as enshrined in the clichés and formulas of popular culture. He is blind to the two major social issues of the play, the Civil War and the Labour movement. (For him there is no future because the future has not yet been recorded, and he lacks the interior consciousness with which to imagine it.) When Mrs. Boyle, shocked by the appearance of Mrs. Tancred, lists those from the house who have been killed or wounded, Boyle responds with a reference to his own fanciful past, while Joxer delivers himself of his most appallingly facetious quotation, this one from Wallace's *Maritana*: 'Let me like a soldier fall—me breast expandin' to th' ball!' [81]. There is no chance of Joxer dying a heroic death. The greatest threats to his life are silence and starvation. Like Boyle, Joxer begins by striking the audience as hilarious to the extent that his ingratiating quotations are relatively harmless, but as the fantasy of the will crumbles into death and desolation, Joxer's absolute selfishness provokes a ferociously bleak black comedy.

Though his speech is clearly marked by the characteristics of an oral culture, Joxer claims to be literate. He expresses his admiration for an old tale, *Elizabeth, or The Exiles of Siberia* [59], and for a popular history, *The Story of Ireland*, (1883), by A. M. Sullivan and not, as Boyle characteristically mistakes it, by J. L. Sullivan, the Irish American boxing champion [69]. His final lines refer to the 'darlin' story' of *Willie Reilly and His Own Colleen Bawn* by William Carleton. But one feels that books, if he has ever read any, have had little effect on his oral mind-set: they remain talismanic, emblems of knowledge and power.

The same could not be said of Mary Boyle, who is, of course, of another generation. The opening stage direction locates her between two cultural forces:

one, through the circumstances of her life, pulling her back; the other, through the influence of books she has read, pushing her forward. The opposing forces are apparent in her speech and her manners, both of which are degraded by her environment, and improved by her acquaintance—slight though it be—with literature. [47]

Being young and ambitious and a friend of Jerry Devine, she supports the organised labour union. The lines that establish her in the opening sequence are characterised by the concept of 'principles' and the 'new' slogans or formulas of industrial resistance. These abstract principles are a product of a literate culture and so attract the younger generation as much as they bemuse their parents.

What's the use of belongin' to a Trades Union if you won't stand up for your principles? Why did they sack her? It was a clear case of victimisation . . . . It doesn't matter what you say, Ma—a principle's a principle. [49]

On these same grounds Mary approves of her brother's refusal to accept that the Treaty has brought an end to the conflict: 'He stuck to his principles, an', no matter how you may argue, Ma, a principle's a principle' [50]. When Bentham enters toward the end of Act One, Johnny repeats this mixture, dismissing his mother's complaint that his patriotism has yet to do him any good.

I'd do it agen, Ma, I'd do it agen; for a principle's a principle . . . . Ireland only half free'll never be at peace while she has a son left to pull a trigger. [65]

The audience will soon discover that the younger Boyles' adherence to these principles is very superficial. Johnny is doomed, having betrayed a comrade; Mary is dressing up not to support her fellow workers but to meet the man who will doom her and the rest of her family to a social perdition from which they will never escape to the 'better' life that all the Boyles aspire to.[5]

O'Casey makes it obvious that the inhabitants of Hilljoy Square generally speak with an uneducated accent, but, as a means of enabling any actor or actress to reproduce the sounds on which the dialogue was based, his efforts at phonetic transcription are inadequate. Take, for example, Boyle's reply to Bentham's remark on Mrs. Boyle's nickname:

Yis, doesn't it? You see, Juno was born and christened in June; I met her in June; we were married in June, an' Johnny was born in June, so wan day I says to her, 'You should ha' been called Juno,' an' the name stuck to her ever since. [65]

O'Casey has transcribed four words in a non-Standard manner: *Yis, an', ha',* and *wan.* If we assume that O'Casey is suggesting a working-class Dublin accent, we do so not because of the evidence of this transcription but on external evidence—historical, biographical, traditional. The preceding four variations from Standard that he advertised are not limited to Dublin or even to Irish dialects of English. More to the point, had he been striving for precision of transcription, O'Casey could have easily indicated other non-Standard features. For example:

Yis, doesn' i'? Y'see, Juno wiz born an' christent in June; I met her in June; we were married in June, an' Johnny wiz born in June, so wan day I sez t' her, 'Ye should 'a' been call' Juno,' an' the name stuck to 'er ever since.

Even this is patently inadequate, for without using the international phonetic alphabet, there is no way of showing, for example, the enormous difference between the Dublin city working-class pronunciation of *I met her* and *June* and the same words in Received Pronunciation. In these plays O'Casey is content merely to indicate the presence of dialect, lower-class Irish and English, or the absence of lower-class dialect. One assumes, for example, that an actual Bentham, for all his studies, would have had a pronounced Irish accent; however, all his lines are written in Standard, and since the play was written for the Abbey, there was no problem. Outside Ireland, if there is an attempt to use Irish accents, presumably Bentham will be played with the local idea of a middle-class (or what the British media refer to as 'an educated') Irish accent.[6] Of course, there is no absolute need for Dublin or even Irish accents: all that is necessary to comply with O'Casey's demands is that there be a distinction between middle-class Bentham and the other working-class characters, just as there was between Davoren and the other inhabitants of Hilljoy Square. Apart from accent, there are other and more interesting linguistic differences between Bentham and the others.

Even if O'Casey had given no indications of accent, only one character could have spoken the following lines: 'Juno! What an interesting name! It reminds one of Homer's glorious story of ancient gods and heroes' [65]. The inhabitants of Hilljoy Square would have immediately recognised the tone as 'higher' than their own, partly because of the reference to Homer and partly, and much more strikingly, because of the forms of expression. They would have said: 'Juno! That's an interesting name. It'd remind you . . .'[7] The phonetics of Bentham's lines do not matter all that much; what is crucial to a production of the play is that the audience recognise that his speech is different from that of the others. His 'educated' use of expressions that are closer to Standard than to Hiberno-English establishes him as culturally alien and socially superior to the Boyles and their neighbours. Bentham is the Davoren of *Juno*, a higher literate among a community that is still overwhelmingly oral.

Before he ever opens his mouth, Bentham's dress advertises his social superiority: he is wearing knee breeches and a tie and carrying gloves and a walking stick. Twelve times in four pages Juno refers to him as *Mister* Bentham. Her deference is emphasised in her initial welcome in which the repetition is set against her working-class grammar and innocence of what is acceptable in polite conversation:

Come in, Mr. Bentham; sit down, Mr. Bentham, in this chair; it's more comfortabler than that, Mr. Bentham. Himself'll be here in a minute; he's just takin' off his trousers. [64]

When her husband offers Bentham a drink, using slang terms that Bentham does not recognise, Juno reminds him that their guest is not only from a different class but speaks a different language: 'Jack, you're speakin' to Mr. Bentham, an' not to Joxer.'

Jerry's efforts to ingratiate himself with the Boyles and defeat Bentham in order to win Mary are particularly inept: while Bentham appears to offer a life of permanent leisure, all Jerry can offer the Captain is work. A union employee, Jerry is painfully aware of the attraction that the well-dressed schoolteacher has for Mary:

I saw yous comin' out o' the Cornflower Dance Class, an' you hangin' on his arm—a thin, lanky strip of a Micky Dazzler, with a walkin'-stick an' gloves! [57]

This is Jerry's best moment in the play because here he gives some idea why he was favourite to be elected secretary of the union. His hostile depiction of Bentham is what one would expect from a jealous lover in a culture noted for verbal abuse; but his image of Bentham as a 'Micky Dazzler' is inspired. The term generally indicates a person (Michael was a common name) who dresses extravagantly to attract female attention. The sexual connotation is strengthened by the fact that 'micky' was slang for penis,[8] but the crucial element is the recognition of Bentham as somebody who is setting out to dazzle (to bewilder and delude with an excess of light, motion, or number or, by extension, prospects) the entire Boyle family by offering the escape they all long for. Onstage, Bentham attracts instant attention with his dress, his news, and, most persistently, his use of language. When Jerry tries to compete with the charms of the well-spoken schoolteacher, he fails:

Have you forgotten, Mary, all the happy evenin's that were as sweet as the scented hawthorn that sheltered the sides o' the road as we sauntered through the country?

This is poor stuff. Compared to the admittedly high standard of Hilljoy Square, it is technically inept. There is no sense of pacing or modulation, and the excessive alliteration spoils the imagery of the country road so that the scent of the hawthorn becomes quite sickly and Jerry the romantic lover quite silly; he is not speaking out of his own oral tradition but striving after effects he has found in romantic novels and verse. Here, as so often in these plays, the unsuccessful aspiration collapses into a species of malapropism. When he makes his last effort—'Let me kiss your hand, your little, tiny, white hand!'—the audience, for once, must agree with Boyle, who asks: 'Your little, tiny, white hand—are you takin' leave of your senses, man?' [57f.].

Boyle's contempt for Jerry's floundering derives from his own confidence in wielding words, as Jerry of all people should know, for he has just had a taste of Boyle's vituperative powers. When Jerry describes how he has been looking everywhere for him to tell him the good news about the job, Boyle reacts memorably:

What business is it o' yours whether I was in a snug or no? What do you want to be gallopin' about afther me for? Is a man not to be allowed to leave his house for a minute without having a pack o' spies, pimps an' informers cantherin' at his heels? [55]

This is splendidly crafted and paced, two relatively short questions followed by a climactic third. The third develops the hunting metaphor suggested in the second by *gallopin'* and creates the image of Boyle (the peacock turned fox) being pursued from the cover of his tenement house through the streets of Dublin, not by a group of red-coated aristocrats but by a gang of furtive blackguards. The development of the imagery is supported by the fabric of alliteration, consonance, and rhythm:

Is a *m*an not to be a*l*l*ow*ed
to *l*eave his h**ou**se for a *m*inute
without having
a *p*ack o' *sp*ies, *p*im*p*s an' informers
cantherin' at his heels?

The alliteration lends energy to the pursuit, while the triple catalogue of persecutors, a standard rhetorical emphasis, underlines the unfairness of the odds, the unjustness of the suffering.[9]

Boyle is a gifted wordsmith, and his masterpiece, dwarfing the fantasies of *Shadow*, is his epic portrait of the artist as a modern Odysseus. To produce and develop this heroic canvas, he must overcome the kind of scathing criticism that was never invoked in *Shadow*.

Everybody callin' you 'Captain,' an' you only wanst on the wather, in an oul' collier from here to Liverpool, when anybody, to listen or look at you, ud take you for a second Christo For Columbus! [54]

Confronted by his willing auditor and inspired by the shouts of a coal-seller on the street, Boyle is undeterred by any memory of his wife's remarks, and he launches into his magnificent fantasies of life at sea, sailing the globe in all weathers, seeing strange things, and pondering the mysteries of creation:

Them was days, Joxer, them was days. Nothin' was too hot or too heavy for me then. Sailin' from the Gulf of Mexico to the Antanartic Ocean. I seen things, I seen things, Joxer, that no mortal man should speak about that knows his Cathechism. Ofen, an' ofen, when I was fixed to the wheel with a marlin-spike, an' the win's blowin' fierce an' the waves lashin' and lashing, till you'd think every minute was going to be your last, an' it blowed—blew is the right word, Joxer, but blowed is what the sailors use . . . . An', as it blowed, I ofen looked up at the sky an' assed meself the question—what is the stars, what is the stars? [61f.]

Joxer, like everybody else, knows that this is all a fantasy, that, in fact, 'a row on a river' would make this would-be sailor seasick [67]. But the Captain rides out these squalls and holds his course. Like all the great live performers, he can improvise to suit the circumstances. When Bentham claims attention with his talk of Yogi, the Captain refuses to be outdone: 'Yogi! I seen hundhreds of them in the streets o' San Francisco' [73].

Initially, his fantasies are hilariously funny, but as the atmosphere of the play darkens, so too does the effect of his remorseless adherence to them. Not even the presence of Mrs. Tancred is allowed to temper his rhapsodies:

When I was a sailor, I was always resigned to meet with a wathery grave; an' if they want to be soldiers, well, there's no use o' them squealin' when they meet a soldier's fate. [81]

This unshakeable faith in his own fiction makes Boyle one of O'Casey's masterpieces and his contribution to the finale so effective. When he has lost everything, and the hangover has begun to intimate itself into his final binge, Boyle refuses to take any responsibility for the collapse: it is the country (and the world) that will have to steady itself [101]. He exists in a time frame of his own in which the past/present/future of common sense does not exist. He redefines his own life in terms of a new past that leads to a new future, both fantasies.

If th' worst comes . . . to th' worse . . . I can join a . . . flyin' . . . column . . . I done . . . me bit . . . in Eassther Week . . . had no business . . . to . . . be . . . there . . . but Captain Boyle's Captain Boyle! . . . . Commandant Kelly died . . . in them . . . arms . . . Joxer . . . Tell me Volunteer butties . . . says he . . . that . . . I died for . . . Irelan'! [101]

This takes us beyond the ludicrous and into the realm of the obscene. It would have been particularly effective in the 1920s, when a special disdain was reserved for those who falsely claimed to have taken part in the national struggle and who consequently prospered 'on another man's wounds.' Local considerations aside, any audience will cringe at the sight of a drunken, apathetic father laying claim to the kind of patriotic commitment that maimed and killed his own son.

It seems inadequate to describe Boyle as a liar, even as a pathological liar. It is difficult to imagine that in a twentieth-century city a man could enact such outrageous roles and have them tolerated, if not accepted, by his family and friends. Psychologists will have their own explanations, but the anthropologist will recognise in Boyle tendencies common in oral cultures. For the Captain words are an event in themselves and have a power over actuality; the world created by words competes with the actual world.[10] Perhaps such faith always inspires pathological liars, enabling them to believe in their own creation at least as much as in their own experience, to believe that fantasy has a fighting chance against fact. Part of his greatness as a dramatic character is his power to convince the audience that he actually believes what he is saying when he says it. Though the audience *knows* that Boyle is lying, they find it impossible not to enjoy the creative power that takes them through raging storms from the equator to the pole, and all without any risk of getting wet.

Boyle is the greatest of those characters created by O'Casey to suggest the capacity for self-delusion that he saw as the fatal weakness of the working-class poor. Boyle is not merely typical of those who failed to see where their political interests lay, not merely of those who failed to take part in the struggle for their country or their class, not merely of those who served their own interests at the expense of those around them, not merely of those who preferred some illusion of self-importance but of those who, when the fighting was over, were capable of claiming that they were among the idealists who had risked all in the fight for freedom.

The man on whom O'Casey based Boyle may well have been morally reprehensible, but he served as the model for a masterpiece. The story is told that the real-life Joxer and Boyle saw *Juno* at the Abbey. Daly was furious and threatened to sue O'Casey. As one might expect, the original Boyle was more agile, simply denying the resemblance that seemed obvious to others.[11]

There are many ways in which *Juno* is an advance on *Shadow*, but the key difference between the two plays is the character of Juno. It may be that in Mrs. Moore's sufferings O'Casey recognised the sufferings of his own mother and that the influence of his beloved mother led him to create a character who, while no allegorical Perfection, is almost free from the vices of Hilljoy Square and is granted virtues unimaginable in the other characters.

To begin with, Juno is defined by her powerlessness, her inability to impose her will on her husband or offspring.

She is forty-five years of age, and twenty years ago she must have been a pretty woman; but her face has now assumed that look which ultimately settles down upon the faces of the women of the working-class; a look of listless monotony and harassed anxiety, blending with an expression of mechanical resistance. Were circumstances favourable, she would probably be a handsome, active and clever woman. [47]

But circumstances are not. Her husband, a member of the long-term unemployed, drinks in the morning while his wife waits to serve him breakfast. (She does this not in a spirit of wifely devotion but because she knows from bitter experience that unless she supervises matters, her husband will lavish on his crony more hospitality than they can afford.) In vain has she gone down on her knees and begged her son to stay out of the Civil War. In vain has she tried to dissuade her daughter from becoming involved with the union. Yet, though unable to influence a world run by men, she is the most powerful presence on the stage, not because of her actions but because of her words.

Juno is a woman whose speech is marked by a lack of formal education; one would not be surprised to learn that she is illiterate. O'Casey advertises her working-class accent in his usual way by eliding final consonants, aspirating dentals, and indicating pronunciations that were archaic in Received English:

Ay, that's what he'd like an' that's what he's *waitin'* for—till he thinks I'm gone to work, an' then sail in with the boul' Joxer, to burn all the coal an' dhrink all the tea in the place, to show them what a good Samaritan he is! But I'll stop here till he comes in, if I have to wait till tomorrow mornin'. [48]

In Irish society, then even more than now, such an accent normally indicated a lack of the power associated with middle-class education and private property. Juno is initially deferential when Bentham arrives on the scene, but, within her own family and class, she shows a critical intelligence and a command of language of which the most highly educated burgher would be proud.

The play has hardly begun when Juno shows her imagination and linguistic dexterity, caricaturing her navvy husband as 'a paycock.' This may seem excessive until we meet Boyle and notice his 'slow, consequential strut.' The more we learn about Boyle, the unemployed navvy whose colourful fantasies are so strikingly at odds with his circumstances, the more we will appreciate the imaginative intelligence that sees him 'struttin' about the town like a paycock.'

Even more striking than her command of metaphor is Juno's ability (which may owe as much to Shaw's paradoxical wit as to Susan Casey's kindness) to subvert those slogans or formulaic statements in which others seek an escape from individual thinking. When asked by her straitened mother why she is on strike, Mary Boyle cites the standard union principle of solidarity: 'It was a clear case of victimization. We couldn't let her walk the streets, could we?' Juno counters by pushing the logic of Mary's principles ad absurdum:

No, of course yous couldn't—yous wanted to keep her company. Wan victim wasn't enough. When the employers sacrifice wan victim, the Trades Unions go wan better be sacrificin' a hundred. [49]

In dramatic terms, a poor mother's instinctive pragmatism castigates the giddy innocence of youth; viewed in the light of cultural history, it may be that Juno, formed in an overwhelmingly oral culture, cannot understand (and maybe even fears) the alien mental process by means of which young people can become passionate about abstractions, about things that do not exist in her world. Toward the end of the first act, when Johnny boasts of his principles, Juno is even more dexterous as she exposes the weakness of his assertions by locating them in the *real* world:

MRS BOYLE. Ah, you lost your best principle, me boy, when you lost your arm; them's the only sort o' principles that's any good to a workin' man.

JOHNNY. Ireland only half free'll never be at peace while she has a son left to pull a trigger.
MRS BOYLE. To be sure, to be sure—no bread's a lot better than half a loaf. [65]

As we might expect, she has vast resources of irony. She blasts Joxer with the ordinary variety:

Pull over to the fire, Joxer Daly, an' we'll have a cup o' tay in a minute! Are you sure, now, you wouldn't like an egg? . . . . people is always far more comfortabler here than they are in their own place. [52]

Juno's double comparative would be heard as a mistake by most members of the audience, but observant listeners learn not to laugh; Juno has a much greater command of language than those who would fault her diction as, in some sense, untutored.

Take, for example, her scathing account of her husband's preparations for work.

Shovel! Ah, then, me boyo, you'd do far more work with a knife an' fork than ever you'll do with a shovel! If there was e'er a genuine job goin' you'd be dh'other way about—not able to lift your arms with the pains in your legs! Your poor wife slavin' to keep the bit in your mouth, an' you gallivantin' about all the day like a paycock! [54]

The word 'shovel' states the subject succinctly in a very sarcastic key. The opening phrase, 'Ah, then, me boyo,' is largely phatic, shifting the focus on to the victim of Juno's scorn and also serving as a simple drumroll prelude to the elaborate musical arrangement of what follows. The first sentence is essentially a three-line stanza:

> *you'd do far more work*
> *with a knife an' fork*
> *than ever you'll do with a shovel.*[12]

The metrical structure

$$\cup \cup - \cup -$$
$$\cup \cup - \cup -$$
$$\cup - \cup \cup - \cup \cup - \cup$$

is instantly apprehended as sufficiently regular to make it memorable, an important function of rhythm in oral culture. The alliterative pattern is also strikingly fricative and offensive: the **f** of f*ar* anticipates the strong repetition in *knife an' fork*, while the voiced versions in *ever* and *shovel* complete the pattern. The assonantal pattern is in perfect harmony with the rhythmical and rhetorical pattern, which is a strong contrast between what **he would do** *with a knife an' fork* and what **he will do** *with a shovel*. The remainder repeats and amplifies the central theme of ironic contrast in two viciously satirical repetitions. In the first, all Boyle's dishonesty and laziness are contained in the ludicrous image of a man who is *not able to lift your arms with* *the pains in your legs*; in the second, the disgracefully incongruous relationship of husband and wife is suggested not only in the conjunction of the images of *slave* and *peacock* but also in the linguistic contrast between the common, concrete vernacular of *your poor wife slavin' to keep the bit in your mouth* and the extravagant fantasy of a poor unemployed Dubliner *gallivantin' about all the day like a paycock!*

The lines are typical of the Hiberno-English oral style and translate effortlessly back into Irish.

Sluasaid! Ar' a bhuachaillín-ó, is mó go mór an obair a dhéanfá le scian agus forc ná le sluasaid! Dá mbeadh post ceart ar fáil, a mhalairt de chuma a bheadh ort—gan a bheith in ann do lámha 'árdú leis an bpian i do dhá chois! Do bhean bhocht ag sclábhaíocht chun an greim a choinneáil i do bhéal agus tusa ag starrfach thart an lá go léir ar nós péacóige!

The characteristics of the Irish and Hiberno-English can be highlighted by transposing, somewhat facetiously, Juno's lines into Standard English.

Work! You are more concerned with consumption than production. If work were available, your attitude would be quite different: you would be incapacitated by rheumatism. While your unfortunate wife labours in order to feed you, you are occupied in idle self-conceit.

The language of modern literates is careful to be correct and tends toward the abstract. For the speakers of Hilljoy Square speech is a performance, an event in itself rather than a mere report: they enjoy it, make it exuberant and memorable by using striking rhythms and an abundance of metaphors derived from physical experience.

We find in Juno's speech an economy of image, rhythm, alliteration, and assonance normally associated with verse. It is superb dramatic writing: memorably vivid, strikingly structured, and tonally in key with the character of Juno. Nobody acquainted with Irish speech would feel that it offended against the basic laws of realism: even today, after sixty years of modernisation, one might be pleased, but certainly not surprised, to hear such a speech from an elderly Irish person of Juno's social location.[13]

But for all her rhetorical prowess Juno still has no real power in the family. When Bentham tells of the will, Juno imagines a relief from the anxiety of poverty, Johnny looks forward to getting away to where they are not known, and Mary can anticipate a life of middle-class respectability with Bentham. Characteristically, Boyle does not wait for the money: he re-creates himself as a captain of commerce, a professional man of business. It should not surprise those who are familiar with *Shadow* that when Boyle encounters Joxer in Act Two, he *'takes a pen in his hand and busies himself with papers'* [68]. For the inhabitants of Hilljoy Square the ultimate authority and social prestige were exemplified by the signature that activated the power of written documents, and so the first things that Boyle acquires are the props he needs for his performance as lawyer-cum-businessman: an old attaché case, paper, and a pen.

Ever since the Will was passed I've run hundreds o' dockyments through me han's—I tell you, you have to keep your wits about you. [68]

Boyle sees Bentham as a competitor for the headship of the household. Bentham brings word of the will, which will enable the family to live at the level Boyle has never achieved for them; Bentham bears himself with, and speaks with, the authority that Boyle feels is the prerogative of the father. Boyle reacts characteristically: if 'his Majesty, Bentham' has decided to study to become a lawyer, Boyle will become a lawyer. Joxer automatically slips into a supporting role, offering to return when Boyle is less busy, but wealth and power have not lessened Boyle's magnanimity:

It's all right, Joxer, this is the last one to be signed today. [*He signs a paper, puts it into the case, which he shuts with a snap, and sits back pompously in the chair.*] Now, Joxer, you want to see me; I'm at your service—what can I do for you, me man? [68]

Now that he is a professional person, Boyle can offer his considered opinion on the two men who wish to become his son-in-law.

[Bentham's] too dignified for me—to hear him talk you'd think he knew as much as Boney's Oraculum. He's given up his job as teacher, an' is goin' to become a solicitor in Dublin—he's been studyin' law. I suppose he thinks I'll set him up, but he's wrong shipped. An' th' other fella—Jerry's as bad. The two o' them ud give you a pain in your face, listenin' to them; Jerry believin' in nothin', an' Bentham believin' in everythin.' [70]

Not that anybody could be more ridiculously 'dignified' than Boyle, who must outdo Bentham on every subject from gramophones to theosophy, from the stock market to ghosts.

The party is a typical working-class affair in which, lubricated by drink, people become merrily voluble and sing. Bentham is obviously the outsider: he doesn't join in the singing, and his major contribution relates to spiritual beliefs that are alien to the Boyles and their other guests. When Mrs. Tancred passes down the stairs on the way to the removal, Juno echoes the words of Mrs. Rocliffe:

MRS BOYLE. He's gone now—the Lord be good to him! God help his poor oul' creature of a mother, for no matther whose friend or enemy he was, he was her poor son.
BENTHAM. The whole thing is terrible, Mrs Boyle; but the only way to deal with a mad dog is to destroy him.
BOYLE. . . . We've nothin' to do with these things, one way or t'other. That's the government's business, an' let them do what we're paying them for doin'.
MRS BOYLE. I'd like to know how a body's not to mind these things; look at the way they're afther leavin' the people in this very house. Hasn't the whole house, nearly, been massacreed? [80]

Juno goes on to name the bereaved of the tenement, identifying the dead by name and family relationship rather than by political affiliation, her physical feeling ('I'd like to know how a *body*'s not to mind') contrasting with Bentham's callousness and Boyle's bluster. Yet Juno is only halfway on the journey that will take her to her final cri de coeur. She is glad they did not have the gramophone playing when the mourning party passed by, and yet she argues that 'in wan way' Mrs. Tancred, because she opened her house to the Diehards, 'deserves all she got.' Shortly afterward she supports Johnny's request that they put a record on the gramophone, and when Nugent chastises them for their lack of 'respect for the Irish people's National regard for the dead,' Juno responds: '*Maybe*, Needle Nugent, it's *nearly* time we had a *little* less respect for the dead, an' a *little* more regard for the livin' [82; emphasis added]. The series of qualifications shows her caught between her sympathy for the bereaved mother and her antipathy to a tradition that elevates the dead above the living. It will take the death of her own son to grant her the enlightenment of her great prayer for peace and love. But first she must deal with the plight of her daughter.

O'Casey opens Act Three with a deft touch when Juno asks Mary if the absent Bentham has done what comes so easily to educated literates: 'An' has Bentham never even written to you since—not one line for the past month?' The reason for his silent absence soon becomes clear. Mary will inherit nothing because 'the scholar, Bentham, made a banjax o' th' will' [93]. His aspirations were beyond his capabilities when it came to legal writing. Thanks to his supermalapropism, all Mary can expect now is a baby whose birth will condemn mother and child to a form of social death.

Boyle's reaction to Mary's pregnancy is characteristic. He shows no sign of being concerned for his daughter's welfare. His wonderful imagination is entirely solipsistic, and he sees Mary's misfortune in terms of his own identity in the oral culture around Hilljoy Square:

An' it'll be *bellowsed* all over th' disthrict before you could *say* Jack Robinson; an' whenever I'm seen they'll *whisper*, 'That's the father of Mary Boyle that had th' kid be th' swank she used to go with; d'ye know, d'ye know?' [92; emphasis added]

As disaster piles on disaster, and the Boyle household crumbles before our eyes, Juno breaks the shackles of received opinion and subverts the most awesome slogan of them all. It was the custom of people like Juno to welcome whatever happened, however terrible, as the will of God. When Mary quotes Jerry Devine's conviction that there was no God, Juno leaps to God's defence:

These things have nothin' to do with the Will o' God. Ah, what can God do agen the stupidity o' men! [99][14]

From one point of view this is the ultimate blasphemy—Juno is suggesting that God is not omnipotent—but we also notice Juno's refusal to take the easy way out by blaming the sins of the world on God. The misfortunes of the Boyles were not a consequence of the *will* of God so much as of the *will*, in both the legal and sexual senses, of men like Bentham and the Captain. With little else to lose at this point she asserts herself for the first time, leaving her incorrigible husband to fend for himself, leaving the house she has kept for him and moving to her sister's, consoling Mary by telling her that her fatherless child will 'have what's far better—it'll have two mothers' [99]. Before she leaves the stage, Juno, now almost possessed with grief, will issue one of the great pleas for peace instead of war.

Part of the power of Juno's speech derives from the fact that it is largely a repetition of Mrs. Tancred's speech in Act Two; now, because of her own personal experience of the loss of her son, Juno *feels* the truth of words that she had not fully understood at the time, and she transfers this shocking awareness to the audience. In her brief appearance Mrs. Tancred had revealed the linguistic talent we associate with Juno. When First Neighbour tried to console her with the slogan that 'the Republicans won't be always down,' Mrs Tancred had dismissed it: 'Ah, what good is that to me now? Whether they're up or down—it won't bring me darlin' boy from the grave.' When assured that her son will be buried 'like a king,' she replies witheringly that she will 'go on livin' like a pauper' [79].

The principal structural element of her threnody is balance: birth and death, beginning and end, Republican and Free Stater. When the following piece is divided, as it might easily be spoken, the pattern of consonance, alliteration, and rhyme becomes clearer.

> Ah, what's the pains I suffered bringin' him into the world
> to carry him to his cradle,
> to the pains I'm sufferin' now, carryin' him out o' the world
> to bring him to his grave!

The same structural elegance is present in the next excerpt. Notice especially how 'her Free State soldier son' ($\cup$ — — — $\cup$ —) is metrically echoed in 'our two dead darlin' sons' and how the alliteration of 'soldier son' is transposed to 'dead darlin'.'

An' I'm told he was the leadher of the ambush where me nex' door neighbour, Mrs. Mannin', lost her Free State soldier son. An' now here's the two of us oul' women, standin' one on each side of a scales o' sorra, balanced be the bodies of our two dead darlin' sons. . . . Mother o' God, Mother o' God, have pity on the pair of us! . . . O Blessed Virgin, where were you when me darlin' son was riddled with bullets, when me darlin' son was riddled with bullets! . . . Sacred Heart of the Crucified Jesus, take away our hearts o' stone . . . an' give us hearts o' flesh! . . . Take away this murdhering hate . . . an' give us Thine own eternal love! [80]

In her anguish at the loss of her own son, Juno realises that she did not share Mrs. Tancred's sorrow sufficiently because she thought of Robbie Tancred as a Diehard:

Ah, why didn't I remember that then he wasn't a Diehard or a Stater, but only a poor dead son! It's well I remember all that she said—an' it's my turn to say it now.

Even at this stage, before she quotes Mrs. Tancred, Juno has struck the rhythmical balance of Mrs. Tancred's delivery. Juno's speech consists of two sections of Mrs. Tancred's with one crucial variation in each section.

What was the pain I suffered, Johnny, bringin' you into the world to carry you to your cradle, to the pains I'll suffer carryin' you out o' the world to bring you to your grave! Mother o' God, Mother o' God, have pity on us all! [100]

In the first important variation Juno addresses her dead son rather than any interlocutor; in the second she asks the Mother of God to have pity on 'us all' rather than on 'the pair of us.' Both changes increase the emotional intensity, and the second widens the focus to include all suffering humanity.

It may seem to some that the structure of these speeches is excessively elaborate and beyond the practice of a working-class woman in Dublin in the 1920s, but there is no basis for such reservations. O'Casey's first audience would have recognised the specific ritual involved. Mrs. Tancred and Juno are keening their sons in a manner that may still be heard in parts of Ireland and is amply recorded in literature. Traditionally, the keeners address the dead persons, praising their virtues and making little of their faults, asking them why they died and left their friends grieving, imploring heaven why such a cruel fate was decreed for them.

As Synge noticed on the Aran Islands, the *caoineadh* is a strange mixture of paganism and Christianity, a Christianised version of an older strategy to deal with death. Synge also felt the force that forms Juno's second variation:

This grief of the keen is no personal complaint for the death of one woman over eighty years, but seems to contain the whole passionate rage that lurks somewhere in every native of the island. In this cry of pain the inner consciousness of the people seems to lay itself bare for an instant, and to reveal the mood of beings who feel their isolation in the face of a universe that wars on them with winds and seas. They are usually silent, but in the presence of death all outward show of indifference or patience is forgotten, and they shriek with pitiable despair before the horror of the fate to which they are all doomed.[15]

In what are probably the three most famous laments in Irish literature, *Caoineadh Airt Uí Laoghaire*, Maurya's lament in Synge's *Riders to the Sea*, and Juno's, there are Christian elements but a remarkable absence of reference to the key Christian belief in an afterlife of heaven or hell. Where the keener is a mother, there is often, as in Synge and O'Casey, a dual allusion to the pains of birth and death:

I've had a husband, and a husband's father, and six sons in this house—six fine men, though it was a hard birth I had with every one of them and they coming into the world—and there were some of them were found and some of them were not found, but they're gone now the lot of them.[16]

Maurya is at least as concerned with the form of the burial as with the Christian theology of death and resurrection, and she sees the cruel sea as an instrument of pagan fate rather than of Christian providence. Similarly, Mrs. Tancred and Juno implore the Blessed Virgin and the Sacred Heart, but their main concern is with the dead bodies of their sons and not with their immortal souls. Mrs. Tancred and Juno are convincing portraits of Irish mothers who, shocked by the loss of a son, express their grief with a passionate eloquence that derives from their own oral tradition.

It is possible that O'Casey was actually influenced by Synge's Maurya but much more likely that he was drawing on his own experience of bereaved mothers; it may even be that the words used by Mrs. Tancred and Juno were those (or close to those) of Mrs. Moore, his unfortunate neighbour who lived in 'the two pair back' above him on the North Circular Road.

Though it generates more horror, fear, and disgust, *Juno and the Paycock* is not as utterly bleak as *The Shadow of a Gunman*. This is not because there is the slightest suggestion that the social structures involved—religious, political, familial, or communal—offer a ray of hope to the people of the tenement. National politics are still surrounded by idealistic slogans and funereal pomp, but the war of liberation has deteriorated into tit-for-tat murder, and, for the people of Hilljoy Square, it consists of treachery, terror, and serial death; the play opens with an account of Robbie Tancred's dead body, and this is balanced toward the end with the discovery of Johnny Boyle's dead body. On the stage we see Johnny Boyle physically and mentally maimed by his involvement in politics. This 'hero' of 1916 has become an informer living in terror of retribution; no reason is given for his treachery, allowing the audience to think the worst, that he did it from envy of one who was still physically whole, that he did it out of some small spite. There is a grim connection between politics and religion. The funeral of Robbie Tancred is represented ironically by the singing of a hymn:

To Jesus' Heart all burning
With fervent love for men. [82]

Johnny Boyle's summons to the Battalion Staff meeting is accompanied by the funeral crowd reciting the rosary: *Pray for us sinners, now and at the hour of our death* [83]. When the Second Irregular asks Johnny if he has his rosary beads, the significance is clear: prayer announces a sentence of death rather than a promise of forgiveness.

Nor does the Labour movement offer much hope. Mary's socialist principles are quickly and quietly cast aside when Bentham arrives; the liberation of the working class is forgotten in the individual dream of escape into middle-class security. Jerry Devine seems at least as interested in the salary with which he could achieve domestic bliss with Mary as in the fate of the workers who might elect him secretary of the union. Though he claims that Labour teaches that 'humanity is above everything' and that he is a leader 'in the fight for a new life,' his humanity does not extend to an unmarried mother or to the new life in her womb: it is one thing to poeticise about the revolution, quite another to risk one's own prospects for it.

The Captain and Joxer are the ultimate representatives of the communal ability to live lives of selfish fantasy in the face of the stark reality that surrounds them. In a sense they have no selves. Nationalism, socialism, and religion are simply grist to their imaginative mills; the Captain's 'negative capability' gives him a role to suit every circumstance, while Joxer has a quotation for all occasions. All the Boyles want to escape: the Captain succeeds most easily because he will settle for a drink, and Joxer will settle for whatever falls from the Captain's table.

What, apart from the structural superiority, makes this a more profound and less pessimistic play than *The Shadow of a Gunman* is the presence of Juno. The Juno, never susceptible to the power of the slogan, recognises the political funeral for what it is, a cultural trap in which mothers must weep and sons die as a divided community continues to find in the same political and religious codes approval of their conflicting objectives. Juno is no saint, but she is the only one who can break through the vicious circle of slogans that condemn the community to self-sustaining suffering and death. She refuses to take the escape routes which enable the others to avoid the facts of life and death around them. She sees that it is 'our business' and is eventually driven to act rather than simply speak. The woman who was initially defined by powerlessness dismisses the ideological distinction in favour of a common humanity. Her final action shows much more heroic courage than poor Minnie's hysterical gallantry: she salvages the next generation from the mess of the past and leaves the braggart and his parasite to their own exquisitely inane devices.

In *The Shadow of a Gunman* we found a community that, because still predominantly oral, was so awed by the powers of literacy that they aspired to fantasy lives largely derived from literary sources. There is no avoiding the connection between writing and death: the final emblem is the bloody piece of paper on which the name of the writer has been blotted out by Minnie's blood. Davoren's reputation as a master of the highest form of literacy (and of the new technology of typewriting) earned him enormous respect in a community where the only equivalent power was that of the gunman, the master of life and death.

There are many similarities between Davoren and Bentham. Both are outsiders whose superior social status is marked by their use of Standard English rather than the dialect of Hilljoy Square; both of them are non-Catholics among primitive Catholics; both of them are 'high' literates in a secondary oral culture; both of them deceive a local girl by feigning love, and both abandon her in her hour of need. Both are guilty of overreaching or 'high' malapropism. Davoren's pathetic efforts to become a poet-philosopher wreak havoc on the house in which he lives. Bentham has given up teaching, the promulgation of basic literacy, in order to administer the 'higher' language of the law, but his writing of the will is even more generally destructive than Davoren's efforts at poetry. Instead of transmitting the legacy to the Boyles, he makes 'a banjax o' th' Will,' encouraging their great expectations and leaving them with less than nothing; 'the scholar' is exposed as 'the thick,' but by then the damage has been done and he has fled to England. If the will is not, like Davoren's page, covered with actual blood, it is charged with 'that energy that lingers' where sensational actions have taken place [73].

As a dramatic emblem, the fascination with literacy is less obvious but more subtly effective than in *The Shadow of a Gunman*. Her *acquaintance—slight though it be—with literature* has brought Mary into trade union politics and a relationship with Jerry Devine. Literature, in the form of the will, is her letter of introduction to the unscrupulous Bentham. When Boyle hears of his daughter's condition, he does not so much blame Bentham as Mary's contact with literature:

Her an' her readin'! That's more o' th' blasted nonsense that has the house fallin' down on top of us! What did th' likes of her, born in a tenement house, want with readin'? Her readin's afther bringin' her to a nice pass—oh, it's madnin', madnin', madnin'! [92]

Bentham has made Mary pregnant and destroyed the Boyle household, but there is something in Boyle's accusation: Bentham's education, his 'high' literacy, made him attractive to Mary and gave him the power to bring such *madnin'* confusion into Boyle's world. But, here as everywhere, Boyle is selfishly shortsighted: when the prospect of money promised him a wider range of options, he chose the trappings of 'high' literacy, pen and paper, an 'attackey case' and 'dockyments,' and played a part very close to that to which Bentham aspires. He has also decided to scale the highest peak of literacy and become a poet. At the party he disdains the customary song in favour of reciting his first poem. (Joxer and Mrs. Boyle refer to his *writing* of poetry, but there is no stage direction to indicate his possession of a text, and he recites rather than reads the doggerel.)

Boyle's lyrical lament for his imprisoned pal is not the only poem quoted. With a vicious irony, Mary reminds Jerry of 'the verses you read . . . Humanity's Strife with Nature' [96]. It is not clear if Jerry was reading his own work or merely quoting that of somebody else. (Most of what Mary quotes comes from an earlier poem by O'Casey; the last four lines are found only in the play.) It would be easy to believe that Jerry composed these lines, but this is not crucial; what is important is that the socially ambitious Jerry, who seems willing to sacrifice all in his ascent, is associated with such aspects of 'high' literacy as reading and lecturing. Devine has no reply to this reminder of the disparity between his claim and his action. He slinks off in silence, exposed to the audience as a hypocrite. He is not a leader of anything, merely another slave of the cliché that condemns the unmarried mother as an untouchable.

O'Casey's plays almost certainly exaggerate the place occupied by books in this society, partly because he himself had grown up among books, partly because his plays dealt with political activists, but most of all because he uses books and writing in general as important metaphors in his dramatisations of the revolutionary phase of modern Irish history as it impinged on the working class. As we have already seen, an education in reading, writing, and 'rithmetic was, short of inheriting money from a long-lost relative, the only means of social mobility available to the poor. This practical respect for formal education was amplified by the fact that so many of the poor were illiterate and tended to invest literacy with almost magical powers of social transformation. In *The Shadow of a Gunman* O'Casey presented a community that was addicted to writing; clearly, his intention was not to belittle literacy but to expose the tendency of the characters to base their lives on ludicrously inept reading.[17] In *Juno and the Paycock* he uses the miswritten will as a metaphor for his central concern, the delusion of the working class by bourgeois Nationalists who promised everything and delivered nothing. An educated outsider whose obvious social superiority dazzles the Boyles, Bentham intends to exploit the family in order to get a share of their due inheritance, but he fails even to do this, and instead of the promised liberation they are left with general desolation.

Boyle is the last rose of an oral summer, blooming all alone in spite of encroaching literacy. He dismisses Mary's books as 'nothin' but thrash,' but it is unlikely that he is capable of reading beyond the title of the Ibsen collection, and he is suspiciously unwilling even to claim the same degree of reading as Joxer:

BOYLE. . . Three stories, *The Doll's House*, *Ghosts*, an' *The Wild Duck*—buks only fit for chiselurs!
JOXER. Didja ever rade *Elizabeth, or Th' Exile of Sibayria*? . . . Ah, it's a darlin' story, a daarlin' story!
BOYLE. You eat your sassige, an' never min' *Th' Exile o' Sibayria*. [59]

His idea of encyclopedic learning is *Boney's Oraculum*, an almanac of fortune-telling and superstitious prophecy, the popularity of which among the poor testified to their lingering association of books and magic.

In this context, as in so many others, Juno is the shining exception. Though she too is probably illiterate, she is content to remain so and makes no claims to be more than an ordinary working-class wife and mother. Despite her lack of education in literature, philosophy, politics, or religion and with nothing to inspire her except her experience as mother, wife and neighbour, she breaks through the mental barriers that imprison the other residents. She alone can see the natural relations that are concealed by ideological division and political slogans: she achieves enlightenment through the medium of her own oral tradition, beginning with the witty subversion of the formulas that govern the lives of her family and ultimately, in the wake of her *caoineadh*, seeing the contemporary model of marriage as figment of male imagination.

Juno and the Paycock depicts a community that is beginning to want something better than the tenement squalor and deprivation they have inherited. Some of the younger generation, notably Mary and Jerry Devine, have glimpsed in their reading a vision of a better life; others, notably the Captain, are too marked by long years of poverty, economic and cultural, to fight for a new future and retreat into fantasies. The community is pathetically amenable to promises of liberation that they do not fully understand and cannot criticise adequately: they are deluded and cheated by 'outsiders,' literally by Bentham, who brings news of the will, metaphorically by politicians who ask them for sacrifices as a necessary preliminary before independence. Another image of their situation is that of an oral community that is dazzled (Jerry calls Bentham a 'Mickey Dazzler') by the arrival of a literacy that they see as a mysterious power. Their only hope is Juno, who is the only one who can offer them a coherent criticism of the crisis *in their own language*. Juno does not aspire to the 'high' style of the outsiders but adapts the traditional style represented by Mrs. Tancred so that, as we have seen, her more penetrating perception is expressed in a form that, going back to pre-Christian times, must be among the oldest in Irish culture.

The first production of *Juno* was a huge success, and the play remains a great favourite with Irish audiences to this day. The only substantial criticism of the first run was directed at the concluding sequence with Boyle and Joxer on the almost empty stage. For example, W. J. Lawrence, in an extremely favourable review, which praised O'Casey's flouting of Aristotelian rules and categorical divisions of tragedy and comedy, wrote that the drunken epilogue was 'artistically indefensible, and cannot be characterised otherwise than a painful mistake.'[18] Few would agree with this view. O'Casey had learned this technique in *Shadow*, where, after the shock of the climax, the dramatist almost dares the audience to laugh at precisely the kind of thing they had been laughing at all night; but the climax has changed everything, and what seemed a safe and harmless joke earlier is now tinged with bitterness and resentment.

NOTES

1. For details see Garry O'Connor, *Sean O'Casey* (London: Hodder and Stoughton, 1988), 148f.

2. Ibid., 146.

3. Discussed in Chapter 3.

4. In his attempts to raise the tone of his allusions, he is only following the example of his master, who, shortly after meeting Bentham for the first time, expresses his solemn sorrow for William Ellison in three languages—English, Latin, and Irish. 'Resquiescat in pace . . . or, usin' our oul' tongue like St. Patrick or St. Bridget, Guh sayeree jeea ayera!' [66]. As almost always happens around Hilljoy Square, the attempt to reach a higher level of language results in malapropism: the Irish phrase means 'God save Ireland.'

5. The aspirations of Juno and Mary predate the arrival of Bentham and news of the will. There is the evidence of Mary's reading of the avant-garde Ibsen, and the song she and Juno sing at the party, from *Il Trovatore*, is a cut above popular ballads.

6. There is a growing tendency among students, both in Ireland and abroad, to assume that Bentham is English.

7. But see Juno's reaction to the Prawna: 'What a comical name!' [72]. O'Casey would have expected the actress to recognise that here Juno is suppressing a snigger and putting on her best linguistic style for *Mister* Bentham.

8. In his note on this term, Ayling quotes an article by Richard Wall which contains the suggestion that the term could also apply to women. See O'Casey, *Seven Plays by Sean O'Casey,* a students' edition, with an introduction and notes by Ronald Ayling (London: Macmillan, 1985), 505. Despite the structure of the term, in common usage it always denotes 'Mickey who dazzles' and not 'She who Dazzles the Penis.'

9. 'Pimp' is here used, as commonly in Dublin at the time, meaning a spy or somebody who takes an improper and furtive interest in somebody else's affairs; there is no suggestion of any activity related to prostitution. See also *The Plough and the Stars,* 160, and *Ulysses,* 93.

10. See Walter Ong, *Orality and Literacy: The Technologizing of the Word* (London: Methuen, 1982), 32f.

11. See Garry O'Connor, 151f., 161f.

12. It also reads well as a quatrain rhyming AABB:

> *You'll do far more work*
> *With a knife and fork*
> *That ever you'll*
> *Do with a shovel!*

13. On the other hand, the use of such striking rhythms and abundant metaphors at a dinner party would be condemned as affected and intrusively ostentatious and most likely due to intoxication.

14. Lines one would not be surprised to hear in, say, Shaw's *St Joan*.

15. J. M. Synge, *Collected Works*, vol. 2, ed. Alan Price (Gerrards Cross: Colin Smythe, 1982), 75.

16. Ibid., vol. 3, book 1, ed. Ann Saddlemyer (London: Oxford UP, 1968), 21. For an Irish text and English translation of *Caoineadh Airt Ui Laoghaire*, see Seán Ó Tuama and Thomas Kinsella, *An Duanaire: Poems of the Dispossessed 1600–1900* (Dublin: Dolmen Press, 1981), 200–219.

17. It is not Shelley's fault that Davoren mistook him as a reflection of his own chosen pose; Shelley was genuinely radical and brave and, as Davoren should have known, was the only English poet who actually went to Dublin to preach revolution.

18. Quoted in Ronald Ayling, ed., *Sean O'Casey, The Dublin Trilogy* (London: Macmillan, 1985), 88.

Chapter 6

The Grammar of Assent

In October 1924, eight months after the hugely successful *Juno*, the Abbey production of *Arms and the Man* was followed by another O'Casey one-act play, *Nannie's Night Out*, which Robert Hogan considers 'one of the superb one-act plays of the modern stage, standing next to the great one-acts of O'Casey's colleagues—Strindberg, Synge and Shaw.'[1]

The action takes place in a dairy in a working-class district where the proprietor, Polly Pender, is courted by three old buffers. When a gunman comes in to steal the takings, the old men are predictably useless; the raid is accidentally foiled by the only substantial figure in the play, Irish Nannie.

She is about thirty years of age, well made, strong and possibly was handsome before she began to drink. Her eyes flash with the light of semi-madness; her hair is flying about her shoulders. Her blouse is open at the neck. A much damaged hat, containing flowers that once were brightly coloured, but are now faded, is on her head. Her manner, meant to be recklessly merry, is very close to hysterical tears; a shawl is hanging over one arm. [307]

The action of the play is in itself uninteresting, but Nannie fascinates partly because of her dramatic energy, partly because of her imperviousness to figurative reduction. She does not seem to be a symbol of anything. She is too detailed merely to represent the degradation of slum poverty. Although still a young woman, she lives in a methylated haze and sleeps rough; there is the suggestion that she is or has been a prostitute and that her drinking is a consequence of this and the death of her father. She has frequently been imprisoned for her breaches of the peace and is proud of her ability to offer physical resistance to policemen.

Nannie doesn't care a curse for anybody . . . . Let them send down their Foot, an' their Calvary—Nannie's waitin' for them; she'll give them somethin' better than cuttin' down th'

Oul' Age Pensions . . . . Republicans an' Free Staters—a lot of rubbidge, th' whole o' yous! Th' poor Tommies was men! [314]

Though her final remark may relate her to Bessie Burgess, Nannie is not a Protestant Unionist; she is, in Brendan Behan's later phrase, one of 'the unregenerate pre-Gaelic League people' of the Northside whose menfolk fought in the British army and who were consequently immune to the appeal of independence. In fact, Nannie would fit in well with the group of riotously witty women who sing and drink their way through Behan's newspaper sketches and his radio play, *The Big House*.[2]

Nannie's Night Out is unfinished in the sense that there are two endings, one in which Nannie dies of a heart attack, another in which she is taken off by the police. Neither is preferable to the other because neither is a resolution of the action; both are merely terminations of what was essentially a soliloquy surrounded by the characteristic O'Casey blend of domestic buffoonery, song, and political jibes. Outside the enigma of Nannie herself (why is a youngish mother given the name associated with a grandparent, and why is she called *Irish* Nannie?[3]), the language is more effective than the action in reproducing the feel of a contemporary working-class district. As had become his wont, O'Casey offsets the tragic poverty of Polly's circumstances with the comic wealth of her language, loading the sketch with the heavily accented slang and linguistic style of the tenements. Polly Pender doesn't have 'what ud jingle on a tombstone,' meaning she has no money. Nannie threatens the police that she will 'swing for wan o' yous yet,' meaning that she is willing to murder them and endure execution by hanging. Best of all, she addresses the police as 'yous gang of silver button'd bouseys,' showing that power of visual imagination and rhythmical alliteration that was a feature of the local speech and was becoming the hallmark of his major plays.

The *Irish Statesman* reviewer described the emotional confusion generated by *Nannie's Night Out*:

He brings us to his plays and then he heaves life at us, with its sharp corners and its untidy jumble of laughter and tears . . . . And the worst of it is, that if we go on allowing him to make us laugh and cry together in this hysterical manner, we may end by insisting that he is a genius.[4]

O'Casey claimed not to think much of the play.[5] Nor was Lady Gregory enthusiastic, finding it 'too short to be of much use' and hoping 'he will make a big play again, perhaps his Labour one.'[6] She would have been pleased to hear what O'Casey told Holloway: his next work would be entitled *The Plough and the Stars*, a reference to the flag of the Irish Citizen Army, and would be 'about Liberty Hall and Easter Week 1916.'[7]

It was almost inevitable that O'Casey should turn his attention to the crucial moment of modern Irish history, the 1916 insurrection. In *Shadow* he had deromanticized the War of Independence and in *Juno* exposed the futile savagery of the Civil War. Now it was time to confront the Abbey audience with his conviction that the Easter Rising had been a ghastly and a costly mistake.

Responsibility lay not only with the Nationalists, who had deluded the working class with their false promises, but also with those socialists, especially Connolly, who had betrayed the workers by leading the Citizen Army into a treacherous alliance with the Irish Volunteers.

It is inconceivable that the inclusion of the Easter Rising in a play submitted in 1921 and 1922 would not have drawn some comment from a reader, and so we may take it that the major difference between *The Crimson and the Tri-Colour* and *Plough* was the setting of the latter immediately before and during what was almost universally considered to be the sacred event in modern Irish history.[8] It is probably impossible for a modern reader to appreciate how daring O'Casey was in his choice of material and how courageous the Abbey was in staging it, both dramatist and management knowing that the vast majority of the audience would consider it politically blasphemous. By 1925 most Irish people, even those who had not supported the military rebellion, had come to believe in the mythic aspects of the Easter Rising: that just as Christ had shed his blood and laid down his life for the salvation of humankind, an act of martyrdom vindicated by his Resurrection, so too the leaders of the 1916 Rising had sacrificed their lives for the freedom of Ireland, a sacrifice vindicated by the achievement of freedom, albeit limited, from the bondage of Britain. O'Casey was one of the small minority that did not share this view, and in his new play he would show members of the Irish Citizen Army and the Irish Volunteers in a poor light and present the words of Patrick Pearse as a call not to glory but to pointless suffering and death. He must have known that many in the audience would consider his version of the Easter Rising almost as offensive as if he had portrayed Christ as a vainglorious coward whose sacrifice was more an act of self-indulgence than unselfish love.

It is ironic that, had O'Casey stuck to his original conception, he would have run less of a risk. The central objective of a play 'about Liberty Hall and Easter Week 1916' would be to dramatise the seduction of the workers and the Citizen Army away from their purely socialist aims and into common cause with the Nationalists. O'Casey could have shown James Connolly making a tactical decision to exploit the Rising as a stepping-stone to furthering the cause of Labour. Connolly's relations with the Nationalists were inconsistent, and at times he outdid them in his desire for military action. In December 1915 Connolly wrote of the growing 'feeling of identity of interests between the forces of real Nationalism and of Labour.' On the other hand, Connolly, however anxious for action, rejected the idea of mass sacrifice and insisted that anybody who supported it was 'a blithering idiot.'[9] Had *Plough* concentrated on the mistaken policies of the Citizen Army, it would have grievously offended only the socialist minority. In the event, he went a great deal further and managed to offend almost everybody.

It is very likely that O'Casey did envisage a play 'about Liberty Hall and Easter Week 1916.' Gabriel Fallon heard O'Casey read early drafts that were 'very funny and mainly concerned the Covey.'[10] But in the play as we have it, apart from an occasional sneer from the Covey, the conflict between Liberty Hall and the Irish Volunteers is avoided. Far from highlighting Connolly's dismissal of symbolic suicide, O'Casey associates Connolly anonymously with the tenor of Pearse's speeches by putting in the mouth of Lieutenant Langon of the Volunteers lines written by Connolly in January 1916: 'the time for Ireland's battle is NOW—the place for Ireland's battle is HERE' [141].[11] The ideological tension in the Citizen Army between those for and those against joining with the Volunteers is only hinted at through the medium of the Covey, who is not even a member. In *Plough* there is no ideological distinction between members of the Citizen Army and the Volunteers, only that of uniforms and banners. To take one example, when the Covey claims that, by marching with the Volunteers, the Citizen Army is disgracing their banner, Clitheroe *remonstratively* asks why; but when the Covey replies that the flag should be used only 'when we're buildin' the barricades to fight for a Workers' Republic,' Clitheroe has nothing to say, and his silence on what was a key issue for the Left is striking. Whatever his original intentions, O'Casey did not write a political 'play of ideas' but used the mode and tone he had discovered in *Shadow* and developed in *Juno*.

Plough is set in, and in the immediate vicinity of, a tenement house. As well as focussing the attention of the audience on the people who, in O'Casey's view, had suffered most and gained least in the Rising, the tenement setting allowed him to present a large group of related characters who represented a wide spectrum of political opinion. A feature of the earlier plays was the endemic tendency of the characters to transcend the limitations of tenement life by creating glamorous fantasies for themselves. Obvious, to a farcical extent, in *Shadow*, this was developed magnificently in Captain Boyle and more subtly in Mary, Johnny, and Jerry. In the earlier plays the principal medium was language itself, but in *Plough* the more experienced dramatist makes extensive use of a wide range of theatrical means, especially costumes and props: Peter's sword, the Covey's Jenersky, Clitheroe's belt, and so on.[12]

The house in which the play is set is a tenement but not yet a slum tenement: *a fine old Georgian house, struggling for its life against the assaults of time, and the more savage assaults of the tenants* [105]. The stage direction cannot refer to all the tenants: the Clitheroe flat is well kept and quite elegant compared to descriptions we have of contemporary slum tenements. Nora has furnished it *'in a way that suggests an attempt towards a finer expression of domestic life'*: the floor is covered in linoleum, and there are flowers and pictures. One assumes that Mrs. Gogan's flat is not as comfortable, and we see later that Bessie's attic flat is quite decrepit, having *'an unmistakable air of poverty, bordering on destitution'* [160]. The difference is, to a great extent, due to economic circumstances: both are widows, Mrs. Gogan a charwoman with a consumptive child, Bessie a street fruit-vendor whose son is away in the trenches with the Dublin Fusiliers [168]. As a Protestant, Bessie does not, as Mrs. Gogan does, take charity from the Vincent de Paul Society, but it seems as if she could do with it [134]. She claims to have known better days—'Poverty an' hardship has sent Bessie Burgess to abide with sthrange company'—and a lingering sense of superiority leads her to put a euphemistic gloss on her looting [152].

Compared to their neighbours (and, indeed, to the tenement dwellers in the earlier plays), the Clitheroes are extremely comfortable. Jack and his cousin, the

Covey, are tradesmen, a bricklayer and a fitter, respectively, better paid and more consistently employed than labourers such as Peter Flynn, Nora's uncle. Nora can look forward to Jack's housekeeping money and the Covey's and Peter's rents when she plans her domestic economy with a view to living decently in the tenement before moving to better accommodation. She dresses well, is polite herself, and insists on politeness and good manners in the others. As the play begins, she is having Fluther, another tradesman, fix the lock of her door, a significant act in a community where doors were always open to neighbours. Such 'notions of upperosity' do not go unnoticed: Mrs. Gogan resents Nora's disdain for the tenements, and even Fluther has to admit that such an insistence on neatness and hygiene is excessive.

The other men in the play are also well above the breadline: Langon is a civil servant, and Brennan a chicken butcher. Leaving Nora and the middle-class woman from Rathmines aside, it is the women who are poor. Mrs. Gogan, Bessie, and Rosie have drinks bought for them in the pub; Fluther buys for Mrs. Gogan and Rosie, and the Covey buys willingly for Bessie and is embarrassed into buying for Rosie.

The extended family of the Clitheroes includes an officer in the Irish Citizen Army, a young socialist, and a middle-aged Nationalist.[13] Mrs. Gogan's Catholic rhapsodies are balanced by Bessie's Protestant raptures. Bessie is the lone Unionist. The bartender and Rosie are, for professional reasons, above politics. British imperialism is represented somewhat uncomfortably by the two soldiers, one of whom claims to be a socialist.

At some stage all the male characters wear recognizable uniforms, either military or civilian. We see two of them, Jack and Peter, change from civilian into military attire, and we notice one of them, Captain Brennan, change back from military to civilian to escape arrest. The Covey advertises his working-class socialism by wearing a vividly red tie with his dungarees.

A tradesman carpenter enjoyed considerable status at the top of the working class. Fluther is generally lackadaisical, *rarely surrendering to thoughts of anxiety*, and his dress expresses this perfectly: apart from his little black bow, the articles that signify his social status—suit (seedy), bowler (faded), apron (soiled)—are not meticulously cared for. He is forty years of age and claims to have taken part in political demonstrations, but one suspects that his Nationalist zeal rises or falls with his alcohol level. He is not associated with any organisation and is more likely to act in defence of his own community rather than risk his life for any abstract cause.

Of particular significance in the play are changes of costume, especially into military uniforms in which every detail (buttons, badges, etc.) is designed to indicate allegiance to a specific cause. The most obvious and the most comic change in the opening act features Peter, who assumes the full 'canonicals' of the Irish National Foresters, a mildly Masonic organisation with a strong Nationalist and Catholic inclination: *green coat, gold braided; white breeches, top boots, frilled shirt. He carries the slouch hat, with the white ostrich plume, and the sword in his hands* [117]. Uncle Peter is not a soldier, but he wears a uniform, and part of the comedy of the first act is his transformation from a small, cantankerous man in a state of semiundress to a ridiculously anachronistic figure who looks more like an army officer in the forces of the United Irishmen (in 1798) or of Robert Emmet (in 1803) than somebody involved in contemporary politics. His sword would be of little practical worth against the steel helmets and rifles of the Wiltshires, to say nothing of the machine guns and artillery which are directed at the General Post Office. Uncle Peter represents a spiritual Nationalism that consists entirely of tradition and has never come to terms with the actuality of a modern urban rebellion. That is the point of the Covey's mockery when he sings extracts from two songs by Thomas Moore: by the turn of the twentieth century Moore's *Irish Melodies* were scorned by militants as genteel parlour music. The Covey quotes from one of Moore's more explicit songs:

> Oh, where's the slave so lowly,
> Condemned to chains unholy,
> Who, could he burst his bonds at first,
> Would pine beneath them slowly?

> We tread the land that bore us,
> The green flag glitters o'er us,
> The friends we've tried are by our side,
> And the foe we hate before us!

This is a typically subtle diplomatic formulation: Liberals could nod agreement to the general principles invoked, while Irish Nationalists could find coded messages in the green flag and the idea of a battle with the hated foe. But Peter's idea of desperate political action is to wave his sword in the air, an idea so ridiculous that even Fluther dismisses it as blather [129]. The ultimate proof of his irrelevance to the revolutionary situation is Nora's threat:

If you attempt to wag that sword of yours at anybody again, it'll have to be taken off you an' put in a safe place away from babies that don't know th' danger of them things [115].

Everybody in the tenement tends to find Peter ridiculous, but nobody enjoys mocking him as much as the Covey does.

On a domestic level this is a case of the young know-all belittling an older man, but more important is the ideological pattern in which modern socialism dismisses obsolete Nationalism. The Covey also figures in the visual symbolism: He is dressed in dungarees, and is wearing a vividly red tie [142]. The cap and dungarees are the uniform of the working man; the red tie, his personal pennant. Whereas Peter transforms himself from individuality to uniformity in the course of Act One, the Covey divests himself of his uniform and asserts his nonparticipation in the alliance of Volunteers and Citizen Army. Having taken off his dungarees, he throws them contemptuously on Peter's dress shirt.

The latter half of Act One is a superb illustration of O'Casey's new way of dealing with one of his favourite themes, the tendency of the working class to create roles for themselves by adapting, with varying degrees of success, a 'higher' vocabulary and style.

According to Mrs. Gogan, Jack Clitheroe drifted away from the Citizen Army because 'he wasn't made a Captain of'; so confident had he been of promotion that he had already bought himself a Sam Browne belt [108]. When, at last alone with Jack, Nora repeats the accusation, Jack quickly changes the conversation to more congenial matters and reminds Nora of the hat he ordered for her birthday and *kisses her rapidly several times* [120]. The sequence seems to suggest the archetypal pattern of romantic comedy: the man and the woman overcome their problems and celebrate their reunion in symbolic marriage. Caught between the attractions of Mars and Venus, Clitheroe, prompted by his wife, chooses Venus: there can be no doubting his physical passion or the symbolism of his song. Singing for Nora for the first time since their honeymoon, he accepts her choice of the song with the refrain:

> When I first said I love'd only you, Nora,
> An' you said you lov'd only me!

As they honour Venus with a kiss, there are two fateful knocks on the door, the second *more imperative than the first*, and Mars appears at the door in the form of a fully uniformed member of the Irish Citizen Army. When he learns of his promotion, Clitheroe reverses his earlier choice and prefers the martial belt to the girdle of Venus, the arms of war to the loving arms of his wife. In his anger, he dismisses Nora's embrace as 'nonsense,' grips her arm so that it hurts her, and speaks to her in tones that are the opposite of the earlier song:

> You deserve to be hurt . . . . Any letter that comes to me for th' future, take care that I get it . . . . D'ye hear—take care that I get it!

Although Nora accuses him bitterly of betrayal and ruinous vanity, the more powerful element of the scene is visual rather than verbal:

> *He goes to the chest of drawers and takes out a Sam Browne belt, which he puts on, and then puts a revolver in the holster. He puts on his hat, and looks towards* NORA. *While this dialogue is proceeding, and while* CLITHEROE *prepares himself,* BRENNAN *softly whistles 'The Soldier's Song.'*
> CLITHEROE [*at door, about to go out*]. You needn't wait up for me; if I'm in at all, it won't be before six in the morning.
> NORA [*bitterly*]. I don't care if you never come back!
> CLITHEROE [*To* CAPTAIN BRENNAN]. Come along, Ned.
> *They go out; there is a pause.* NORA *pulls her new hat from her head and with a bitter movement flings it to the other end of the room. There is a gentle knock at door, right, which opens, and* MOLLSER *comes into the room. She is about fifteen, but looks to be about ten, for the ravages of consumption have shrivelled her up. She is pitifully worn, walks feebly, and frequently coughs. She goes over to* NORA. [124f.]

The symbolism of this sequence is obvious enough, but its full effect depends on an elaborate context, largely visual.

The first words of the act are unspoken, and we guess at them through the replies of Mrs. Gogan. They are the words of the man who is delivering the new hat that Clitheroe has ordered from Arnott's for Nora's birthday. Mrs. Gogan displays the expensive hat, *black, with decorations in red and gold,* and associates it with Nora's 'notions of upperosity,' her desire for a better life than that of the tenements. When Nora appears, we are immediately aware of her expensive taste in clothes: *she is dressed in a tailor-made costume, and wears around her neck a silver fox fur* [114]. As we have seen, Jack uses the gift of the hat to turn Nora's thoughts away from the Citizen Army and toward sexual desire. Despite his apparent lack of enthusiasm for seeing Nora in the hat, she puts it on, and it has its effect:

CLITHEROE. It suits you, Nora, it does right enough. [*He stands up, puts his hand beneath her chin, and tilts her head up. She looks at him roguishly. He bends down and kisses her.*] [121]

Almost immediately afterward, he sings the song while (still wearing the hat) she *nestles her head on his breast and listens delightedly* [122].

When Brennan enters, he is identified by the fact that he is wearing *the full uniform of the Irish Citizen Army—green suit; slouch green hat caught up at one side by a small Red Hand badge; Sam Browne belt, with a revolver in the holster* [123]. As far as the audience is concerned, this fateful presence *is* the uniform of the Citizen Army, and perhaps the most unusual aspect of the uniform, and thus the most striking, is the slouch hat. Clitheroe's decision to return to the Citizen Army is not expressed verbally but mimed by his putting on the uniform, including the belt he had bought in anticipation of being promoted to officer status. The stage direction indicates that when Clitheroe has put on his hat, he *looks towards* NORA, and this invites the audience to note, consciously or subconsciously, that his putting on the military hat is a further rejection of the love he had symbolised with the Arnott's hat. This pattern is completed when Nora tears off her hat and flings it from her.[14]

There is also a musical strain in the pattern. Brennan's insistent knocking had come at the romantic climax of Clitheroe's song. To accompany Clitheroe's change from husband to uniformed soldier, Brennan had whistled 'The Soldier's Song.' Shortly afterward we hear a regiment of the British army on their way to the front singing 'It's a Long Way to Tipperary.' On the stage all the songs are symbolic in that they represent not only the human delight in music but a range of allegiances: to domestic love, Irish nationalism, and British imperialism. By having Brennan whistle 'The Soldier's Song,' O'Casey may well have been making a rather subtle point. This marching song, later to become the Irish national anthem, was a Nationalist song and almost totally identified with the Volunteers: it was sung many times during the Easter Rising, most notably before the attempted retreat from the GPO. Brennan's whistling may indicate the extent to which the Citizen Army had been subsumed into the Volunteers or, on a more general level, the extent to which Clitheroe the individual is transformed into a uniformed soldier. The scene that began with loud knocking ends with Mollser's gentle knock. The exiting soldiers are replaced by the entering Mollser, who, ravaged by consumption, is, within the patterned action, symbolic of early death. The dramatic conjunction is ominous, especially when supported by Bessie's apocalyptic vision of bodies 'scattered abroad, like th' dust in th' darkness' and by the coughing Mollser's inquiry: 'Is there anybody goin', Mrs. Clitheroe, with a titther o' sense?' [126].

The visual pattern of this sequence is part of a wider pattern. Act Two will conclude with Clitheroe's rejecting his wife again, this time for the more pressing claims of Ireland. Toward the end of Act Three he will yet again, although with nothing like his earlier conviction, throw his wife aside and stay loyal to his military comrades. As a consequence of his final roughness, his child is born dead and shares a coffin with Mollser.

The two characters who are most dependent on O'Casey's earlier, largely verbal technique are the characters who existed in some form in earlier plays and who are the least attracted to the role of military hero, the Covey and Fluther.

In his wealth of references, his susceptibility to malapropism, and his quasi-religious attachment to Jenersky's *Thesis,* the Covey is typical of a community in which literacy has only recently arrived. He is a theatrical descendant of Tommy Owens and Jerry Devine in that his professed commitment, in his case to socialism, is exposed when confronted by Rosie's material needs.[15] The justness or otherwise of his socialist criticism is reduced to the level of malapropistic farce by his tendency to parrot undigested ideas and to use his 'high' learning as a means of establishing himself as intellectually superior to all around him; even more than Jack Rocliffe, he lacks the intelligent sympathy that is the professed basis of socialism.

His opening lines are characteristically rich in implicit references. His criticism of the Nationalists as deluded by the opium of the people may not be without its point, but it is weakened by the first of many malapropisms: 'Didn't you hear them cheerin', th' mugs! They have to renew their political baptismal vows to be faithful in seculo seculorum.'[16] He seems oblivious to the fact that he relies on his infallible book as least as much as the most deluded Christian relies on Scripture.

Look here, comrade, there's no such thing as an Irishman, or an Englishman, or a German or a Turk; we're all only human bein's. Scientifically speakin', it's all a question of the accidental gatherin' together of mollycewels an' atoms. [111]

His pronunciation of 'molecules' may indicate no more than his working-class accent, but his selfishness and arrogance are beyond question, his use of the term 'comrade' hilariously incongruous in the circumstances: 'There's no use o' arguin' with you; it's education you want, comrade' [111f]. The Covey is much more interested in advertising his own 'big brain' than in educating those less enlightened than himself. So engrossed is he in his own infallibility that this materialist is in danger of losing contact with humanity and living in the spiritual atmosphere of Jenersky's *Thesis.* This is the point of his ludicrous exchange with Rosie.

Rosie is, from economic necessity, the ultimate materialist. She has empirical, rather than theoretical, evidence of the spiritualisation of Irish life:

They're all in a holy mood. Th' solemn-lookin' dials on the whole o' them an' they marchin'
to th' meetin'. You'd think they were in th' glorious company of th' saints, an' th' noble
army of martyrs thrampin' through th' sthreets of paradise. They're all thinkin' of higher
things than a girl's garthers. [127]

Rosie is quite happy to go along with the Covey's views for as long as he is a
prospective customer. She shows more tolerance than does the audience, especially
when the Covey responds to Rosie's charms with characteristic callowness:

[*Tapping* ROSIE *on the shoulder*] Look here, comrade, I'll leave here tomorrow night for
you a copy of Jenersky's *Thesis on the Origin, Development, an' Consolidation of the
Evolutionary Idea of the Proletariat.* [131]

There is worse to follow when the Covey dismisses Rosie as a prostitute, a lapse
from which he never recovers.[17] He is less strident in the second half of the play,
but his unwillingness to shelter Brennan is typically selfish. The Covey offers a
pertinent criticism of Corporal Stoddart's socialism, but even Irish audiences tend
to agree with the British corporal when he tells the Covey to shut up: 'Ow, cheese
it, Paddy, cheese it!' [167]. The Covey is as imprisoned in the formulations of the
Thesis as any Nationalist in the songs and ceremonies of traditional Nationalism:
he is no longer in intellectual control of the quotations and had become a mere
mouthpiece. He is much more adept using his knowledge of Nationalist ballads to
annoy Peter.

The Covey's attitude to Jenersky's *Thesis* seems to fit the pattern of the earlier
plays, where books (and literacy) enjoyed enormous prestige in a community that
is a mixture of the old oral and the new literate cultures, but, as in other respects,
the *Plough* develops, rather than conforms to, the pattern.

Neither illiteracy nor semi-illiteracy plays any part; in fact, the world of the
Plough is strongly literate. The first action in the play is that of writing: Mrs.
Gogan, the least obviously educated member of the community, signs for the parcel
from Arnott's and confidently asks if she should use 'Maggie or Mrs.' [106]. The
next sequence begins when Fluther produces the handbill for the Great
Demonstration from his pocket and reads it for Mrs. Gogan, who, while speaking
of Clitheroe's disappointment, *takes up book after book from the table, looks into
them in a near-sighted way, and then leaves them back* [109]. When the Covey
enters, he first of all advertises his own reading and later draws attention to Peter's
ability to read (and mock) extracts from Jenersky's *Thesis* [148]. The final
sequence of Act One is focussed on the letter that Brennan brings for Clitheroe,
which draws attention to the previous letter, which Nora has destroyed.

Again, the earlier pattern of characters beguiled by the power of books
survives only in the case of the Covey, who regards the *Thesis* with primitive awe
and is as deluded by his misreading of Jenersky as ever Davoren was by Shelley's
poetry or the Boyles by Bentham's miswritten will.

The major technical development, which subsumes the earlier writing motif,
just as the use of costumes, emblems, and flags subsumed most of the tendency to
create roles through language, is the employment in Act Two of what is described

in the list of characters as *The Figure in the Window*. By means of this strikingly visual device O'Casey seeks to present with great theatrical force what led Clitheroe to leave his loving wife and dedicate his life to war. It is a dramatic formulation of what he had been preaching in the *Irish Worker* as far back as January 1914 in 'An Open Letter to the Workers in the Volunteers': 'Many of you have been tempted to join this much talked of movement by the wild impulse of genuine enthusiasm. You have again allowed yourselves to be led away by words—words—words.'[18]

Thanks to their general knowledge (or the theatre programme) few people witness Act Two of the *Plough* without being aware that the words of the orator are those of Patrick Pearse, the idealistic teacher and writer who had read the Proclamation outside the GPO and who had been subsequently executed by the British. Early Abbey audiences would certainly have recognised Pearse's words, and O'Casey was anxious as to how they would react because in the years since the Rising, Pearse had achieved the status of a secular Christ among Nationalists.[19] However, for whatever reason, O'Casey refused to identify the orator as Pearse, and the failure of any of the characters to do so tends to suggest that it is *not* Pearse; after all, in Act Three the Covey recognises General Pearse reading the Proclamation outside the GPO, and the casual acceptance of his report suggests that Pearse was well known to the others. O'Casey's refusal to identify the orator as Pearse (or as anybody else) adds greatly to the effect. Before the first extract the stage direction states: *Through the window is silhouetted the figure of a tall man who is speaking to the crowd*. The words are attributed to *The Voice of the Man*. More or less the same notation is used before the later extracts, and the evidence of the stage directions would produce a tall, dark shadow that was obviously male but utterly impersonal and devoid of individuality.[20]

In the 1991 Abbey production, the Figure was placed in the audience, and a large reflecting screen was dropped at the back of the stage to enable the audience to see themselves and the Figure. The actor did not offer a physical resemblance of Pearse. If the objective was to suggest some sort of identification between the Speaker and the Abbey audience, it succeeded to an extent: some members of the audience were reminded at times that they, members of a cultivated community with the means and leisure to attend the Abbey, felt closer to the Figure than to the brawling boozers of the public house. The relocation of the Figure was an interesting idea but, as I argue presently, sacrificed something central to the play as written.

The extracts from Pearse's speeches highlight his concept of blood sacrifice, which he expressed most succinctly in a famous sentence that O'Casey chose not to quote: 'Life springs from death; and from the graves of patriot men and women spring living nations.'[21] The Voice proposes a series of transformations or transubstantiations: death in war is not horrible but glorious and preferable to living in slavery; war does not involve the loss of young men but is redemptive and necessary for the manhood of a nation; blood spilled in battle is wine poured in sacrifice to God; Ireland should not fear war because of its terrors but should welcome it as a means of experiencing the mystical exhilaration of heroism; Ireland may be physically weaker than its enemies but will always derive a spiritual superiority from the graves of those who have died for Ireland in the past.

The mode of the orator might be described as a 'Christo-heroic' idealism that uses the death and Resurrection of Christ to validate a war of liberation: the spiritual is elevated above the physical, the symbolic above the actual, the eternal above the temporal. Though the words of the Voice are startling in their absolute clarity, this is not the first time that the idea of a holy war has occurred in the play. The handbill that Fluther produces at the beginning of Act One called for a demonstration in explicitly religious terms, a *torchlight procession around places in th' city sacred to th' memory of Irish Patriots, to be concluded be a meetin', at which will be taken an oath of fealty to th' Irish Republic* [108]. Though, in an Irish context, the idea of blood sacrifice was and is identified with Pearse, it had a tradition at least as old as Christianity, was widespread in Europe at the time, and underpinned a good deal of the rhetoric of both sides in the Great War.

The character who most obviously counterpoints the Voice of the Man is Rosie, the young woman who lives by offering her body to men and whose livelihood is seriously threatened by the seductive powers of the Voice. In this contrast we notice O'Casey's insistence on the Voice as shadow rather than a substance, spirit rather than flesh, an annunciating angel: 'When war comes to Ireland she must welcome it as she would welcome the Angel of God!' [134]. Those in the audience and those in the bar *see* through a glass darkly what the faithful outside *see* as God's messenger come to bless the call to arms; but the dramatist takes great care to guide the audience to the conclusion that the faithful are deluded, that the words they hear are not those of the God of Life but those of a false prophet who lures them into the arms of the Angel of War and Death.

In *Shadow* and *Juno* working-class people were deluded by outsiders whose styles of speech were 'higher' than those of the tenement dwellers and who were associated with the 'power' of writing. The Voice is the outsider of *Plough*, the only character whose speech is free from the aspiration and loss of final consonants with which O'Casey marks the dialect of Hilljoy Square. If Davoren, himself a 'shadow,' and Bentham are metaphors for the political fantasies that delude the working class, the Voice is the phantom itself, projected as a ghastly apparition that leads the men to their doom and heaps the horrors of loss on the women, especially on Nora and Bessie.

Though O'Casey presents the Voice as diabolical rather than divine, he does not deny its potency. His early immersion in religion had marked him to the extent that he always accepted a spiritual dimension: communism was, for him, a perfection rather than a rejection of Christianity. His mockery of the Voice is that of an exorcist rather than an unbeliever. The uniformed men are clearly possessed and given the gift of prophecy: in Act Three we see Langon wounded, in Act Four we hear of Clitheroe's death, and an attentive audience may assume that, after the final curtain, Brennan was imprisoned. In *Plough* there is no resurrection to compensate for the sacrifice: the implication is that the spirit that possessed them was not that of Life but of Death.[22]

Fluther and Peter had been temporarily excited by the Voice; when the uniformed men enter the bar with their banners, they are in a trance:

They are in a state of emotional excitement. Their faces are flushed and their eyes sparkle; they speak rapidly, as if unaware of the meaning of what they said. They have been mesmerized by the fervency of the speeches.
CLITHEROE [*almost pantingly*]. Three glasses 'o port! [*The* BARMAN *brings the drinks.*]
CAPT. BRENNAN. We won't have long to wait now.
LIEUT. LANGON. Th' time is rotten ripe for revolution.
CLITHEROE. You have a mother, Langon.
LIEUT. LANGON. Ireland is greater than a mother.
CAPT. BRENNAN. You have a wife, Clitheroe.
CLITHEROE. Ireland is greater than a wife.
LIEUT. LANGON. Th' time for Ireland's battle is now—th' place for Ireland's battle is here.
The tall, dark figure again is silhouetted against the window. [141]

It is as if they have been hypnotised. The spirit that spoke through the Voice now speaks through the soldiers. As with subjects of hypnotism, they are no longer freethinking individuals but automatons controlled by external suggestions: their former selves no longer know what they are saying or why, but the audience knows that they have been possessed by the spirit of war, whose greatest enemy is the love that binds men to women. The Voice returns to contrast the physical strength of the enemy with the spiritual strength of the Irish, in whose hearts God is miraculously ripening 'the seeds sown by the young men of a former generation.' This is a typical adaptation to Irish politics of the common Christian belief that 'the blood of martyrs is the seed of saints,' and the soldiers respond automatically and, figuratively, with one voice:

CAPT. BRENNAN [*catching up the Plough and the Stars*]. Imprisonment for th' Independence of Ireland!
LIEUT. LANGON [*catching up the Tricolour*]. Wounds for th' independence of Ireland!
CLITHEROE. Death for th' Independence of Ireland!
THE THREE [*together*]. So help us God!
They drink. A bugle blows the Assembly. They hurry out. A pause. FLUTHER *and* ROSIE *come out of the snug;* ROSIE *is linking* FLUTHER *who is a little drunk. Both are in a merry mood.* [141f.]

The framing device serves not only to set the mystical sequence in a comic context but also, by contrast, to explain the nature of the mysticism.

The Voice is the Voice *of the Man.* It is male and homosexual to the extent that it bonds men together and is opposed to heterosexual love. In choosing Ireland, traditionally represented as a woman, the men reject the women in their lives. Instead of Guinness or whiskey, the water of life, they call for port, the red wine already equated with bloodshed and death. The Voice claims that only through war can a nation preserve its manhood. The heroism proclaimed here is exclusively male, a virtue descended from the Latin *virtus*, manliness, and there is a suggestion in the play, from Jack's desertion of Nora, to the death of their child and Nora's insanity, that the Voice perverts the love within men from life to death, from erotics to politics, and that men who put on uniforms are literally in love with death.[23] There is a striking statement of this motif in Mrs. Gogan's early lines concerning Clitheroe and his gun:

He was so cocksure o' being made [a Captain] that he bought a Sam Browne belt, an' was always puttin' it on an' standin' at th' door showing it off, till th' man came an' put out th' street lamps on him. God, I think he used to bring it to bed with him! But I'm tellin' you herself was delighted that the cock didn't crow, for she's like a clockin' hen if he leaves her sight for a minute. [108f.]

The image of Clitheroe taking his belt and, presumably, his gun to bed with him acquires an even stranger aura when surrounded by the stridently sexual imagery of cocks and hens. A man who preferred the weapons of war to those of love was predisposed to the belief that Ireland was more important than a wife.

Of course, a predisposition to fantasies of power or heroism is, on the evidence of the earlier plays, endemic in Hilljoy Square. From Tommy Owens to the Covey we see a line of dreamers who imagine themselves as more consequential than they really are and try to speak accordingly. Generally, these men preserve their dreams from the grim actualities of war, but those who, like Minnie, fail to respect the crucial line between heroic aspiration and heroic action pay with their lives. Fluther, Peter, and the Covey are susceptible to political excitement, but they don't confuse it with real-bullet battles. The more idealistic in *Plough* not only play the part by dressing for battle but also go into battle and soon discover the difference between blood and wine.

The Voice, the outsider who appeals to the heroic imaginations of these dreamers, does not merely speak a language that is unmarked by the 'flaws' of those who have received little formal education; the words spoken by the Voice are instantly recognisable as rhetoric, the traditional emblem of European education since the time of Plato. The original Greek denoted the art of using persuasive speech, but, with the development of literacy, rhetoric came to include the art of eloquent writing. Even in the 1920s it was impossible not to see the connection between rhetoric and power. Politicians and lawyers depended on their powers of verbal persuasion and abuse. The greatest leader of Nationalist Ireland, Daniel O'Connell, had spellbound tens of thousands, mostly illiterate, at his monster meetings. Robert Emmet would live forever because of the power of his speech from the dock. Pearse had galvanised Irish separatism by his oration at the grave of O'Donovan Rossa.[24] Ironically, especially given the fact that the masses were still in direct contact with the tradition that had produced and elevated the art of public speech, these leaders owed their power to the rhetorical skills they acquired during their higher education, because, by another historical irony, shortly after the arrival of literacy, the art of public speaking was taught and learned through books and, before long, the skills applied to the written language, *ars grammatica*.[25] I have argued that the rhetorical powers displayed by such uneducated (and probably illiterate) characters as Juno and Boyle were as admirable in their way as anything in the line of orators from Demosthenes to Burke, but nobody could fail to see the differences between the passionately pleonastic rhapsodies of the working-class word-spinners and the more logically balanced propositions of the Voice. The Voice exudes the power that the uniformed men estimate so highly and desire so intensely that it mesmerises them until, in the most frightening development of the farcical malapropisms of *Shadow*, they sentence themselves unwittingly to their doom: *Their faces are flushed and their eyes sparkle; they speak rapidly, as if unaware of the meaning of what they said.*

There is also a suggestion in the play that the task of the Voice is made easier by the existence in this community of a pronounced death wish and not only in those who obey the Voice. Mrs. Gogan is obsessed with death, partly because she is a widow and the mother of a dying child but also, because the dramatist presents her visions in a comic mode, we feel that, like a tenement Romantic, she prefers to luxuriate in the sensuous surrender of death rather than continue the uneven struggle for life. In Act One she allows herself to see death in the midst of life; in Act Three she recounts her dream of Fluther's death:

an' then it got so dark that nothin' was seen but th' white face of th' corpse, gleamin' like a white wather-lily floatin' on th' top of a dark lake. Then a tiny whisper thrickled into me ear, sayin', 'Isn't the face very like th' face of Fluther?' [145]

But this is a fantasy rather than a vision: Fluther arrives on the scene seconds later, having rescued Nora. Early in Act Two Fluther himself was sufficiently possessed by the spiritual cocktail of whiskey and the Voice to break the barriers of ordinary perception. Listening to the speeches, his mind was purged of the commonplace:

Every derogatory thought went out o' me mind, an' I said to meself, 'You can die now, Fluther, for you've seen the shadow-dhreams of th' past leppin' to life in th' bodies of livin' men that show, if we were without a titther o' courage for centuries, we're vice versa now!' Looka here. [*He stretches out his arm under* PETER'S *face and rolls up his sleeve.*] The blood was BOILIN' in me veins! [129]

But Fluther's excitement is temporary, as is his interest in ghostly men: he prefers livelier spirits and living women.

The dominant structural device of the play is, as so often in the early O'Casey, contrast or counterpoint. In Act Two the mystical utterances of the Voice are counterpointed by the mundane farce of the bar in such a manner as to provoke subversive laughter. For example, as Fluther and Covey drink their whiskeys with patriotic zeal, the Voice speaks of blood as 'the red wine of the battlefields,' and, as Bessie brawls with Mrs. Gogan and the Covey sneers at Peter, the Voice interrupts them to announce that 'heroism has come back to the earth.' As far as the audience is concerned, everything in the construction of the act is designed to subvert the awesome authority of the Voice. Though Fluther and Peter are obviously excited by the Voice, they are not transfixed. Their quick visit to the bar suggests that they consume the words of the Voice as they consume their whiskey, for the same reasons and with the same effect: it brings some temporary exhilaration into their otherwise unexciting lives. The Barman and Rosie are primarily concerned with trade. The Covey and Bessie are immune to the appeal of the Voice, while Mrs. Gogan is more interested in her battle with Bessie. The Voice has almost been forgotten, and Act Two seems set for a warmly comic conclusion when Fluther chivalrously defends Lady Rosie's honour against the slights of the Covey, and the loving couple then adjourns to the snug; but, in a minor echo of Act One, the romantic comedy is interrupted by the arrival of the men in uniform.

Fluther is the most attractive of the male characters. In the oral tradition, he learned the principles of Nationalism from lore and ballads and can remember as a child 'bein' taught at his mother's knee to be faithful to the Shan Van Vok' [138]. One is inclined to believe his claims to have been injured by a dragoon in O'Connell Street and by a policeman at a Labour meeting in the Phoenix Park, partly because his boasts are restrained—'Maybe, then, I done as much, an' know as much about the Labour movement as th' chancers that are blowin' about it!' [138]—and partly because of his maverick heroism. He is not without convictions, but his loyalties are local and personal. He risks his life for his neighbour Nora, and, even when the bullets are flying, and a British soldier is killed in Act Four, he will not be bullied or abused by Sergeant Tinley.

FLUTHER. Eh, who are you chuckin', eh?
SERGEANT TINLEY [*roughly*]. Gow on, git aht, you blighter.
FLUTHER. Who are you callin' a blighter to, eh? I'm a Dublin man, born an' bred in the city, see?
SERGEANT TINLEY. I don't care if you were Broin Buroo; git aht, git aht.
FLUTHER [*halting as he is going out*]. Jasus, you an' your guns! Leave them down, an' I'd beat th' two o' yous without sweatin'! [171]

O'Casey has caught the indomitable truculence of Fluther to perfection, especially in his final 'eh' and 'see.'[26] Part of Fluther's appeal is his unquenchable individualism. Despite his temporary possession by the Voice, Fluther's preferred spirits are whiskey, the water of life as opposed to the wine/blood of death, and physical sex (spirit in the archaic sense of 'semen'), the source of life, which transcends individual death. The audience also warms to Fluther's language, especially those phrases that are redolent of the old oral style of the city: 'Put up your mits now, if there's a man's blood in you! Be God, in a few minutes you'll see some snots flyin' around . . . . I hit a man last week, Rosie, an' he's fallin' yet' [140]. Fluther, fond of his 'oil' and 'a terrible man for the women,' is relatively content with his lot and lacks the susceptibility to dangerously heroic fantasies that the Voice exploits.

A good deal of the counterpoint humour in the play is generated by the skilful delight of the tenement dwellers in flyting. The Covey drives Peter to paroxysms of rage and retaliation:

I'll make him stop his laughin' an' leerin', jibin' an' jeerin' an' scarifyin' people with his corner-boy insinuations! . . . . He's always thryin' to rouse me: if it's not a song, it's a whistle; if it isn't a whistle, it's a cough. But you can taunt an' taunt—I'm laughin' at you, he, hee, hee, hee, hee, heee! [114]

When Mrs. Gogan gets stuck into Bessie in Act Two, she shows more energy that ever she did in her morbid fantasies:

Y' oul' rip of a blasted liar, me weddin' ring's been well earned be twenty years be th' side o' me husband, now takin' his rest in heaven, married to me be Father Dempsey, in th' chapel o' Saint Jude's, in th' Christmas Week of eighteen hundhred an' ninety-five; an' any kid, livin' or dead, that Jinny Gogan has since, was got between th' bordhers of th' Ten Commandment! [135]

But perhaps the outstanding performer in this area is Bessie.

It may initially seem strange that Bessie, the Protestant Unionist whose son is fighting with the British army on the continent, is rhetorically or spiritually close to the Voice and the concept of divinely sanctioned sacrifice in battle.

There's a storm of anger tossin' in me heart, thinkin' of all th' poor Tommies, an' with them me own son, dhrenched in water an' soaked in blood, gropin' their way to a shattherin' death, in a shower o' shells! Young men with th' sunny lust o' life beaming in them, layin' down their white bodies, shredded into torn an' bloody pieces, on th' althar that God Himself has built for th' sacrifice of heroes! [133]

Though this differs in accent and personal energy from the speeches of the Voice, the sentiments are identical. Bessie has every reason to have death on her mind: her own son is in mortal danger, while she sees death all around her in the form of little Mollser and the inevitable wrath of the British army on the treacherous rebels. As an older inhabitant of the tenements, she was formed in a predominantly oral tradition; as a Protestant she has (like her creator) absorbed and interiorised the figures, phrases, and rhythms of the King James version of the Old Testament. In moments of high passion, whether in drink or in dispute or in her moment of death, she sings hymns and quotes from the more sublime books of the Bible in a way none of her neighbours could manage. Her education has made her the most gifted of all the characters in orchestrating passages of finely modulated rhetoric such as her apocalyptic climax to Act One:

There's th' men marchin' out into th' dhread dimness o' danger, while th' lice is crawlin' about feedin' on th' fatness o' the land! But yous'll not escape from th' arrow that flieth be night, or th' sickness that wasteth be day . . . . An' ladyship an' all, as some o' them may be, they'll be scattered abroad, like th' dust in th' darkness! [125]

In her vindictive abuse of the retreating rebels she exploits her familiarity with the Nationalist tradition in the form of Moore's *Melodies* as well as with more vernacular forms of mockery:

Th' Minsthrel Boys aren't feelin' very comfortable now. Th' big guns has knocked all th' harps out of their hands. General Clitheroe'd rather be unlacin' his wife's bodice than standin' at a barricade . . . . And the professor of chicken-butcherin' there, finds he's up against somethin' a little tougher even than his own chickens, an' that's sayin' a lot! [155]

When Fluther arrives back with the demented Nora, Bessie continues to abuse the Nationalists and provokes even Fluther by singing 'Rule Britannia'. Yet, unnoticed by the others, *she gives a mug of milk to* MOLLSER *silently*. In a comic variation on the theme of expressing their fantasies in uniforms, Bessie covers herself in looted luxuries and makes common cause with Mrs. Gogan. But she hasn't changed: minutes later she is mocking the rebels. Nor has she changed in another respect: when Nora is left lying on the street, Bessie transcends her personal dislike of her and carries her into the house. There are for Bessie, it seems, forces greater than sectarian ideology. Unlike the men, who in time of relative peace proclaim a heroism they cannot maintain in battle, Bessie acts heroically despite herself. The stage direction indicates that she looks at Nora *for a few minutes* before coming to her aid. She is genuinely frightened as she goes out for a doctor and has only *Psalms* to protect her and save Nora:

the sound of some rifle shots, and the tok, tok, tok of a distant machine-gun brings her to a sudden halt. She hesitates for a moment, then she tightens her shawl round her, as if it were a shield, then she firmly and swiftly goes out.
BESSIE [*as she goes out*]. Oh, God, be thou my help in time o' throuble. An' shelter me safely in th' shadow of Thy wings! [159]

When Brennan tells her that news of Clitheroe's glorious death will turn Nora's grief to joy, Bessie is sardonically succinct: 'If you only seen her, you'd know to th' differ' [163]. Whatever heroism Bessie exemplifies is not the manly *virtus* preached by the Voice and absorbed by the soldiers but a female version that is characterized by a willingness to transcend ideology to help a neighbour. For Bessie, 'love thy neighbour' is a very clear and direct commandment. Her reaction to being shot is the opposite to that attributed to Clitheroe. The fatally wounded Clitheroe had been burned in the Imperial Hotel, an end described by his commanding officer as 'a gleam of glory' [163]; Bessie experiences a burning sensation that she would love to extinguish.

Merciful God, I'm shot, I'm shot, I'm shot . . . . I've got this through you . . . through you . . . through you, you bitch, you! . . . O god, have mercy on me! . . . This is what's afther comin' on me for nursin' you day an' night . . . . I was a fool, a fool, a fool![27] Get me a dhrink o' wather, you jade, will you? There's a fire burnin' in me blood! . . . . Jesus Christ, me sight's goin'! It's all dark, dark! Nora, hold me hand . . . .

I do believe, I will believe
That Jesus died for me;
That on th' cross He shed His blood,
From sin to set me free. [173][28]

The same sacrifice on the cross inspired Bessie and the men who set out to free Ireland from those Bessie supported. Within the play, Bessie's death is more genuinely and admirably heroic. There is evidence that the men who put on uniforms were deluded by their own desires and the mesmeric power of the disembodied Voice. Bessie, born a Protestant in a predominantly Catholic society and brought up to associate her sense of difference and of superiority with the Bible, was nonetheless formed in a culture that depended on communal support and taught by the Bible to love others as she loved herself. In her language she integrated the characteristics of the old oral culture with the Word of God as translated into the solemn cadences of early modern English. In her life she showed that she had the moral resources to do what none of the men could do: to have the courage to love those she didn't like, to have the courage to admit she was afraid, to have the courage to rage at her own death and then accept it in the spirit of a love higher than human love. Her heroism is all the more moving because, like Juno, with only the instincts of a poor working-class woman, she transcends the controlling ideology of sectarian hatred and in death shows an alternative to the alien Voice, which brings nothing but delusion and death to the people of Hilljoy Square.

My reading of these three plays has stressed the manner in which O'Casey implies that the illiterate or recently literate tenement dwellers were dazzled and deluded by outsiders whose 'high' language and literary skills they associated with power. In this context, one of Bessie's tirades acquires an extra significance. The conversation in the pub pauses while the Voice encourages Ireland to welcome the coming of war 'as she would welcome the Angel of God.' The Covey dismisses this as 'dope,' the opium of a hallucinating people. Bessie appears to disregard the Voice and resume her attack on Mrs. Gogan, but her language picks up the reference to 'angel.'

They [people like Mrs Gogan] may crow away out o' them; but it ud be fitther for some o' them to mend their ways, an' cease from havin' scouts out watchin' for th' comin' of th' St Vincent de Paul man, for fear they'd be nailed lowerin' a pint of beer, mockin' th' man with an angel face, shinin' with th' glamour of deceit an' lies! [134]

Was it O'Casey's immersion in the Authorised Version that generated the final phrase in which 'deceit an' lies' are identified with the word that records the popular association of literary education with dangerous powers of delusion? However it came about, it makes for a chord of significance in which Bessie, consciously accusing Mrs. Gogan of deceit, unconsciously draws attention to the Voice of the Speaker that has just been using *ars grammatica* to lure his audience to their doom.

NOTES

1. Sean O'Casey, *Feathers from the Green Crow: Sean O'Casey 1905–1925*, ed. Robert Hogan (London: Macmillan), 302. Numbers in square brackets refer to pages in this edition.

2. See Brendan Behan, *Hold Your Hour and Have Another* (London: Hutchinson, 1963), 31f.; Brendan Behan, *Brendan Behan's Island* (London: Hutchinson, 1962), 93–112.

3. O'Casey's fellow-labourers on the Great Northern Railway had mocked his membership of the Gaelic League by calling him 'Irish' Jack.

4. *Feathers from the Green Crow*, 300f.

5. See, for example, Sean O'Casey, *The Letters of Sean O'Casey*, ed. David Krause, vol. 1, 1910–1941 (London: Cassell, 1975), 69. *Letters*, I, 119.

6. Augusta Gregory, *Lady Gregory's Journals,* ed. Daniel J. Murphy, 2 vols. (Gerrards Cross: Colin Smythe, 1978), I, 586.

7. See Garry O'Connor, *Sean O'Casey* (London: Hodder and Stoughton, 1988), 166.

8. O'Casey took the figure of a carpenter from *The Crimson in the Tri-Colour* and made him the basis for Fluther. He identified the Covey with the 'noble proletarian' of that play. Act Two of *Plough* drew on *The Cooing of Doves*, which was, in turn, indebted to Michael Dolan's advice to change the location of a scene in the second version of *The Crimson in the Tri-Colour* from outside a convent to inside a pub. See earlier, 84–88.

9. See Ruth Dudley Edwards, *Patrick Pearse: The Triumph of Failure* (London: Gollancz, 1977), 245.

10. Fallon in *Modern Drama*, vol. 4 (1961), quoted by Garry O'Connor, 169.

11. Dudley Edwards, 246.

12. See Bernice Shrank, "'Th' nakedness o' th' times:" Dressing-Up in *The Plough and the Stars,' Canadian Journal of Irish Studies*, 7, 1981, 5–20.

13. There is no stage direction or other compelling reason for the usual casting of Peter as an elderly man; as Nora's uncle he need be only in his forties. The opening stage direction describes him as 'a little, thin bit of man,' but he is presumably vigorous enough to work as a labourer. En passant it might be noted that giving Bessie a northern accent is not only without a basis in the text but also misleading; as O'Casey knew, there were poor Dublin Protestants with strong Unionist views, and Bessie represents this aspect of the political spectrum.

14. In traditional Abbey productions, Clitheroe puts on his civilian hat, but the stage direction [124] would allow him to use a slouch hat, and this would, perhaps, add to the force of the sequence.

15. His relationship with Jerry Devine reminds us that the Covey is the character in the play whose ideological stance regarding the Rising would have been very close to O'Casey's in 1916, and to this extent he continues O'Casey's particularly savage treatment of socialist materialists in these plays.

16. The correct form is 'in secula seculorum.'

17. In the dialect of Hilljoy Square, 'prostitute' was an alien, middle-class term of moral denigration. Locals, more charitably, preferred to refer to the many prostitutes as 'unfortunate girls.'

18. For context, see chapter two, page 27.

19. Gabriel Fallon, *Sean O'Casey: The Man I Knew* (London: Routledge and Kegan Paul, 1965), 73. Notice that in Fallon's account O'Casey says that there might be people in the audience who had 'heard Pearse speak and they might easily be offended at my use of his words', with the implication that O'Casey was not portraying Pearse, merely using his words.

20. As a matter of fact, Pearse was not remembered or represented as particularly tall: he was slightly above average height and of compact build. The height of the Figure may be O'Casey's unconscious addition of the dominant physical feature of De Valera, a surviving idealist whom O'Casey detested more vehemently than he did the dead Pearse.

21. From the oration at the grave of O'Donovan Rossa. The last of the Voice's passages is taken from the same speech. See Dudley Edwards, 236f.

22. In *The Silver Tassie* O'Casey frequently 'reverses' Scripture. For example, the opening speech of the Croucher in Act Two is a reversal of Ezekiel 37:1–10.

23. 'So he managed, and with genius, to incorporate into the play's conception the opinion of his old Citizen Army commandant, Captain White, that "the Irish question was the sexual problem writ large."' See Garry O'Connor, 173.

24. Larkin was a brilliant public speaker, but though he showed force and passion and wit, he lacked the aura of 'higher' education associated with middle-class Nationalists such as Pearse. It is difficult not to suspect that political resentment lay behind O'Casey's loathing of the educated middle class in these plays.

25. Something of this paradox lingers in English, for example, where 'speech' may indicate either the act of orality or a written text of such an act.

26. An Irish audience almost always shows its approval of Fluther's stance, in marked contrast to its lack of support for the Covey's efforts to educate Corporal Stoddart.

27. The double repetition of 'fool' recalls the Voice of the Man: 'but the fools, the fools, the fools!—they have left us our Fenian dead, and, while Ireland holds these graves, Ireland, unfree, shall never be at peace' [141].

28. Bessie is killed as she pulls Nora away from a window at the back of her room. It would be interesting to design a production that led the audience to see a visual connection between this window and the larger pub window through which the tall, dark male shadow was seen.

Chapter 7

Beyond the Beyonds

As we have seen, such was the delight of early reviewers in the language of the Abbey plays that they were willing to overlook what they saw as weakness of structure. Some of the reviews seem strange today, but that is only to be expected: we have had the best part of a century to familiarise ourselves with these plays. Given later developments in realism, especially in the cinema, we would be slow to describe the characters of *Shadow* as photographs.[1] The Abbey plays have been for so long such a permanent part of the Irish theatre that it is impossible for us to imagine the language in which they are written as a shock, however pleasant, to the ears. Perhaps that is why there is no comprehensive analysis of O'Casey's language: maybe there is an unconscious assumption that it must have been done a long time ago.

Robert Hogan has written:

O'Casey chose the raciest of what people said; a photographic realist chooses whatever people say, whether it be witty or boring. Such a writer is the naturalist of the drama, the inheritor of the mantle of Zola. He uses words for their reality to a real-life situation rather than for their dramatic effect . . . . The dialogue of O'Casey's early Dublin plays is probably at the very outer edge of comic realism. O'Casey's dialogue is rooted in reality, but, as with Dickens' dialogue, there is an inordinate profusion of roots. O'Casey's dialogue is usually much funnier than [Lennox] Robinson's, as Dickens' dialogue is usually much funnier than Jane Austen's; but it is so funny that it calls attention to why it is funny.[2]

Though he is properly distrustful of absolute divisions in a writer's work, Hogan accepts the popular view that, beginning with *The Silver Tassie*, O'Casey's dramatic mode changed from a kind of realism to a more poetic form.

Broadly speaking, dramatic realism involves a representation that entails the illusion of actuality. The audience at a realist play will expect visual accuracy in setting, costume, and movement; psychological probability in character and action; and language such as men and women in those circumstances might use. The three

Abbey plays meet these requirements provided our definition of realism is not applied with absolute rigidity. (Even the most realist plays avoid 'candid camera' details such as long pauses in which nothing at all or nothing interesting happens. Even the most realist plays telescope time in order to represent a time frame of more than two or three hours.)

Shadow is convincing in setting and action. Nothing happens that might not have happened in the circumstances. The dramatic transmission strains our ideas of probability if we wonder how likely it was that the various characters should arrive in Shields' room in such a convenient sequence, but we tend to overlook this (and even the difficulty Maguire would have in getting out of Hilljoy Square and into the evening newspaper in less than an hour) because we sense that we are dealing with a comic realism in which a series of characters come on and perform like vaudeville 'turns.' Every mature person has encountered a poseur like Davoren and a cynic like Shields in one form or another. Most of the more broadly comic characters—Tommy Owens, Mr. Gallogher, Mrs. Henderson, Mr. Grigson—are credible only if we allow for a degree of exaggeration. Psychologically and linguistically, they are recognisable types: all casual details have been removed so that only the most striking elements remain.

The dialogue involving the broadly comic characters generates a laughter of recognition in the audience and also draws attention to its own composition. Whatever about their international counterparts, Irish audiences recognise the language as simultaneously familiar and strange.[3] Many of them will associate it with elderly relatives and acquaintances whose language escaped the flattening influence of education or the international media. Consciously or unconsciously, they will know that the dramatist has sought to include in the dialogue as much as possible of the older and more colourful forms of expression; some may even sense that these forms are characteristic of the oral tradition. Yet nothing is said that would strike the native speaker of Hiberno-English as false. Davoren's final lines are extremely artificial, but we have no difficulty in believing that such an artificial character as Davoren would use them in the circumstances.

The same is largely true of *Juno* if, again, we allow the dramatist the right to impose a significant shape on the action and, for example, to indicate the passage of time by dropping a curtain in Act Three. The setting is convincing, and all the characters and their actions well are within the bounds of probability—even Boyle and Joxer. The dialogue is, for a native speaker, a superb representation of actual speech. It is, of course, in the nature of a written play to select, and the editing out of casual chat leaves behind a speech that is a refined version of the vernacular, richer and denser but still recognisably vernacular. (Similarly, we accept that while the realist play represents the actual, it does not represent all of the actual, and, consequently, we do not fault the play because, for example, there is no talk of emigration, no mention of football or the music hall, and no young children in a setting that teemed with them.) Bentham, like Davoren, is convincingly different, as is Jerry Devine when he affects a lyrical mode. We accept Mrs. Tancred's and Juno's exceptional eloquence because they are in exceptional emotional states and automatically speaking within the conventions of the traditional *caoineadh*.

While there is nothing in *Juno* to trouble an audience, there is at least one element in the language to raise the eyebrow of a hypercritical reader. The character of Maisie Madigan consists almost entirely of three long, rhapsodic quasi soliloquies at the party in Act Two. Given the setting in a semioral culture, her tendency to fill her life with words is not surprising. She is a version of that type of person who luxuriates in recollection, and her detailed compositions are perfectly in character, as is her favourite song, 'And You'll Remember Me.'

I remember as well as I remember yestherday, at a party given to celebrate the comin' of the first chiselur to Annie an' Bennie Jimeson—who was the barber, yous may remember, in Henrietta Street, that, afther Easter Week, hung out a green, white an' orange pole, an' then, when the Tans started their Jazz dancin', whipped it in agen, an' stuck out a red, white an' blue wan instead, givin' as an excuse that a barber's pole was strictly non-political—singin' 'An' You'll Remember Me' with the top notes quiverin' in a dead hush of pethrified attention, folleyed be a clappin' o' han's that shuk the tumblers on the table, an' capped by Jimeson, the barber, saying that it was the best rendherin' of 'You'll Remember Me' he ever heard in his natural! [78]

This is brilliantly realised in image and sound, especially the inset of the Henrietta Street barber and the explosion of applause for Maisie's song; she has a skill that has obviously been polished by a lifetime of performance and appreciation. The audience revels in the flights of Maisie's fancy but the native speaker will read the phrase 'with the top notes quiverin' in a dead hush of pethrified attention' and will reread it and probably decide that this is not vernacular, however heightened by an oral rhapsodist. The description of high notes as quivering is common, as is 'dead hush,' but there is something fundamentally false about 'petrified attention.'

Even if 'dead hush' was not recorded elsewhere, it would be accepted because 'dead' is a common qualifier of silence and stillness—for example, dead centre, dead heat—and when, in common usage, 'dead' is used instead of 'deadly,' it produces 'dead quiet,' 'dead still,' 'dead serious,' and so on. 'Petrified attention' is another matter. The intended meaning is clear: *the people were so attentive that they seemed afraid to move.* In a more literary or poetical text intended for more educated listeners it might be that *the people were so attentive they seemed as still as stones*, but, whatever about the theatre audience, neither Maisie nor her neighbours would be aware of this. They would have spoken of being 'frozen with [the] fear' but not of being 'in frozen fear.' They would have spoken of being 'in the frozen cold' as well as the more common 'in the freezing cold'; but the metaphorical transference of personal stillness to the abstract 'attention' would be unlikely in vernacular speech. It would, of course, pass unnoticed in Shakespeare or in Synge, but they were writing dialogue based on speech, not transcribing speech. Because it is a tiny discord in a speech (and a play) characterised by colourful speech, it passes unnoticed in a production of *Juno*.

The language of *Plough* is another matter because extravernacular forms occur frequently and from the very beginning. The setting and opening are typical of O'Casey's comic realism. Mrs. Gogan, a rhetorical relation of Maisie Madigan, is a voluble woman of morbid imagination and expresses herself in language that is copious and colourful and redolent of oral usage:

I dunno: there's many a man this minute lowerin' a pint, thinkin' of a woman, or pickin' out a winner, or doin' work as you're doin', while th' hearse drawn be th' horses with the black plumes is dhrivin' up to his own hall door, an' a voice that he doesn't hear is mutterin' in his ear, 'Earth to earth, an' ashes to ashes, an' dust to dust.'

Fluther, anxious about his cold, responds: 'A man in th' pink o' health should have a holy horror of allowin' thoughts o' death to be festherin' in his mind.' 'A man in the pink of health' is a common expression. 'Holy terror' is also common but lacks the alliterative appeal of 'holy horror.' 'Thoughts festering in the mind' may not be common but, again, is striking and instantly accessible because of many analogies. The same cannot be said of one phrase in Mrs. Gogan's next speech.

It always gives me a kind o' threspassin' joy to feel meself moving along in a mournin' coach, an' me thinkin' that, maybe, th' next funeral 'll be me own, an' glad, in a quiet way, that this is somebody else's. [109f.]

The rhythm and pacing evoke the improper pleasure she derives from the experience, but the phrase 'threspassin' joy' is another example of metaphorical transference that is common in poetry but unusual (if not nonexistent) in the vernacular. Many simpler structures exist—'fleeting pleasure,' 'fading joy,' 'rising optimism,' and so on—but 'threspassin' joy,' in the sense of 'sinful pleasure,' is more complex. In the three examples, the participle is a simple adjective qualifying the noun; in the O'Casey phrase, it is not the joy that trespasses but the person who experiences it.

Seconds later Fluther reacts *vehemently* when Mrs. Gogan refers to Peter's shirt as a 'Lord Mayor's nightdress': 'Blast you an' your nightshirt. Is a man fermentin' with fear to stick the showin' off to him of a thing that looks like a shinin' shroud?' [110]. This has many of the characteristics associated with the speech of the tenements. There is an elaborate system of alliterations, the most extravagant involving 'showin' . . . shinin' . . . shroud.' The metaphorical use of 'fermenting' is bold but not without many analogies that indicate the transforming power of emotions: 'seething with rage,' 'boiling with anger,' and so on. The comparison between Peter's shirt and a shroud is just about acceptable, given that the speaker is gripped by a sudden fear of death, but the idea of a luminous shroud is extreme; a white shirt might look like a shining shroud to somebody whose grip on actuality is tenuous, but Fluther doesn't seem quite that shaken, and one feels that the adjective owed as much to alliteration as to anything else, a feeling that becomes progressively more common in the later plays. The accumulation of these rhetorical effects in a five-second speech would certainly push against the parameters of common speech; the phrase 'to stick the showin' off to him of a thing' probably breaches them. If Fluther had said 'to stick the sight of a thing,' nothing would have been lost except perhaps the sense of Fluther losing control expressed by his transcendence of the vernacular.

   O'Casey was better placed than any modern reader to recognise the limits of
the vernacular, and his decision to breach them must have been deliberate. In doing
so, he was, of course, merely claiming the traditional right of the dramatist to edit
current speech in order to create a literary language.

   There was little in O'Casey's literary education to incline him toward realism.
He had been raised on the rhetorical fluency and imagery of the Bible. In terms of
drama his early masters had been Shakespeare and Boucicault; the novels of
Dickens also influenced his sense of comic characterisation and dialogue. The
appeal of realism for a youngish socialist dramatist was that it was still new, was
still considered refreshingly radical, and, perhaps most attractive of all, had not yet
been directed at the Dublin working class as well as O'Casey thought he could do
it. O'Casey wanted to show conditions as they actually were, to expose, rather than
romanticise, economic and intellectual poverty. Irish melodramatists, including
Boucicault, tended to stress the spiritual nobility of the poor and transform their
poverty in time for the final curtain. Having seen the tenements at first hand,
O'Casey did not believe that poverty and hunger were spiritually elevating. Raw
realism must have seemed the obvious medium, and yet, as we know, he chose a
kind of comic realism in which lighthearted comedy is punctuated by moments of
terror. There was little sense of physical hunger or poverty in *Shadow*, certainly not
enough to disturb an audience. His next play was more hard-hitting (Juno worries
about being able to make ends meet, and eventually the entire family disintegrates),
but the central family in *Plough* is relatively well-off, and the only poor characters
are Bessie and Mrs. Gogan. By the time he came to write *Plough*, O'Casey was
already allowing into his comic realism the older influence of Boucicault and the
newer influence of expressionism as practised by, say, Toller, whose plays O'Casey
admired as much as he admired the author's left-wing politics.[4] It was inevitable
that criticism would identify Toller's expressionism as a key factor in O'Casey's
rejection of realism, but against this should be placed his innate tendency toward
poetic and melodramatic forms and also his later insistence that he had never
embraced expressionism.

Never had any personal contact with Toller, George Kaiser, Piscator or any other plunger
into Expressionism, German or otherwise. Don't know what it means; nor do I yet know
what 'Realism' is either. Heard the name of Piscator, but don't know what he does or did.
Saw Toller's Masse-Men done by the Dublin Drama League years ago (25 or so), read his
HOOPLA, and saw his DRAW THE FIRES in London, long after W. THE GATES and
SILVER TASSIE had been written.[5]

It is likely that the experience of Toller's play influenced the conclusion of the
second acts of *Plough* and *Tassie*, but it is difficult to believe that O'Casey's
development would have been radically different had he never seen any of the
Drama League's productions. Given his early addictions to the Bible, Shakespeare,
Dickens, and Boucicault, it was inevitable that such an awkward individualist, who
had broken with almost every organisation he had ever joined, would resent the
shackles of realism.

The early Abbey was antirealist and never produced a body of drama in the Ibsenite tradition. Yeats was essentially a verse dramatist, and the plays of Lady Gregory were closer to folktales than slices of life. The one popularly acknowledged genius of the early Abbey was Synge. Synge's objective was 'the reality, which is the root of all poetry,' but he had no time for the 'realist' language of Ibsenite drama.

> In the modern literature of towns, however, richness is found only in sonnets, or prose poems, or in one or two elaborate books that are far away from the profound and common interests of life. One has, on one side, Mallarmé and Huysmans producing this literature; and on the other, Ibsen and Zola dealing with the reality of life in joyless and pallid words.[6]

Synge believed that art involved a collaboration between poet and people, with writers neither disregarding the vernacular nor confining themselves within its limits. His claim that in writing *The Playboy*, as with his earlier plays, he had used only one or two words that he had not heard spoken in Ireland may mislead some into believing that the language of the plays was the language of rural Ireland. Synge was insisting that his vocabulary was that of rural Ireland, not that his syntax and rhythmical structure were always based on popular speech. Synge's dialogue is not a transcription of any Irish speech. Synge took the language of rural Ireland and edited it in order to highlight certain qualities (strikingly concrete imagery, rhetorical delight in metaphor, alliteration, assonance, and rhythm) that he identified as deriving from Gaelic and that we would see as characteristically oral. (In passing, it might be noted that the language of the Abbey plays translates into Irish more readily than the language of Synge or of the later O'Casey.) Synge felt that, living where and when he did, he enjoyed many of the advantages that Shakespeare exploited.

> It was part of Synge's greatness that he realized . . . that the future of poetic drama did not lie within the limits of the traditional blank-verse form—that a new poetic medium needed to be forged, one which would combine the vigour and intensity of poetry with the flexibility and naturalism of prose. He found the makings of such a medium in the Anglo-Irish dialect, and he exploited them to the full.[7]

O'Casey discovered in the conversation of the Dublin working class the same kind of naturally flavoured and imaginative speech, ideal for the stage, that Synge had previously found in Wicklow, West Kerry, and the Aran Islands and made the basis of his dialogue. (It is important to remember that it was only after *Shadow* and *Juno* that O'Casey actually saw a Synge play, that is, heard the language in performance;[8] he had, of course, read Synge before that.) The more he wrote, the more O'Casey tried to create a dramatic speech that would be to working-class Dublin what Synge's was to the peasant communities on the west coast. Some would argue that he succeeded, and others, that he never quite managed Synge's harmony of poetic splendour and natural vigour.

The moral problems that certain Abbey actors had with the 'strong' language of *Plough* have tended to overshadow the fact that from the very beginning some people had aesthetic qualms about the writing. Late in rehearsals Lennox Robinson, the producer, thought it 'the worst written' of O'Casey's plays but was confident that 'good characters and good acting' would carry it through. The first night was a great success, and Robinson thought it 'a better play as a whole than *Juno*' but 'seriously hampered by long rambling speeches': 'Some I cut a bit but Casey doesn't like drastic cutting and the speeches are so much part of the style of the play—as much its style as Synge's but he hasn't got Synge's clarity of expression.'[9] The expression 'as much its style as Synge's' is not absolutely clear, but one understands Robinson to be making two main points: that the rhetoric of the play is an inherent part of its style and, second, that this linguistically 'rich' style lacks the translucence of Synge's equally 'rich' style. Lest his remarks be associated with his own antipathy to rhetoric, Robinson mentioned that 'other people' felt the same. Among them might have been Holloway, who casually noted that the dialogue 'at times seems too long and wordy, kept back the action, and will have to be tightened up.'[10] The *Irish Times* carried the most favourable review of the opening night, which, inter alia, made the following points:

Mr. O'Casey's play is more than realism; it is naturalism—a faithful reproduction of what happened, with the truth of the picture apparent to the dullest imagination . . . . The play is remarkable for the sparkle of its dialogue, even when, as often happens, character after character has to speak long-drawn out sentences. When these miniature speeches have been trimmed a little, *The Plough and the Stars* will be a better work.[11]

A few nights later such quibbles seemed irrelevant as rioters guaranteed play and playwright their place in history. In the intervening years the status of the play has continued to rise, accelerated by the political revisionism that followed the outbreak of civil war in Northern Ireland.

As we have seen, from the very beginning of Act One, O'Casey gave Mrs. Gogan and Fluther lines that transcend the Dublin vernacular on which they were based. It is extremely difficult to establish a correlation between the pitch of passion and the level of elaboration, partly because the horrors imagined by Mrs. Gogan and Fluther are always safely set within the conventions of comedy. When the language of Mrs. Gogan and of Bessie is, for different reasons, flavoured with religious references, we find it convincing because both women are, in their different ways, obsessed by religion; but Fluther's retort to the Covey is less immediately coherent: 'There's no necessity to be raisin' your voice; shoutin's no manifestin' forth of a growin' mind' [111]. Perhaps we should understand this to be the language of a man who consciously parades high-faluting biblical phrases as a retort to the Covey's belligerent atheism. At any rate, one feels the need to find a reason.[12]

Most of Act One consists of abuse, and so the language comes within the conventions and traditions of flyting, where words are heaped and hurled like weapons. Fluther bombards the Covey with language:

You'll be kickin' an' yellin' for th' priest yet, me boyo. I'm not goin' to stand silent an' simple listenin' to a thick like you makin' a maddenin' mockery o' God Almighty. It 'ud be a nice derogatory thing on me conscience, an' me dyin', to look back in rememberin' shame of talkin' to a word-weavin' little ignorant yahoo of a red flag socialist. [112]

This works well, partly because of the barrage of alliterations. Perhaps 'makin' a maddenin' mockery' tests the limits of realist dialogue; 'in rememberin' shame of talkin' to' breaches them. Here again the intended meaning is clear enough—'to look back with shame as I remember talking to'—but the use of a present participle to qualify an abstract noun rings as false as 'threspassin' joy' and for the same reasons.

O'Casey delighted in the binding force of alliteration. Though he may sometimes overdo it, there is no doubt that he is drawing on a tradition of rhetorical abuse that includes Mrs. Gogan's pithily elegant 'there's always th' makin's of a row in th' mention of religion' [113] as well as Peter's ranting catalogues.

I'll leave you to th' day when th' all-pitiful, all-merciful, all-lovin' God 'll be handin' you to th' angels to be rievin' an' roastin' you, tearin' an' tormentin' you, burnin' an' blastin' you! [113]

In a culture where verbal abuse was a cultivated form, this combination of divine forgiveness and human malice is wonderfully convincing; seconds later Peter continues, but less convincingly:

Isn't it a poor thing for a man who wouldn't say a word against his greatest enemy to have to listen to that Covey's twartin' animosities, shovin' poor, patient people into a lashin' out of curses that darken his soul with th' shadow of th' wrath of th' last day! [114]

Again one notices that the biblical coda, while perfect for Bessie, seems to be part of a general style rather than written with the specific character of Peter in mind. But more discordant than the biblical influences is the structure of 'shoving poor people into a lashing out of curses.' There does not seem to be any analogy for this in common speech. There are some that are reasonably close—'talking people into throwing away their money/giving up their rights'—but they are all well short of what will become one of O'Casey's favourite structures in which the prepositions 'in' and 'into' are followed by a verbal noun or participle or related structure.

Take Nora's lines.

Are yous always goin' to be tearin' down th' little bit of respectability that a body's thryin' to build up? Am I always goin' to be havin' to nurse yous into th' hardy habit o' thryin' to keep up a little bit of appearance? [115]

Again, the second sentence seems to founder on the use of the preposition 'into' after the verb 'to nurse.' In common speech one nurses somebody *back to* health. It is possible to follow the metaphorical use of 'nurse' to mean 'gradually bring to the point of doing something properly,' but the effort is not helped by the choice of the alliterative 'hardy' to qualify 'habit.' One might say a person given to early morning cold showers had 'hardy habits,' but the adjective, in that sense, is incongruous when applied to refined domestic manners. Perhaps by 'hardy'

O'Casey intended the meaning found in the phrase 'hardy annuals,' so that Nora expects Peter and the Covey to preserve their habits forever despite all provocation. Perhaps. The reader may muse, but for the audience the moment is already gone. It is difficult to avoid the suspicion that O'Casey is being drawn off course by the pull of alliteration, that in heightening common usage, he has left the clarity of the vernacular but failed to achieve the coherence of poetical realism.

Nora's next speech prefigures developments after *Plough*.

If th' two o' yous don't thry to make a generous altheration in your goin's on, an' keep on thryin' t' inaugurate th' customs o' th' house into this place, yous can flit into other lodgin's where your bowsey battlin' 'll meet, maybe, with an encore. [115]

'Generous alteration' would not occur in vernacular speech with reference to behaviour. It is difficult to know what O'Casey gains by this combination other than to draw attention to a 'higher' use of language. Nor is this change part of a consistent raising of vocabulary because 'alteration' and 'inaugurate' are balanced by 'flit' and 'bowsey.' The phrase 'inaugurate the customs of the rest of the house into this place' is striking, partly because 'inaugurate' is not a word in common usage and even more because 'inaugurate [object] into' has no basis in English, written or spoken, educated or common. If these lines were given to, say, Mr. Gallogher in *Shadow*, we would understand them as symptomatic of malapropistic aspiration, but nothing in *Plough* encourages such a reading of Nora's character. On the other hand, 'bowsey battling' is both admirably concise and convincing. The noun 'bowsey,' meaning 'an obnoxious, troublesome male,'[13] can be used as an adjective in a phrase like 'bowsey behaviour' and, when linked alliteratively to 'battling,' is a fine description of the constantly bickering Peter and the Covey. 'Encore' would not be used in this way in common speech. Boxing fans would find the cry of the opera house unacceptably effete. Maybe we are to understand the discord as suggestive of Nora's refined reaction to the uncouth behaviour of the men, but, coming at the end of a short speech that has already tested the audience, the potential force of the contrast is likely to be lost in the swirl.

One is reminded of Robinson's comment that O'Casey lacked Synge's 'clarity of expression.' Robinson was a successful playwright and experienced producer. Even those who criticised him had to admit that 'the word was all important for Lennox' and that 'vocally he was absolutely splendid.'[14] He knew that the play would succeed despite the wordiness, that there was enough in the characters to win and hold an audience; yet one can understand his problems with much of the opening act and especially with some of Nora's lines, which could not be played, like those of Peter, at farcical speed: 'An', once for all, Willie, you'll have to thry to deliver yourself from th' desire of provokin' oul' Pether into a wild forgetfulness of what's proper an' allowable in a respectable home' [115]. A man offstage delivered Nora's hat *from* Arnott's, but in the lines just quoted the verb 'deliver' is used in a way Nora would have known only in prayers where God is asked to 'deliver us from evil.' Once again, this usage would not seem out of place in Bessie's lines or even in Mrs. Gogan's, but in Nora's it sounds simply pretentious. The use of 'desire' (rather than 'desirous') followed by 'of' is strikingly odd; 'a wild forgetfulness' seems, at best, paradoxical, the energy of the adjective contradicting the absence connoted by 'forgetfulness.' At this point one senses that the constraints of comic realism have been dispensed with, that the dramatist is experimenting freely with poetic realism, but with no obvious pattern or rationale.

Just as the dramatist is entitled to experiment, so the reader is entitled to ask what has been gained. What, for example, would have been lost had Nora said something like this? 'And, once and for all, Willie, you'll have to resist the temptation to provoke old Peter into such a temper that he loses all sense of what's proper and allowable in a respectable home.' The most obvious difference is that of linguistic mode, the difference between O'Casey's *poetry* and my *prose*. The quality of O'Casey's writing is another matter. If his intention was to create a speech in which the rhetorical structure complemented the emotional charge, then he succeeded, but at a considerable cost: what the speech gains in comic energy it loses in clarity of expression.

The exchange between Nora and Jack at the end of Act One is conducted almost entirely within the conventions of realism, even if Jack's romantic depiction of his 'little, little red-lipped Nora' strikes most people as mawkish or unconvincing or both. When Nora removes his arm from around her, Jack is irritated:

CLITHEROE [*with a pause of irritation*]. Oh, well, if we're goin' to be snotty! [*A pause.*]
NORA. It's lookin' like as if it was you that was going to be . . . snotty! Bridlin' up with bittherness, th' minute a body attempts t' open her mouth.
CLITHEROE. Is it any wondher, turnin' a tender sayin' into a meanin' of malice an' spite!
NORA. It's hard for a body to be always keepin' her mind bent on makin' thoughts that'll be no longer than th' length of your own satisfaction. [*A pause. Standing up*] If we're goin' to dhribble th' time away sittin' here like a pair o' cranky mummies, I'd be as well sewin' or doin' something about the place . . . . Ah, Jack, don't be so cross!
CLITHEROE [*doggedly*]. Cross? I'm not cross; I'm not a bit cross. It was yourself started it. [120f]

Though both characters are emotional at this point, Clitheroe's first and final speeches are models of realist dialogue, the first for his use of a word so obsolete in polite usage that the original actor resented having to use it on the stage, the final for the sense of spontaneity generated by the repetition of 'cross.' 'Bridling up with bitterness' shows the oral delight in concise alliteration phrases; in the premotor era everybody would have been familiar with bridles and associated metaphors. Clitheroe's next lines are more recognisable as O'Casey's new dialogue than as working-class speech. '*T*urning a *t*ender saying into a **m**eaning of **m**alice and spi*t*e' sounds well, and the general sense is clear, but the arrangement of the sound sacrifices something of the clarity when the ear asks the brain to imagine a physical act of speech, *a saying*, turning into a concept, *a meaning*. The first sentence of Nora's retort is no more demanding than an imaginative passage in Shakespeare, but it lacks the elegant coherence that is normally the reward for such difficulties in Shakespeare, and it remains hazy. Her next sentence is at least as demanding but is instantly rewarding in its transformation of the uncompromising couple into a pair of cantankerous mummies, their tight-lipped exchanges brilliantly captured in Nora's use of 'dribbling away the time.'

Here, as elsewhere, it is difficult to discover a consistent pattern in O'Casey's introduction of poetic structures into a dialogue that is still predominantly realist. The most obvious reason for 'raising' the level of the language would be to suggest a 'raising' of emotions (as in Mrs. Gogan's fantasies or in the men's flytings), but when, with the revelation concerning his promotion, tempers really flare between Jack and Nora, there is no commensurate transcendence of realist language.

CLITHEROE [*removing her arms from around him*]. None o' this nonsense, now; I want to know what you did with th' letter?
[NORA *goes slowly to the lounge and sits down.*]
CLITHEROE [*angrily*]. Why didn't you give me th' letter? What did you do with it? . . . . [*He shakes her by the shoulders*] What did you do with th' letter?
NORA [*flaming* up]. I burned it, I burned it! That's what I did with it! Is General Connolly and th' Citizen Army goin' to be your only care? Is your home goin' to be only a place to rest in? Am I goin' to be only somethin' to provide merry-makin' at night for you? Your vanity'll be th' ruin of you an' me yet . . . . That's what's movin' you: because they've made an officer of you, you'll make a glorious cause of what you're doin', while your little red-lipped Nora can go on sittin' here, makin' a companion of th' loneliness of th' night!
CLITHEROE [*fiercely*]. You burned it, did you? [*He grips her arm.*] Well, me good lady—
NORA. Let go—you're hurtin' me!
CLITHEROE. You deserve to be hurt . . . . Any letter that comes to me for th' future, take care that I get it . . . . D'ye hear—take care that I get it! . . . . You needn't wait up for me; if I'm in at all, it won't be before six in th' morning. [124]

The sequence works very effectively, the realist dialogue conveying Nora's desperation and Clitheroe's brutality. In the context, Nora's image of herself 'makin' a companion of th' loneliness of th' night' sounds false and contrived, but the producer could disregard the fortissimmo of the exclamation mark and contrast Nora's poetic vision of loneliness with the vernacular directness of her abuse.

On the other hand, in the brilliant finale of Act One, which follows almost immediately, Mollser's melancholic isolation is expressed in realist language, while Bessie's angry belligerence is orchestrated with biblical extravagance

There's th' men marchin' out into th' dhread dimness o' danger, while th' lice is crawlin' about feedin' on th' fatness o' the land! But you'll not escape from th' arrow that flieth be night, or th' sickness that wasteth be day . . . . An' ladyship an' all, as some o' them may be, they'll be scattered abroad, like th' dust in th' darkness! [125]

This works in the same way as Juno's lament works. In the fervour of her passion she draws on the words of her god and on her own locally learned oral skills. Her flights of imagination, from marching men, to crawling lice, to flying arrows, to mysterious sickness, to general pulverisation, are wonderfully clear. The alliteration emphasises without disturbing the focus, and the whole passage is modulated with great rhetorical skill.

Some of the compositional skills (rhythm, balance, alliteration and rhyme) emerge more clearly when the speech is written out in a way that visualises its structure.

> *There's th' men marchin' out*
> *into th' dhread dimness of danger,*
> *while th' lice is crawling about*
> *feedin' on th' fatness o' the land!*

> *But you'll not escape*
> *from th' arrow that flieth be night,*
> *or th' sickness that wasteth be day . . . .*

> *An' ladyship an' all,*
> *as some o' them may be,*
> *they'll be scattered abroad,*
> *like th' dust in th' darkness!*

The element of rhyme in each section shows how carefully constructed the sections are: modelled on the music of the psalms rather than on any strict stanza, their power is in their measured threats. The climactic third section, brandishing the self-satisfaction of a perfect stanza, owes at least as much to the flyting of Hilljoy Square as it does to the Bible:

$$\smile - \smile \smile \smile -$$
$$\smile - \smile \smile \smile -$$
$$\smile \smile - \smile \smile -$$
$$\smile \smile - \smile \smile - \smile$$

Having hit the high notes with Bessie's speech, we are returned to earth with Mollser's question: 'Is there anybody goin', Mrs Clitheroe, with a titther o' sense?'

Despite the intensity of the atmosphere in the bar in Act Two, the language is generally comic realist. Rosie's opening remarks about the men who are 'thinkin' of higher things than a girl's garthers' is typically imaginative and colourful and consistent with vernacular usage. Excited by drink and the Man's rhetoric, Peter and Fluther express their Nationalist zeal without recourse to alien syntax or vocabulary. Even when Fluther reacts *fiercely* to Peter's, he does so with vernacular intensity: 'Sure, I don't give a damn if you slep' in Bodenstown! You can take your breakfast, dinner, an' tea on th' grave in Bodenstown, if you like, for Fluther.' [132]. Even when, defending Rosie against the Covey's abuse, he is *roaring at the top of his voice*, he contents himself with a battery of familiar formulas: 'Come on, come on, you lowser; put your mits up now, if there's a man's blood in you! Be God, in a few minutes you'll see some snots flyin' around, I'm tellin' you' [140]. Only when the row between Bessie and Mrs. Gogan is warming up do Peter and Fluther, trying to calm things down, flirt with prepositions in a way we have noticed before:

PETER [*anxiously*]. Take no notice of her; pay no attention to her. She's just *tormentin' herself towards havin'* a row with somebody . . .

FLUTHER. . . . The safest way to hindher her from havin' any enjoyment out of her spite, is *to dip our thoughts into the fact of her bein'* a female person that has moved out of th' sight of ordinary sensible people. [133; emphases added]

Apart from these examples, the principal agents of extravernacular forms are, again, Bessie and Mrs. Gogan.

At this stage we have come to expect from these women expressions of passion that derive as much from their religious obsessions as from their material lives. A skilled oral rhapsodist with the entire Bible at her disposal, Bessie is predictably powerful. Mrs. Gogan matches her in malice but not in rhetorical control: when she speaks of her children being 'got between th' bordhers of th' Ten Commandments,' the audience is left to resolve the conjunction of bedclothes and tablets of stone. Only when they row again in Act Three does Mrs, Gogan lose contact with vernacular usage:

an', steppin' from th' threshold of good manners, let me tell you, Mrs. Burgess, that it's a fat wondher to Jennie Gogan that a lady-like singer o' hymns like yourself would lower her thoughts from sky-thinkin' to stretch our her arm in sly-seekin' way to pinch anything dhriven asthray in th' confusion of th' battle our boys is makin' for th' freedom of their counthry! [152]

'Sky-thinkin',' especially when echoed by 'sly-seekin',' is too far from the structures of common speech to ring true in a realist, even a comic realist play.

By Act Three, however, the audience has come to realise that the language of the play is a mixture of realism and extrarealism. It is neither consistently realist, as was *Juno*, nor as consistently heightened as in Shakespeare or Synge or even the later O'Casey. There is no pattern: supercharged emotions do not always produce a similarly charged language. Surprisingly, the incidence of extravernacular forms decreases as the play progresses from domestic bickering to the mortal terrors of battle. Even more surprisingly, perhaps, Nora takes more liberties with common usage in Act One, when she is sane, than she does in Acts Three and Four. The consequence is that the audience distinguishes between the flamboyantly self-advertising language of the first part and the more restrained language of the second, and the critic may see this as part of O'Casey's contrast between the bravery of heroic anticipation and the chastening experience of a real battle where men are wounded and killed.

What is undeniable is the dramatist's unwillingness to be confined by the restrictions of the mode, comic realism, in which he had established himself. The move toward expressionism is obvious in the sequence where the soldiers enter the bar in Act Two. A modern audience would have little difficulty in accepting this as an expressionist vignette that contrasts with Fluther's comic courtesy, just as the heroic idealism of the soldiers contrasts with the actuality of physical life in the Dublin tenements; but not everybody in the Abbey audiences attended the plays put on by the Dublin Drama League, and O'Casey felt obliged to naturalise the expressionist elements of Act Two by offering an elaborate explanation for the periodic intrusion of the Voice and by emphasising that the soldiers 'have been mesmerised by the fervency of the speeches' [141].

The transition to extrarealist modes is also detectable in the characterisation. All dramatic characters are mixtures of elements that may be termed 'individual' and 'typical.' In realist drama the characters are predominantly individual. The characters of allegorical plays, such as moralities, are predominantly typical and the same is true of their descendants in expressionist drama. While they exist as strong individuals, characters like Clitheroe, Peter, the Covey, and Bessie clearly represent points on the political perspective: revolutionary Nationalism, obsolete romantic Nationalism, international socialism, and anti-Nationalist Protestant Unionism. This function of characters is emphasised by each of them being linked with uniforms and banners and emblems. Mollser has hardly any individuality: she is more emblem than person, symbolising the sickness and early death that were endemic in the tenements.

The conclusion of *Plough* is reminiscent of the earlier plays in that the climax of Bessie's death is followed by a postclimactic sequence in which the soldiers make tea and join in the singing of 'Keep the Home Fires Burning.' But there is nothing to tempt the audience to laugh, as there was at the end of *Juno* and, perhaps to a lesser extent, at the end of *Shadow*. The finale is dominated not by speech but by sound and light effects.

CORPORAL STODDART *pours out two cups of tea, and the two soldiers begin to drink. In the distance is heard a bitter burst of rifle and machine-gun fire, interspersed with the boom, boom of artillery. The glare in the sky seen through the window flares into a fuller and deeper red.* [175]

The final moments are closer to opera or melodrama than to realist drama. *Plough* is the most patterned of O'Casey's works, a series of contrasts so effectively integrated that audiences have always noted and always disregarded the absence of a traditional realist plot. O'Casey had successfully dramatised the heroic catastrophe of 1916, had learned a great deal of stagecraft in the process, and would extend himself and the stage even further in his next play, which would seek to dramatise the even greater catastrophe of the Great War. Unfortunately, the tension between him and the Abbey, which had produced some unpleasantness during the *Plough* rehearsals, exploded when the Abbey rejected *The Silver Tassie* and resulted in a schism between O'Casey and the Abbey.

The later plays fall outside the scope of this study, but it is perhaps relevant to note that the expressionist second act of the *Tassie* could be seen as a development of the inspiration that produced the second act of the *Plough*. (O'Casey's original idea had been to locate the political discussion outside a convent.) There is no longer any pretence at realism: the soldiers speak and chant and sing in a manner that needs no 'explanation' because the mode is expressionist. O'Casey gives full vent to his anger not by having a spokesman onstage but by using a wide range of nonrealist devices. Nobody, to my knowledge, has ever faulted the second act or such fully expressionist sequences as the conclusion of Act One; what some people find difficult to admire are the semirealistic elements in the play, especially the language, which was to become the house style for the latter part of his career.

We get a taste of it at the very beginning in the exchange between Sylvester and Simon. Sylvester recalls the night when Harry punched a policeman.

SYLVESTER. An' the hedges by the roadside standin' stiff in the silent cold of the air, the frost beads on the branches glistenin' like toss'd-down diamonds from the breasts of the stars, the quietness of the night stimulated to a fuller stillness by the mockin' breathin' of Harry, an' the heavy, ragin' pantin' of the Bobby, an' the quickenin' beats of our own hearts afraid, of hopin' too little or hopin' too much. [*During the last speech by* SYLVESTER, SUSIE *has come in with a bayonet, and has commenced to polish it.*]
SUSIE. We don't go down on our knees often enough; that's why we're not able to stand up to the Evil One: we don't go down on our knees enough . . . . I can hear some persons fallin' with a splash of sparks into the lake of everylastin' fire. [182]

Susie is a religious hysteric, and her extravernacular language presents no problem. It could be argued that Sylvester is an old blatherer, but his blathering takes him beyond the range of ordinary working-class speech. Susie's language, like that of many characters in O'Casey from Bessie onward, is dramatically powerful because it is based on a style, that of the Bible, that O'Casey had absorbed with his mother's milk. Sylvester's language may strike some as weak: it is, so to speak, to Shakespeare's verse what O'Casey's poetry was to Shelley's.

Reading a play like *Red Roses for Me*, one is struck by the extent to which O'Casey's extrarealist dialogue lacks the bite of his earlier realism without achieving the compensatory intensity of poetry. Ayamonn's soulful rhapsodies, though tending to become tedious, are in character. But what is the point of the imagery in this exchange between him and a local landlord who interrupts a conversation between Ayamonn and his girlfriend?

AYAMONN [*going over and catching him by an arm to guide him out*]. I can't see you now, old friend, for the pair of us are heavily harnessed to a question that must be answered before either of us is a day older.
BRENNAN. Sure I know. An' isn't it only natural, too, that young people should have questions to ask and answers to give to the dewy problems that get in th' way of their dancing feet? [271]

('Heavily harnessed to a question' is awkward, 'dewy problems' opaque; it is difficult to avoid the suspicion that the adverb and adjective were begotten by the alliterative compulsion.) O'Casey has his moments in these later plays, especially when he uses a wide range of theatrical devices; but the overall effect of his poetic language is not to increase the range of expression but to reduce it and homogenise it into something smooth, sentimental, and sometimes even cloying. His later developments are much more suited to comedy than to tragedy, to whimsical fantasy, as in *Cock-a-Doodle Dandy*, than to works that make overtly 'serious' claims on the audience's attention.

But all that is far beyond the range of this inquiry. By the time *The Silver Tassie* was premiered in London in October 1929, O'Casey was a dramatist of international reputation. Half communist, half fundamentalist preacher, he was now speaking to the world rather than the city of Dublin, urging universal revolution rather than the liberation of a few thousand Irish people. There is nothing in his later writings to relate to the oral/literate motif of the Abbey plays: books are now a major expression of the Good, lovingly studied by the virtuous, repressed by the vicious.

The major creative effort of his years in England was his *Autobiographies,* begun in the early 1930s and concluded in 1954, in which he gave the authorised version of his life and times, treating himself with a tolerance and understanding he afforded very few others. To read the *Autobiographies* is to hear O'Casey speak. It is very much the voice of the sound-recordings he made. It is also, one is convinced, the voice that rhapsodised on salvation in St. Barnabas' Church and later, in smoke-filled rooms, on Irish freedom and the emancipation of the workers. It is essentially the inspired voice of the Protestant preacher formed by the early modern English of the King James Bible, pulsing with rhythms, flashing with colours, driven by a self-delight that would be deemed improper in private conversation or in conventional English prose. It draws its audience in with its constant stream of references, no acknowledgment required, to a shared tradition that includes Gaelic mythology, Irish history, and literature in English. It is, in many ways, the voice of a modern performer who enhances the oral mode with the riches of literary culture, including, for example, the impressionism of Romantic poetry and the neologisms of *Finnegans Wake*. It is the voice that is first heard in Jack Rocliffe in *The Harvest Festival* and heard more clearly twenty years later in Ayamonn in *Red Rose for Me*. It is also the dominant in the music in all of O'Casey's plays with the exception of three, the Abbey plays, and even there it struggles to be heard in *Juno* and is clearly heard in *The Plough*. The more we set these plays in the context of O'Casey's career and output, the more exceptional they seem, not only in subject but in dramatic mode and in language, his only major works that are, predominantly, written within the confines of a vernacular, that of the oral culture of the Dublin working class.

NOTES

1. See Robert Hogan and Richard Burnham, *The Years of O'Casey, 1921–1926: A Documentary History* (Gerrards Cross: Colin Smythe, 1992), 145.

2. Robert Hogan, *'Since O'Casey' and Other Essays on Irish Drama* (Gerrards Cross: Colin Smythe, 1983), 44f.

3. Perhaps this feeling of nostalgic familiarity with the older language, at least in part, makes Irish audiences more uneasy with and less receptive to the later plays than their non-Irish counterparts.

4. After the success of *Shadow*, O'Casey regularly attended the Dublin Drama League productions of plays by such dramatists as Pirandello, Kaiser, Strindberg, Toller, Eugene O'Neill, and Shaw. O'Casey greatly admired Strindberg and was greatly influenced by Toller's *Masses and Man*. See Gabriel Fallon, *Sean O'Casey: The Man I Knew* (London: Routledge and Kegan Paul, 1965), 47.

5. Sean O'Casey, *The Letters of Sean O'Casey*, ed. David Krause, vol. 3, 1955–1958 (Washington, DC: Catholic U of American P, 1989), 497f.

6. J. M. Synge, *Collected Works,* vol. 4, ed. Ann Saddlemyer (London: Oxford UP, 1968), 53f.

7. Alan J. Bliss, 'The Language of Synge,' in *J. M. Synge: Centenary Papers*, ed. Maurice Harmon (Dublin: Dolmen Press, 1971), 54.

8. David Krause, *Sean O'Casey: The Man and His Work* (London: MacGibbon and Kee, 1960), 36.

9. Hogan and Burnham, 294.

10. Ibid., 287. Holloway then went on to make the strange claim that the 'second act carries realism to extremes.'

11. Ibid., 289.

12. Ayling deemed it necessary to explain 'manifestin' forth' as 'proof of'. See O'Casey, *Seven Plays by Sean O'Casey,* a students' edition, with an introduction and notes by Ronald Ayling (London: Macmillan, 1985), 513.

13. Nannie referred to the police as a 'gang of silver button'd bouseys.' See discussion in beginning of Chapter 6.

14. Shelagh Richards, quoted in Hogan and Burnham, 293.

Selected Bibliography

Andrews, C. S. *Dublin Made Me*. Cork: Mercier Press, 1979.

Ayling, Ronald. 'A Note on Sean O'Casey's Manuscripts and His Working Methods.' *Bulletin of the New York Public Library*, June 1969, 359–367.

———. 'Detailed Catalogue of Sean O'Casey's Papers at the Time of His Death.' *Sean O'Casey Review*, Spring 1975, 48–64.

———. 'Detailed Catalogue of Sean O'Casey's Papers at the Time of His Death. Part II.' *Sean O'Casey Review*, Fall 1975, 64–77.

———. 'Detailed Catalogue of Sean O'Casey's Papers at the Time of His Death. Part III.' *Sean O'Casey Review*, Fall 1976, 58–70.

———. 'Popular Tradition and Individual Talent in Sean O'Casey's Trilogy.' *Journal of Modern Literature*, 2, 1972, 491–504.

———, ed. *Sean O'Casey, The Dublin Trilogy: A Casebook*. London: Macmillan, 1985.

———, ed. *Sean O'Casey: Modern Judgements*. London: Macmillan, 1969.

Behan, Brendan. *Borstal Boy*. London: Hutchinson, 1958.

———. *Brendan Behan's Island*. London: Hutchinson, 1962.

———. *Hold Your Hour and Have Another*. London: Hutchinson, 1963.

Benstock, Bernard. *Paycocks and Others: Sean O'Casey's World*. Dublin: Gill and Macmillan, 1976.

Bushrui, Suheil, ed. *Sunshine and the Moon's Delight: A Centenary Tribute to John Millington Synge*. Gerrards Cross: Colin Smythe, 1972.

Carleton, William. *Traits and Stories of the Irish Peasantry*. With a foreword by Barbara Hayley. 2 vols. Gerrards Cross: Colin Smythe, 1990.

Collis, Robert. *Marowbone Lane*. Dublin: Runa Press, 1943.

Corkery, Daniel. *The Labour Leader*. Dublin: Talbot Press, 1927.

Daly, Mary E. *Dublin, the Deposed Capital, a Social and Economic History*. Cork: Cork UP, 1984.

Deane, Seamus. 'Irish Politics and O'Casey's Theatre.' *Threshold*, 24, Spring 1973, 5–16.

de Blaghd, Earnán. *Trasna na Bóinne*. Áth Cliath: Sáirséal agus Dill, 1957.

de Búrca, Séamus. *The Soldier's Song: The Story of Peadar Kearney*. Dublin: P. J. Bourke, 1957.

Dudley Edwards, Ruth. *Patrick Pearse: The Triumph of Failure*. London: Gollanz, 1977.

Ellmann, Richard. *James Joyce*. Rev. ed. Oxford: Oxford UP, 1982.

Fallon, Gabriel. *Sean O'Casey: The Man I Knew*. London: Routledge and Kegan Paul, 1965.

Finnegan, Ruth. *Oral Poetry*. Cambridge: Cambridge UP, 1977.

Fox, R. M. *Jim Larkin: The Rise of the Underman*. London: Lawrence and Wishart, 1957.

Goody, Jack. *Literacy in Traditional Societies*. Cambridge: Cambridge UP, 1968.

Gregory, Augusta. *Lady Gregory's Journals*. Edited by Daniel J. Murphy. 2 vols. Gerrards Cross: Colin Smythe, 1978.

Harmon, Maurice, ed. *J. M. Synge: Centenary Papers*. Dublin: Dolmen Press, 1971.

Hogan, Robert. *'Since O'Casey' and Other Essays on Irish Drama*. Gerrards Cross: Colin Smythe, 1983.

Hogan, Robert and Burnham, Richard. *The Years of O'Casey, 1921–1926: A Documentary History*. Gerrards Cross: Colin Smythe, 1992.

Holloway, Joseph. *Joseph Holloway's Abbey Theatre*. Edited by Robert Hogan and Michael J. O'Neill. Carbondale: Southern Illinois UP, 1967.

Hunt, Hugh. *Sean O'Casey*. Dublin: Gill and Macmillan, 1980.

Innes, Christopher. 'The Essential Continuity of Sean O'Casey.' *Modern Drama*, 33, 1990, 419–433.

Jordan, John. 'The Passionate Autodidact: The Importance of *Litera Scripta* for O'Casey.' *Irish University Review*, Spring 1980, 59–76.

Joyce, James. *Dubliners*. Harmondsworth: Penguin Books, 1992.

———. *Ulysses*. Harmondsworth: Penguin Books, 1992.

Joyce, Stanislaus. *My Brother's Keeper*. New York: Viking Press, 1958.

Kearney, Colbert. *The Writings of Brendan Behan*. Dublin: Gill and Macmillan, 1977.

Kearns, Kevin C. *Dublin Pub Life and Lore: An Oral History*. Dublin: Gill and Macmillan, 1996.

———. *Dublin Tenement Life: an oral history*, Dublin: Gill and Macmillan, 1994.

Kelly, James and Mac Gearailt, Uaitéar. *Dublin and Dubliners*. Dublin: Helion, 1990.

Kiberd, Declan. *Synge and Anglo-Irish Literature*. London: Macmillan, 1979.

Kosok, Heinz. *O'Casey the Dramatist*. Gerrards Cross: Colin Smythe, 1985.

Krause, David. *Sean O'Casey: The Man and His Work*. London: MacGibbon and Kee, 1960.

Krause, David and Lowery, Robert G., eds. *Sean O'Casey: Centenary Essays*. Gerrards Cross: Colin Smythe, 1980.

Larkin, Emmet. *James Larkin: Irish Labour Leader 1876–1947*. London: Routledge and Kegan Paul, 1965.

Leach, Edmund. *Lévi-Strauss*. London: Fontana, 1970.

Lowery, Robert, ed. *Essays on Sean O'Casey's Autobiographies*. London: Macmillan, 1981.

———. *O'Casey Annual Nos 1, 2, 3,* London: Macmillan, 1982/1983/1984.

Magee, Heno. *Hatchet*. Dublin: Gallery Press, 1978.

Margulies, Martin B. *The Early Life of Sean O'Casey*. Dublin: Dolmen Press, 1970.

Maxwell, D.E.S. *A Critical History of Modern Irish Drama 1891–1980*. Cambridge: Cambridge UP, 1984.

McCann, Sean, ed. *The World of Sean O'Casey*. London: New English Library, 1966.

Mikhail, E. H. and O'Riordan, John., eds. *The Sting and the Twinkle*. London: Macmillan, 1974.

Murray, Christopher. *Twentieth-Century Irish Drama: Mirror up to Nation*. Manchester: Manchester UP, 1997.

Ó Cadhain, Máirtín. *The Road to Brightcity*. Translated by Eoghan Ó Tuairisc. Dublin: Poolbeg, 1981.

O'Casey, Sean. *Autobiographies*. 2 vols. London: Pan Books, 1980.

———. *Feathers from the Green Crow: Sean O'Casey 1905–1925*. Edited by Robert Hogan. London: Macmillan, 1963.

———. *The Green Crow: Selected Writings of Sean O'Casey*. London: Virgin, 1994.

————. *The Harvest Festival*. Foreword by Eileen O'Casey and introduction by John O'Riordan. Gerrards Cross: Colin Smythe, 1980.

————. *The Letters of Sean O'Casey*. Edited by David Krause. Vol. 1. 1910–1941. London: Cassell, 1975.

————. *The Letters of Sean O'Casey*. Edited by David Krause. Vol. 2. 1942–1954. New York: Macmillan, 1980.

————. *The Letters of Sean O'Casey*. Edited by David Krause. Vol. 3. 1955–1958. Washington, DC: Catholic U of America P, 1989.

————. *The Letters of Sean O'Casey*. Edited by David Krause. Vol. 4. 1959–1964. Washington, DC: Catholic U of America P, 1992.

————. *Seven Plays by Sean O'Casey*. Selected with an introduction and notes by Ronald Ayling. London: Macmillan, 1985.

O'Connor, Garry. *Sean O'Casey*. London: Hodder and Stoughton, 1988.

O'Connor, Ulick. *Oliver St. John Gogarty*. London: Jonathan Cape, 1963.

Ó Muirithe, Diarmuid, ed. *The English Language in Ireland*. Dublin: Mercier, 1977.

Ong, Walter. *Orality and Literacy: The Technologizing of the Word*. London: Methuen, 1982.

Ó Tuama, Seán and Kinsella, Thomas. *An Duanaire: Poems of the Dispossessed 1600–1900*. Dublin: Dolmen Press, 1981.

Purdom, C. B. *A Guide to the Plays of Bernard Shaw*. London: Methuen, 1964.

Robbins, Frank. *Under the Starry Plough: Recollections of the Irish Citizen Army*. Dublin: Academy Press, 1977.

Ryan, Desmond. *Remembering Sion*. London: Arthur Barker, 1934.

Schrank, Bernice. *Sean O'Casey: A research and production sourcebook*. Westport, CT: Greenwood Press, 1996.

————. "'Th' nakedness o' th' times": Dressing-Up in *The Plough and the Stars*.' *Canadian Journal of Irish Studies* 7, 1981, 5–20.

————. "'You needn't say no more": Language and the Problems of Communication in *The Shadow of a Gunman*.' *Irish University Review*, VIII, 1978, 23–37.

Schrank, Bernice and William W. Demastes. *Irish Playwrights, 1880–1995: A Research and Production Sourcebook*. Westport, CT: Greenwood Press, 1997.

Shaw, G. B. *The Doctor's Dilemma*. Harmondsworth: Penguin Books, 1946.

Smith, Paul. *The Countrywoman*. London: Heinemann, 1962.

Stephens, James. *The Charwoman's Daughter*. Introduction by Augustine Martin. Dublin: Gill and Macmillan, 1972.

————. *Uncollected Prose of James Stephens*. Edited by Patricia A. McFate. 2 vols. London: Macmillan, 1983.

Synge, J. M. *Collected Works*. Vol. 2, ed. Alan Price. Gerrards Cross: Colin Smythe, 1982; Vol. 4, book 2. Edited by Ann Saddlemyer. London: Oxford UP, 1968.

Thornton, Weldon. *Allusions in Ulysses*. Chapel Hill: U of North Carolina P, 1968.

Watt, Stephen. *Joyce, O'Casey and the Irish Popular Theatre*. Syracuse, NY: Syracuse UP, 1991.

Williams, Raymond. *Drama from Ibsen to Brecht*. Harmondsworth: Pelican Books, 1973.

————. *Drama from Ibsen to Eliot*. Rev. ed. Harmondsworth: Peregrine Books, 1964.

Index

About the Author

COLBERT KEARNEY is Professor of Modern English at University College Cork. He has published widely on Irish literature.